Handbook on Clinical Legal Education

The daring publisher, Universal Law Publishing Company, among the foremost in the law publishing field and progressive in venturing to bring out rare legal literature of avant garde *character has rightly enriched the* corpus juris *of India*

Justice V R Krishna Iyer
Random Reflections, page 14

Handbook on Clinical Legal Education

Maj Gen Nilendra Kumar

Director, Amity Law School, NOIDA

Neha Chaturvedi

Advocate, High Court of Delhi

Universal

Law Publishing Co. Pvt. Ltd.

NEW DELHI - INDIA

2013 Edition

ISBN: 978-93-5035-319-6

Published by
UNIVERSAL LAW PUBLISHING CO. PVT. LTD.
C-FF-1A, Dilkhush Industrial Estate,
(Near Azadpur Metro Station) G.T. Karnal Road,
Delhi-110 033
Tel.: 011-47082254, 27438103, 27215334
Fax : 011-27458529
E-mail *(For sales inquiries)* : unilaw@vsnl.com
(For editorial inquiries) : edit@unilawbooks.com
Website : www.unilawbooks.com

Join us on Facebook
www.facebook.com/unilawbooks

Recommended citation: Maj Gen Nilendra Kumar, *Handbook on Clinical Legal Education* (New Delhi: Universal Law Publishing Co. Pvt. Ltd., 2013).

Computer Typeset at Aesthetic and *Printed* at Kailash Graphics, Delhi.

Preface

Clinical legal education as a mode of instruction is vital to inculcate legal skills in law students to make their studies meaningful. It is a step to make them efficient practitioners of law and also to equip them to contribute significantly to the community and society needs. Not much attention was paid to the Clinical legal education in the curriculum of most of the law schools so far particularly as regards preparation of a manual or handbook to guide the students.

An effort has been made in this book to describe a few modes of legal skills which the law students can conveniently grasp, practice and put to use during their tenure of stay in law schools. The faculty would also find it helpful to plan dissemination of their instructions facilitate application of law.

The work, first of its kind, has been undertaken to make law curriculum more practical. The authors will be grateful for any comments or suggestions aimed at improving its contents so as to be more useful to the students.

Noida　　　　Authors

April, 2013

Acknowledgement

We are deeply obliged to all our friends, colleagues and students who have directly or indirectly contributed in various ways for this book.

We place on record our sincere thanks to Dr. Arun Mohan, Senior Advocate for helping with the definition of various words and terms included for the purpose of viva voce examination.

Special thanks to Advocate Kush Chaturvedi for his constructive suggestions that were sought at different stages. Thanks to Mr. Ved Prakash Sharma, Advocate and President, Delhi Bar Association and Mr. G. S. Chaturvedi, Advocate for providing us the forms used in various courts and tribunals.

Help from Dr. J. S. Nair and Ms. Sheetal Singh is acknowledged with regard to the material included concerning moots and legal aid. Law students Faraz Khan and Aakriti Mathur are thanked for helping with the problem relating to mock trial. Faraz, Maitraeyi Bordoloi, Akbar Ahmad and Avinash K. R. for their assistance with regard to the moots.

Wikipedia, the free encyclopedia and legal search engines, legalpundits.com, indiankanoon.org etc. deserve our thanks for the information compiled and made accessible by them.

Mr. M. Sasidharan owes special thanks for helping in a big way with the manuscript.

Lastly, the publishers for all their interest in bringing out the book in this form. Dr. Manish Arora deserves our gratitude for all his assistance and keen interest in its timely publication.

Contents

CHAPTER 1

Broad Outline of Clinical Legal Education

What it is?

Legal education involves study of technical and complex subjects having practical relevance. Clinical Legal Education (in short CLE) is an innovative approach to legal education, which seeks to compliment the theoretical knowledge students gain in class rooms with practical hand-on experience in 'real world' situations.

CLE is directed towards developing the perception, attitudes, skills and sense of responsibilities which law professionals are expected to assume when they complete their professional education.

CLE was evolved as a popular route for preparing a career in law. The earlier concept with regard to CLE was to rely on a case book and case law method. Case book method was used as the primary mode of teaching law in the United States. It followed the principle that rather than studying highly abstract summaries of legal rules, a simple way to comprehend law would be to read the actual judicial decisions which become the law under the rule of *stare decisis*. For this purpose, most illustrative cases concerning a particular area of law were collected in special text books called case books. Case studies then came to be put to use for scrutiny of lessons learnt or experiences gained.

Yet another mode of CLE involved making use of Socratic method of legal analysis. Socratic method involved use of questions to develop a latent idea, as in the mind of a pupil or to elicit admissions, tending to establish a proposition. The process was carried out to reach at truths which the instructor considered to be easily known by all rational minds.

In those days the apprentice system was favoured to enable students in law schools emerge as legal practitioners. It involved co-option with a practicing counsel. The pupil was part of the team of the counsel. He spent time with his senior in the interview of clients, preparation of the case and the actual court proceedings. By observation he slowly gained an insight into practical legal skills. Thus it was based on applied skill training method.

The law teachers in the earlier days thus made use of legal dispensaries and legal aid bureaus.

Need for CLE was felt when the law teachers were found to be ill-equipped to teach students how to practice law. This was perhaps due to law teaching becoming a full-time and the faculty being recruited from those who had no prior exposure to law practice. The faculty was not in a position to help the students develop practical skills necessary for competent undertaking of lawyer's functions. It was also required due to immaturity and incapacity of students to think within and about the role of lawyers.

The underlying aim and purpose of legal education is to prepare a person to serve and help the society or community. The assistance expected from them may be towards a segment of society (read industry, corporate or organization).

CLE provides students with suitable opportunities for professional and intellectual development. It prepares them for the practice of law, as competent law personnel as well as socially responsible citizens.

The absence of proper attention to CLE has led to a deplorable state of legal professionals. According to former Solicitor General of India Jagdish Swarup,

> *"Too many lawyers come into Court today with only a law degree to justify their claims to be advocates. They are untrained and unsupervised in the immensely practical work of litigation.*
>
> *It is doubtful if the University system of education is particularly favourable to all or indeed to any of them. A lawyer really learns most of his law at the expense of his clients. No matter what his preparation is, he is not much when he starts practicing and he either learns or he does not learn from them.*
>
> *Our law schools are library-law schools, book-law schools. They are not as they should be, lawyer's schools. There is, to be sure, a limit on what can be achieved in the surroundings of the law-school. The student must finally depart the class room to refine his advocacy skills.*
>
> *Success as a student does not always ensure success in practice. In the strife and turmoil of the Courts, the great lawyer is evolved.*
>
> *Our law schools do virtually nothing to help a man try a case; with the practical work of the law, the law graduate has little or no familiarity. He comes to the Bar almost ignorant of how the law should be applied and is applied in daily life. It is, therefore, not unusual to find the brightest students the most helpless practitioners, and the most learned surpassed in the profession by one who does not know half as much."*[1]

Mandate by the Bar Council

Bar Council of India Rules enacted under the Advocates Act, 1961 have addressed the aspect of Clinical Legal Education. Rules of Legal Education, 2008 framed by the BCI are relevant in this regard. Under the said Rules of Legal Education, all University Departmental Centres, Faculty, constituent and affiliated centres of legal education proposing to offer law courses under the three years or five years streams are to possess facilities for imparting practical legal education

---

1. Making of a Good Lawyer by Jagdish Swarup (Universal Law Publishing Co. Pvt. Ltd., Delhi, 2nd Edn., 2005), pp. 42-43.

specified in the curriculum under the Rules and Legal Aid Clinic, Court Training and Moot Court exercises. Under the Rules, it is provided that:

(a) The last six months of the three years of the law course shall include a regular course of practical training.

(b) The course of study in law would be by regular attendance for the requisite number of lectures, tutorials, moot courts and practical training given by a college.

(c) At least 30 hours of working per week would include contract and correspondence programme, tutorials, home assignments, library, clinical work etc.

It is also mandated that a law college shall be located at a place where there is at least a District Court or a Circuit District Court or within such distance thereof as the Bar Council of India permits.

Six months of Practical Training to be imparted as indicated above will include following four compulsory papers:—

1. Drafting, Pleading and Conveyance.
2. Professional Ethics and Professional Accounting System.
3. Alternate dispute resolution.
4. Moot Court exercise and internship.

Public interest lawyering relates to the process of legal empowerment aimed at capacity building of common people towards use of law and institutions to bring about social change.

The Bar Council has laid down following practical training scheme for above four papers which is to be adopted by the Universities:—

Compulsory Clinical Courses

1. Drafting, Pleading and Conveyance

Outline of the course:

(a) Drafting:—General principles of drafting and relevant substantive rules shall be taught.

(b) Pleadings:—

(i) Civil: Plaint, Written Statement, Interlocutory Application, Original Petition, Affidavit, Execution Petition, Memorandum of Appeal and Revision, Petition under Articles 226 and 32 of the Constitution of India.

(ii) Criminal: Complaint, Criminal Miscellaneous petition, Bail Application, Memorandum of Appeal and Revision.

(iii) Conveyance: Sale Deed, Mortgage Deed, Lease Deed, Gift Deed, Promissory Note, Power of Attorney, Will, Trust Deed.

(iv) Drafting of writ petition and PIL petition.

The course will be taught class instructions and simulation exercises, preferably with assistance of practicing lawyers/retired judges.

Apart from teaching the relevant provisions of law, the course may include not less than 15 practical exercises in drafting, carrying a total of 45 marks (3 marks for each) and 15 exercises in conveyancing, carrying another 45 marks (3 marks for each exercise) remaining 10 marks will be given for *viva voce.*

2. *Professional Ethics and Professional Accounting System*

Outline of the course: Professional Ethics, Accountancy for Lawyers and Bar-Bench Relations.

This course will be taught in association with practicing lawyers on the basis of the following materials:

(i) Mr. Krishnamurthy Iyer's book on "Advocacy".

(ii) The Contempt Law and Practice.

(iii) The Bar Council Code of Ethics.

(iv) 50 selected opinions of the Disciplinary Committees of Bar Councils and 10 major judgments of the Supreme Court on the subject.

(v) Other reading materials as may be prescribed by the University.

Examination rules of the University shall include assessment through case-study, *viva,* and periodical problem solution beside the written tests.

3. *Alternate Dispute Resolution (ADR)*

Outline of the course:

(i) Negotiation skills to be learnt with simulated program.

(ii) Conciliation skills.

(iii) Arbitration Law and Practice including International arbitration and Arbitration rules.

The course is required to be conducted by senior legal practitioners through simulation and case studies. Evaluation may also be conducted in practical exercises at least for a significant part of evaluation.

4. *Moot Court Exercise and Internship*

This paper may have three components of 30 marks each and a *viva* for 10 marks.

(a) Moot Court (30 Marks)

Every student may be required to do at least three moot courts in a year with 10 marks for each. The moot court work will be on assigned problem and it will be evaluated for 5 marks for written submissions and 5 marks for oral advocacy.

(b) Observance of Trial in two cases, one Civil and one Criminal (30 marks)

Students may be required to attend two trials in the course of the last two or three years of LL.B. studies. They will maintain a record and enter the various steps observed during their attendance on different days in the court assignment. This scheme will carry 30 marks.

(c) Interviewing techniques and Pre-trial preparations and Internship diary (30 marks)

Each student will observe two interviewing sessions of clients at the Lawyer's Office/Legal Aid Office and record the proceedings in a diary, which will carry 15 marks. Each student will further observe the preparation of documents and court papers by the Advocate and the procedure for the filing of the suit/petition. This will be recorded in the diary, which will carry 15 marks.

(d) The fourth component of this paper will be *Viva Voce* examination on all the above three aspects. This will carry 10 marks.

Advocates Act, 1961 is intended to cover all aspects of legal education relating to entry into the Bar.

The above scheme also finds mention in the Bar Council of India Rules approved and adopted by the Bar Council of India at its meeting held on 14 September 2008, *vide* resolution No. 110/2008.

It is also significant that in *Sobhana Kumar* v. *Mangalore University*,[1] it was held that the BCI can only prescribe minimum standards for entry into Bar whereas the Universities or the law colleges can prescribe higher standards.

The National Knowledge Commission in its recommendations has stated that the legal education must aim at preparing legal professionals who will play decisive leadership roles, not only as advocates practicing in courts, but also as academics, legislators, judges, policy makers, public officials, civil society activists as well as legal counsel in the private sector, maintaining the highest standards of professional ethics and a spirit of public service.

Today, therefore, the legal education has to meet not only the requirements of the Bar but also cater for the expectations of industry, trade and commerce in the context of growing internationalization of the profession.

---

1. AIR 1985 Kant 223.

CHAPTER 2
Internship

Concept

An internship is a period of training whereby students work off-campus under supervision so as to learn practical applications of class room material.

Internship is one of the modes of practical training in the sphere of legal education. Apart from the moots, legal aid and legal writing forms the core component of practical acquisition and assimilation of law teaching syllabus for the students. This mode is also known as placement training. This is a programme carried outside the campus for different durations each year.

The process of internship enables an actual study of the purpose of statutory and procedural laws. It provides the students with an opportunity to understand and examine the structure and behaviour of organizations. It shows to them the nature of legal framework of the institutions and concerned issues. Students get the benefit of an exposure to law in action rather than law in books (as acquired in class rooms) and thus help them in due acquisition of legal expertise. Internship provides a glimpse into the daily routine of a law professional on a learning-friendly and stimulating platform.

The tool of internship for law students has followed varying forms, duration and stages in the past. This had been the actual practice in majority of the law schools. Often the students used to choose to intern on their own by selecting the place, organization and duration of internship. These were decided by them at their discretion. They used their personal contacts and initiative to arrange the internship of their liking. A progressive and well designed approach will help them in proper utilization of their efforts.

It is advisable to design internship process to proceed in a graduated pattern so as to keep a relationship with the class room curriculum. The students should be allowed to choose from a variety of fields to match their interest and aptitude. Internship pattern should relate to and be compatible with the educational history of the students and their academic progression. Otherwise, the students would not be able to grasp the applicable laws in practice at the place of internship. It is also to be ensured that internship does not clash or overshadow academic programme. Of course, if the students can conveniently manage to attend the class room teaching to cope up with the syllabus while also carrying out internship, the practice could be permitted by the Law School. In other cases, the internship should be undertaken during the winter and summer breaks between the academic semesters. For the ease of logistics and family considerations, it would be advantageous for the students to undertake internships at or near their home stations.

Where to Intern

The suggested policy for carrying out internship could be designed as given below for the five year law programmes.

Semester	Minimum Duration (One Week)	Place
I	One week	Information Commission/Library of a University/College/Institute
II	Six weeks	Local Court/Consumer Forum/Local Body
III	One week	Prison/NGO/Police/Social activists
IV	Six weeks	PSU/Govt. office/Judicial office/State HRC/NHRC
V	One week	Industry/Bank/Embassy/Hospital/think tank/Foundation/offices of the United Nations agencies
VI	Six weeks	District Court/Tribunal/Undertaking/Corporate Law Office/the office of a political party or a trade union
VII	One week	Media/Law Publishing/Regulating Authority/IGO/Bar Council
VIII	Six weeks	High Court/Supreme Court/National Authority/Legal branches of military or paramilitary forces/Lokayukta/MACT
IX	One week	Post Graduate Teaching Institution in Law/Legal Aid Authorities
X	Twelve weeks	Any of the above or at the discretion of students

For a three year law degree course, the pattern suggested below could be considered.

Semester	Minimum Duration (One Week)	Place
I	One week	Information Commission/Consumer Forum/Law Library of a court or post graduate law college/Foundation
II	Six weeks	Prison and Police Station/social activist and child, women, disabled or SC/ST/OBC Commission/Industry or a Bank/NGO or IGO/Lokayukta/Commission

1	2	3
III	One week	Media/Law Publishing/Bank/Embassy/Bar Council/ offices of the United Nations agencies
IV	Six weeks	District Court or Tribunal, Corporate Law Office or Law offices of military/CBI/Legal Aid Authority/the office of a political party or a trade union
V	One week	High Court/National Authority/National Commission/Supreme Court
VI		Any of the above or at the discretion of the students

In five years, every student would have completed at least forty-one weeks of field work (internship) in different types of environment under guidance. Care is to be taken to transact the internship process with requisite flexibility. Otherwise, the process may appear to be rigid and stereotyped. The students should select the place and retain the option to change the nature, type and duration of internship. However, prior approval of the Director Law School should be taken in this regard.

Not more than two students should carry out internship at the same office. Such an approach would introduce variety and avoid a stereotyped pattern. The students of one law school should not approach the same library, office, advocate or organization for internship. Further, the students are expected to approach and obtain the prior consent for internship from the organizations concerned. Previous communication and efforts may be helpful in this regard. However, for the purpose of record and where required, a letter of introduction may be issued to them by the law school.

To avoid any subsequent embarrassment and inconvenience, the students must confirm the date, time and the official whom they are required to report and the place of his internship. Students are expected to enquire the timings, dress code, discipline, reporting channel and other instructions from the organization for due adherence. Normally no payment, compensation or remuneration is disbursed to the students.

It is important that prior to commencement of their internship, the students discuss with their faculty and mentors the approach, process and modalities involved.

During the internship, the students may like to study and examine the following:—

(a) **Role and function of the organization/office/set up.**—To understand the basic purpose, its objective, need for the society and relevance.

(b) **Statutory base for the same.**—What is the law, rule, ordnance or authority under which it has been set up and operates?

(c) **Public activity undertaken.**—What type of diverse functions it performs or the role it plays. How it meets the needs of the community or a particular section of the society?

(d) **Organisation tree/structure.**—To understand the different layers of control, supervision and decision making processes.

(e) **Type of legal issues.**—Whether there are any legal or judicial difficulties, bottlenecks or legal obligations that require a careful examination with a view to improve?

(f) **Type of litigation, if any.**—Has the role and functioning led to any judicial intervention, whether initiated by the internal work force or by any of the beneficiaries, users or activists etc.?

(g) **Consumer protection/consumer awareness/human rights.**—Issues observed which are suggestive of defects, deficiencies or complaints as regards its role and functioning etc.

A number of organizations/offices chosen for internships are not equipped with law officers and their role is unconnected to law directly. They perform their assigned role despite severe constraints of manpower, resources and time. Students, therefore, will have to take care not to cause any impression that they are expected to check its functioning, find faults or that the internship may result in any legal complications to the hosts, or that it may delay their functioning.

The students will be required to submit a report about their internship to cover the aspects listed above. The report may also include their recommendations and suggestions, if any. Usually, it will be desirable for the student's report to be communicated to the organisation concerned unless for any reason they would not like to do so.

Internship, if carried out diligently and with adequate interest would bring multiple advantages. The students will gain useful knowledge about the organisations and their functioning. The exposure may help in forming their everlasting ties with influential persons. It would greatly assist them in understanding teaching of substantive and procedural laws in class rooms. In many cases, the contacts developed would help the students directly or indirectly in their placements.

How to Get Internship

The first step for the law student is to find out with whom and where he is supposed to intern.

'Where' refers to the location. It may be based on the personal and individual choice or financial compulsions within the time period constraints. The students may seek help of their parents, relatives, neighbours, friends or teachers to get suitable recommendations.

The next step would be to approach the particular person, office or organization after ascertaining the correct contact details. It would be advisable for the student to formally apply for an internship. A letter sent by e-mail or by courier or presented personally may be necessary.

The letter must indicate the name of the student and the particulars of the law school, programme, semester and the batch. It should display his keenness for the internship. It may be desirable to mention any special academic achievements *e.g.*, a high SGPA/CGPA, articles or other publications, performance in moots or debates or previous internships etc. Request for any particular period during which internship would be preferred may also be indicated.

An example of an application is given below.

Letter to get internship Date :..............

To

....

....

....

Sir/Madam

I, ... (name), s/o .... (name) am a student of .... semester in .... programme of .... batch at ....Law College .... under ....University.

As part of internship for the Clinical Legal Education Policy of our institution, I am very keen to undergo internship under you.

I have so far acquired reasonably well in academics with a CGPA of .... I have participated in moots/am actually associated in legal aid clinic of my college/have contributed .... articles to law journals/(or .... , indicate actual activity).

An internship under you would greatly enhance my capacity to apply academic contents to real life situations involving legal education. May I therefore, request you to allow me to intern for.........................weeks in your office, preferably from.........................to ....(indicate period). A letter of recommendation from the head of my college is enclosed.

Thanking you,
Yours truly,

Name :

Address :
Mobile :
E-mail :

It is suggested that the above application should be sent by way of mail or couriered. This should be forwarded in advance, preferably at least three weeks prior to the commencement of internship. The same would help due processing and intimation of decision. If a favourable reply is received, the student should ask the date, time, place and the name of the person to whom to report.

A **letter of recommendation** may be sent along with the above application, if so desired by the particular office/agency/organization.

Letter of Recommendation

Date :.............

To

....

....

....

Internship

Sir/Madam,

This is to certify that ...., S/o, D/o .... is a *bona fide* student of......................... semester .... in .... Law School,......................... University,......................... . His/Her Enrollment No. is ....He/She has been assigned internship under the ________________ during the summer break. You are requested to kindly allow him/her to intern according to the policy as applicable.

Director
................Law School,
...................University, ...

Where and what to do there?

Explained below are the specific areas of study for the students to undertake at different internships.

Libraries

What is the target membership or readership. Categorization of publication into text books, reference books, Bare Acts, commentaries, journals and periodicals. Mode of display of latest and new books, journals and availability of e-books. Suggestions and complaints by the users of the library. Preparation and updating of index cards. How to further upgrade and improve the facilities provided. System in place for procuring new titles and time involved therein.

Address of a few leading law libraries in Delhi are given below. This list may help students to contact libraries at other places.

1. Indian Law Institute Library,
   Bhagwan Das Road,
   New Delhi – 110 001
   www.ilidelhi.org

2. Indian Society of International Law Library,
   Krishna Menon Bhavan,
   Bhagwan Das Road,
   New Delhi – 110 001
   E-mail : info@isil-aca.org

3. Supreme Court Bar Association Library,
   Supreme Court of India,
   New Delhi – 110 001

4.	Delhi High Court Bar Association Library, High Court of Delhi, New Delhi – 110 001
5.	National Human Rights Commission Library, Faridkot House, Copernicus Marg, New Delhi – 110 001 E-mail : covdnhrc@nic.in
6.	Law Faculty Library, Delhi University, Delhi – 110 007
7.	Centre for the Study of Law & Governance Law Library, Jawahar Lal Nehru University, New Delhi – 110 067 E-mail : chair_cslg@mail.jnu.ac.in
8.	Law Faculty Library, GGSIP University, Sector 16-C, Dwarka, New Delhi – 110 078 E-mail : apsingh@yahoo.com
9.	Faculty of Law Library, Jamia Millia Islamia University, Mohd Ali Johar Marg, Jamia Nagar, New Delhi – 110 025
10.	School of Law Library, IGNOU, Maidan Garhi, New Delhi – 110 068 E-mail : directorsol@ignou.ac.in
11.	Amity Law School Library, Amity University Uttar Pradesh, I-2, Block, Sector-125, Noida – 201 303
12.	Amity Law School, Centre-II Library, Amity University Uttar Pradesh, I-2 Block, Sector-125, Noida – 201 303
13.	Amity Law School Library, GGS IP University, F Block, Sector-125, Noida – 201 303

14.	Observers Research Foundation Library, 20, Rouse Avenue Institutional Area, New Delhi – 110 002 E-mail : contactus@orfonline.org
15.	American Centre Library, 24 K.G. Marg, New Delhi – 110 001 E-mail : libdel@state.govt
16.	British Council Library, 17 K.G. Marg, New Delhi – 110 011 E-mail : delhi.enquiry@inbritishcouncil.org
17.	Nehru Memorial Museum and Library, Teen Murti Bhawan, New Delhi – 110 011 E-mail : nmmiccs@gmail.com
18.	Parliament House Library, Library and Reference Research Documentation and Information Service, Parliament House, New Delhi – 110 001
19.	National Archives Library, Janpath, New Delhi – 110 001 E-mail : archives@nic.in
20.	Justice T.P.S. Chawla Library, National Law University, Sector-14, Dwarka, Delhi – 110 078 E-mail : info@nludelhi.ac.in
21.	India International Centre Library, 40 Max Muller Marg, New Delhi – 110 003 E-mail : info@nludelhi.ac.in
22.	Ministry of Law & Justice Library, Government of India, Shastri Bhavan, New Delhi – 110 001
23.	Department of Law, Justice and Legislative Affairs Library, 8th Level, C Wing, Delhi Secretarial, I.P. Estate, New Delhi – 110 001 E-mail : slaw@nic.in

24.	India Habitat Centre Library, Lodi Estate, Lodi Road, New Delhi
25.	Centre for Policy Research Library, Dharam Marg, Chanakyapuri, New Delhi – 110 021 E-mail : cprindia@vsnl.com
26.	Indian Institute for Public Administration Library, Indraprastha Estate, Ring Road, New Delhi – 110 002 E-mail : diriipa@bol.net.in

Local Court

Composition and number of courts. Generally types of litigation. Procedure to file plaints and written statements. Role of a notary public/oath commissioner. Cause list, removal of objections, issue of summons and cross-examination procedure. Size of pendency.

Bar Associations and their role, Bar library.

Consumer Forum

Composition of the forum where interning. Type of complaints generally. Procedure to make a complaint and also to give a reply on behalf of respondents. Time taken usually for disposal of a case. Reasons for delay in completion of a complaint. Feedback of the complainants. Suggestions for greater user satisfaction.

Local Body

Examples of local body are Delhi Development Authority, Ghaziabad Development Authority, Lucknow Development Authority and NOIDA etc.

While interning with a local body, the students should ascertain what are the statutory laws, rules or regulations relating to it? What are its roles and functions? What services does it offer to the residents? What is the total number of employees? What is the type of litigation against it. Is there any case law from the Supreme Court?

Prison

How are the inmates lodged. Number of under trials and convicts, facility of legal aid for inmates, facility of visitors to meet the inmates, meeting with relations and lawyers, lodging of women and children inmates. The daily routine, scope for counselling and reforms of prisoners, procedure for release on parole, medical and health care facilities. It would also be useful for the students to visit juvenile homes or remand lodges.

Non-Governmental Organisations (NGO)

Non-Governmental organizations are legally constituted entities created by natural or legal persons that operate independently from any government. Such bodies are not conventionally for-profit business. These organizations usually pursue some wider social aim. NGOs maintain their non-governmental status by excluding government representatives from their membership. These are social action groups involved in public causes including legal action.

The internees may examine as to what is the aim, charter and composition of the NGO? What are its main objectives? Sources of its funding and target beneficiaries. Do its activities get support under any legal provisions? Court cases, pending or decided, related to its reports or achievements and also if any, to oppose its operations.

Some of the active NGOs are named below. The students may choose the NGO depending upon their area of interest, location and availability.

1. Aadhar – New Delhi.
2. Aahwaan – New Delhi.
3. Abhigyan – New Delhi.
4. Action for Autism – New Delhi.
5. Adhikar – New Delhi.
6. Amnesty International.
7. Aarohan – New Delhi.
8. Asha Deep Foundation.
9. Azim Premji Foundation.
10. Bombay Natural History Society.
11. Centre for Media Studies.
12. Centre for Women's Development Studies.
13. Care India.
14. Centre for Law and Environment.
15. Centre for Science and Environment.
16. Darpan Academy of Performing Arts.
17. Development Alternatives.
18. Dastkar.
19. Delhi Association of the Deaf.
20. Disha.
21. Gandhi Peace Foundation.
22. Go Rural India.
23. Greenpeace.
24. Gandhi Peace Foundation.
25. Human Rights Group.
26. Help Age India.

27. Indian Spinal Injury Centre, Sector-C, Vasant Kunj, New Delhi – 110 070, Website : www.isiconline.org.
28. Indian Red Cross Society.
29. Indira Gandhi Memorial Trust.
30. INTACH, Nizamuddin, New Delhi.
31. Manushi, C 1/3 Sangam Estate, 1, Under Hill Road, Civil Lines, Delhi – 110 054.
32. Narmada Bachao Andolan.
33. National Association for the Blind.
34. Nilgiri Wildlife and Environment Association.
35. Ratan Tata Trust.
36. Srishti, 22, K.G. Marg, New Delhi – 110 001.
37. Spastic Society of India.
38. Society for Cultural and Social Upliftment.
39. Sulabh International.
40. SEWA Lucknow.
41. Transparency International.
42. TERI, IHC Complex, Lodhi Road, New Delhi.
43. Theatre in Education Company, New Delhi.
44. Vatavaran, Asiad Games Village, New Delhi.
45. World Wide Fund for Nature, Lodhi Estate, New Delhi.

Police

In regard to a police station, the total area covered by it and the population in comparison to the number of police personnel posted. The main type of crimes generally reported, the procedure for filing a complaint and lodging FIR. How the initial investigation or inquiry is held. Facilities for detaining suspects and accused persons. Storage of material exhibits. Procedure to hold in custody women or minor suspects. Manner of maintaining old records, sharing of information with other police stations and media.

Social Activists

Activism means the use of direct, often confrontational action, such as demonstration strike, hunger strike or fast, in opposition to or support of a cause.

Social activists are individuals who, for a variety of reasons, have been active to promote public cause. Through the analogy, social activists often try to persuade people to change their behaviour directly or may go to influence governments to change laws.

The internship will expose the students to examine. What is the area of interest and work? How and why was the activist drawn to take up the cause? What are the social problems or ills being addressed. Is there any inadequacy, shortfall or gap in statutory law, rules or procedures. Who are the target group of persons affected? Which Ministry or department of the government is concerned with its activities? What is the approach or plan devised by the activist? How has been the approach of media or civil society?

A few prominent social activists are named below:—

1. Mr. Abid Surti.
2. Mr. Arun Shourie.
3. Mr. Anna Hazare.
4. Mr. Arvind Gaur.
5. Ms. Arundhati Roy.
6. Ms. Aruna Roy.
7. Mr. Ayaz Mughal.
8. Baba Ramdev.
9. Dr. Binayak Sen.
10. Mr. Bittu Sahgal.
11. Mr. C.R. Neelakandan.
12. Mr. Dilip D'Souza.
13. Mr. Girdhari Lal Kedia.
14. Mr. G.R. Khairnar.
15. Mr. Karem Shivaji.
16. Ms. Kiran Bedi.
17. Mr. Kulandei Francis.
18. Ms. Maneka Gandhi.
19. Ms. Medha Patkar.
20. Ms. Mira Nair.
21. Ms. Mirai Chatterjee.
22. Mr. Mahesh Chandra Mehta.
23. Ms. Mallika Sarabhai.
24. .Mr. Nafisa Ali.
25. Mr. Pandit Hulasa Ram Dutta.
26. Mr. Rahul Bose.
27. Mr. Rajendra K. Pachauri.
28. Ms. Rashida Bee.
29. Justice Rajinder Sachar.
30. Ms. Reetika Khera.
31. Mr. Satish Sheetty.
32. Ms. Shabana Azmi.
33. Mr. Sunder Lal Bahuguna.
34. Swami Agnivesh.
35. Mr. Shanti Bhushan, Senior Advocate.

36. Justice N. Santosh Hegde.
37. Ms. Sunita Narain.
38. Mr. Tarun Tejpal.
39. Ms. Vandana Shiva.
40. Mr. Vidyaben Shah.
41. Mr. Subhash Chandra Agarwal

Public Sector Undertakings

Public Sector Undertakings (in short PSU) are government owned corporation. In a PSU, the majority (51% or more) of the paid up share capital is owned by the Central Government or by any State Government or in some cases partly by the Central Government and partly by one or more State Governments.

PSUs have laid a strong foundation for the industrial development of the country. Since the public sector is not overly influenced towards profit generation hence it can play an active role in national building activities.

The students during their internship may wish to familiarize themselves with the role, purpose or objectives of the undertaking. Statutory laws, rules and procedure applicable. Composition and organization. Its legal department and type of cases dealt by it or assigned to it. Any noteworthy case law. Any changes in law introduced as a result of litigation.

Name of a few PSUs

1. Airports Authority of India
2. Andrew Yule & Company Ltd.
3. Artificial Limbs Manufacturing Corporation of India
4. Balmer Lawrie & Co. Ltd.
5. Bharat Bhari Udyog Nigam Ltd.
6. Bharat Coking Coal Limited
7. Bharat Dynamics Limited
8. Bharat Electronics Limited
9. Bharat Heavy Electricals Limited
10. Bharat Heavy Plate & Vessels Ltd.
11. Bharat Sanchar Nigam Limited
12. Cement Corporation of India Limited
13. Coal India Limited
14. Central Coalfields Limited
15. Central Cottage Industries Corporation of India Ltd.
16. Central Electronics Limited
17. Container Corporation of India
18. Cochin Shipyard Limited
19. Central Warehousing Corporation
20. Damodar Valley Corporation

21. Dredging Corporation of India
22. Eastern Coalfields Ltd.
23. Engineers India Ltd., Engineers India Bhavan, 1, Bhikaji Cama Place, New Delhi – 110 066.
24. Educational Consultants India Ltd.
25. Electronics Corporation of India Ltd.
26. Export Credit Guarantee Corporation of India Ltd.
27. Ferro Scrap Nigam Limited
28. Food Corporation of India
29. Gas Authority of India Ltd.
30. Goa Shipyard Ltd.
31. HMT Limited
32. Heavy Engineering Corporation
33. Helicopter Corporation of India
34. Hindustan Aeronautics Ltd.
35. Hindustan Cables Limited
36. Hindustan Insecticides Ltd.
37. Hindustan Latex Ltd.
38. Hindustan Paper Corporation
39. Hindustan Petroleum Corporation Ltd.
40. Hindustan Shipyard Ltd.
41. Housing and Urban Development Corporation Ltd.
42. Hindustan Vegetable Oils Corporation Ltd.
43. Hotel Corporation of India Ltd.
44. Air India
45. Indian Oil Corporation
46. India Trade Promotion Organisation
47. ITI Ltd.
48. India Infrastructure Finance Co. Ltd.
49. India Tourism Development Corporation
50. Indian Drugs & Pharmaceuticals Ltd.
51. Indian Railway Catering and Tourism Corporation
52. Indian Rare Earths Ltd.
53. Indian Telephone Industries
54. Indian Vaccine Corporation Ltd.
55. Instrumentation Ltd.
56. Jute Corporation of India Ltd.

57. Khadi and Village Industries Commission, Gramodaya, 3, Iria Road, Ville Parle (West), Mumbai – 400 056.
58. Konkan Railway Corporation Ltd.
59. Life Insurance Corporation of India
60. Minerals & Metals Trading Corporation
61. Mazagon Dock Limited
62. Metro Railway Kolkata
63. National Fertilisers Ltd.
64. National Hydro Power Corporation
65. National Highway Authority of India
66. National Film Development Corporation
67. National Textile Corporation
68. Oil & Natural Gas Corporation
69. Pawan Hans Helicoptres Ltd.
70. Power Grid Corporation
71. Rashtriya Chemicals & Fertilizer
72. Rural Electrification Corporation
73. South Eastern Coalfields Ltd.
74. Sponge Iron India Ltd.
75. State Trading Corporation of India Ltd.
76. Steel Authority of India Ltd.
77. Shipping Corporation of India
78. Telecommunications Consultants (India) Ltd.
79. Triveni Structurals Ltd.
80. Tungabhadra Steel Products Ltd.
81. United India Insurance Company
82. Uranium Corporation of India
83. Western Coalfields Ltd.

Similar State Government and Union Territories have a number of PSUs under them.

Government Offices

The Ministry or department to which it belongs. Statutory laws, rules and regulations relating to it. The public function that it performs. Its organization. System of complaints and grievances redressal. Court cases relating to its functioning audit and accounting mechanism.

Some of the Government Departments (Central Governments) are listed below.

1. Airports
2. Agriculture
3. Central Bureau of Investigation

4. Chemicals and Fertilizers
5. Child & Women Development
6. Culture
7. Civil Aviation
8. Communications
9. Coal
10. Commerce and Industry
11. Corporate Affairs
12. Culture
13. Development of North Eastern Region
14. External Affairs
15. Earth Sciences
16. Food Processing Industries
17. Health and Family Welfare
18. Human Resources Development
19. Home Department
20. Housing and Urban Poverty Alleviation
21. Khadi and Village Industries Commission, Gramodaya, 3, Iria Road, Ville Parle (West), Mumbai – 400 056.
22. Labour and Employment
23. Law & Justice
24. Mines
25. Minority Affairs
26. Micro, Small and Medium Enterprises Steel
27. New and Renewable Energy
28. Overseas India Affairs
29. Parliament Affairs
30. Personnel, Public Grievances and Pensions
31. Petroleum and Natural
32. Railways
33. Reserve Bank
34. Road Transport and Highways
35. Rural Development
36. Science and Technology
37. Shipping and Transport
38. Social Justice and Empowerment
39. Textiles

40. Tourism
41. Tribal Development

Government Departments (State Governments)

1. Administrative Forms
2. Agriculture
3. Animal Husbandry
4. Backward Classes Welfare
5. Cane Development
6. Civil Aviation
7. Community Development
8. Co-operative
9. Education
10. Energy
11. Environment
12. Excise
13. Factories
14. Fisheries
15. Forests
16. Flood Control
17. General Administration
18. Home
19. Home Guards
20. Housing
21. Industrial Development
22. Infrastructure and Investment
23. Irrigation
24. Industries
25. Law & Justice
26. Lift Irrigation
27. Local Self-Government
28. Medical and Health
29. Minor Irrigation
30. Minorities Welfare
31. Panchayati Raj
32. Planning
33. Police
34. Primary Education
35. Prisons
36. Public Works Department
37. Roads
38. Revenue
39. Secondary Education
40. Sericulture

41. Social Welfare Department
42. State Water Resources Agency, Lucknow
43. State Society for Ultra Poor & Social Welfare, Bihar
44. Technical Education
45. Tourism
46. Tubewells
47. Town Planning
48. Vigilance
49. Youth Advancement

Judicial Offices and Law Offices

Example of judicial or law offices could be District Government Standing Counsel, Advocate General, Legal Remembrancer and Law Secretaries of the States. Additional Solicitor General, Solicitor General of India, Attorney General for India, etc. Internees should observe the layout and organization of their offices, and organization of their offices, briefing and drafting process, settlement of briefs, arguments and intervention in courts, conferences and maintenance of dockets etc.

Human Rights Commission

The student must study the Protection of Human Rights Act and go through the composition, role and function of the Human Rights Commission. What are the officers and staff available. What is the procedure to lodge a complaint? What type of cases are usually lodged and entertained? How are the cases registered? The procedure followed for investigation of cases. Time taken to investigate. What is the follow-up action and the reports of the Commission? Are there any suggestions or scope to make its functioning more effective. Included in this category would be Delhi Commission for Women, C-Block, Vikas Bhawan, I.P. Estate, New Delhi – 110 002.

Industry

The nature and type of industry, the statutory, tax and procedure laws governing it. The legal division of such a corporate enterprise. Organisation of the management and employees Regulations applicable to wage structure, leave, maternity leave, provident fund and workmen's compensation, safety norms, worker's participation in management and unions, if any. Type of product or service provided by the industry, consumer relations and satisfaction, corporate social responsibility, litigation if any, its nature and pendency, case law, if any concerning the industry, rules relating to export and imports where applicable. Shareholders, Annual General Meetings, environmental aspects, where applicable.

Bank

The major function of the particular office or branch. The applicable law relating to the type of banking carried out, rules and regulations in regard thereto the clients and beneficiaries. Nature and type of complaints and disputes the procedure for their settlement. Appeals against their decisions. Statutory and procedural laws in relation to advances and loans. Recovery procedures. Schemes for weaker and marginalized sections.

Embassy

The laws and rules concerning diplomatic privileges and immunity; the bilateral and regional legal instruments, the procedures concerning issue of visa, extradition. Rules and procedures for bi-lateral trades and commerce.

Hospital

The rules and procedures relating to medico-legal cases, donation and retrieval of organs, issue of birth certificates, record of birth and death, sex determination, rules concerning Medical Council of India, treatment and admission of weaker sections of the society, disputes in the nature of consumer grievances.

Think Tanks

A think tank is an organization that conducts research and engages in advocacy in areas such as social policy, political strategy, economics, national or global security concerns and in the creative or cultural spheres. A few examples of think tanks active in India are given below.

1.	Indian Institute of Dalit Studies, D-II/1, Road No. 4, Andrews Ganj, New Delhi – 110 049. Tel : 011-26252082 E-mail : asmita@dalitstudies.org.in
2.	United Service Institution of India, Rao Tula Ram Marg, Opposite Signals Enclave, PO Vasant Vihar, New Delhi – 110 057 Tel : 011-26148682 E-mail : director@usiofindia.org
3.	Centre for Land Warfare Studies, RPSO Complex, Parade Road, Delhi Cantt – 110 010 Tel : 011-25691308 E-mail : landwarfare@gmail.com
4.	Institute for Defence Studies and Analysis, 1, Development Enclave (near USI), Rao Tula Ram Marg, Delhi – 110 010 Tel : 011-26717983 E-mail : idsa@vsnl.com
5.	Control Arms Foundation of India, B-5/146, First Floor, Safdarjung Enclave, New Delhi – 110 029

Tel : 011-46018541
E-mail : contact@cafi-online.org
Web : www.cafi-online.org

6. National Maritime Foundation,
Varuna Complex,
Airport Road, NH-8,
New Delhi – 110 010
Tel : 011-26156520
E-mail : Nmf@maritimeindia.org

7. Delhi Policy Group,
Core 5A, First Floor,
India Habitat Centre,
Lodhi Road,
New Delhi – 110 003
Tel : 011-24649571
E-mail : office@delhipolicygroup.com

8. Centre For Security Analysis,
9B, Ninth Floor,
Chesney Nilgiri, Chesney Lane,
71, Ethiraj Salai, Egmore,
Chennai – 600 008
Tel : 044-65291889
E-mail : office@csa-chennai.org

9. Centre For Civil Society,
A-69, Hauz Khas,
New Delhi – 110 016
Web : www.ccs.in

10. Institute of Economic Growth,
University Enclave,
University of Delhi (North Campus),
Delhi – 110 007
E-mail : system@iegindia.org

11. Observer Research Foundation,
20, Rouse Avenue Institutional Area,
New Delhi – 110 002
Tel : 011-43520020
E-mail : contactus@orfonline.org

12. Transparency International,
Qr. No. 4, Lajpat Bhawan, Lajpat Nagar-IV,
New Delhi – 110 024, Tel : 011-26460826

13. Delhi Commission for Protection of Child Rights,
5th Floor, ISBT Building,
Kashmere Gate,
Delhi – 110 006.

14.	Animal Welfare Board of India, 13/1, Third Seaward Road, Valmiki Nagar, Thiruvanmiyur, Chennai – 600 041.
15.	Vivekananda International Foundation, 3, San Martin Marg, Chanakya Puri, New Delhi – 110 021.
16.	Indian Council on Global Relations, Cecil Court, 3rd Floor, Next to Regal Cinema, Colaba, Mumbai – 400 005.
17.	Lawyers Collective, 63/2, First Floor, Masjid Road, Bhogal Jangpura, New Delhi – 110 014.
18.	Centre for Policy Research, Dharam Marg, Chanakya Puri, New Delhi – 110 021.
19.	Institute for Peace and Conflict Studies, B-7/3, Lower Ground Floor, Safdarjung Enclave, New Delhi – 110 029.
20.	South Asia Analysis Group, P.O. Box 175, Noida – 201 301. E-mail : saag17@yahoomail.com south@southasiaanalysis.org
21.	National Foundation for India, India Habitat Centre, Core 4A, Upper Ground Floor, Lodi Road, New Delhi – 110 003.
22.	Centre for Asian Strategic Studies, Strature Group, A-86, Second Floor, Malviya Nagar, New Delhi – 110 017. E-mail : director@cassindia.com

23.	Institute of Asian Studies, Sholinganallur, Chennai – 600 019 E-mail : ias@xlweb.com Tel : 044-24502212
24.	National Institute of Open Schooling, A-24/25, Institutional Area, Sector-62, Noida – 201 309.

List of Institutions

1. Cyber Appellate Tribunal
2. Indian Council for Child Welfare
3. Indian Council of Forestry Research & Education, Dehradun
4. Indian Council of Social Sciences Research
5. Indian Institute of Public Administration
6. India Islamic Centre, Lodhi Road, New Delhi
7. Industrial Development Bank of India
8. Indian Statistical Institute, 203 B.T. Road, Kolkata – 700 018
9. National Commission for Women
10. National Human Rights Commission
11. Prasar Bharti Board
12. Press Council of India
13. Uttarakhand Environment Protection & Pollution Control Board, Dehradun

District Court

All matters relating to civil and criminal nature, organization and set up, filing of cases, registry, cause list, framing of issues, copies of orders and judgments, appeals, applications for bail, court fee. This would also include internships with Labour Courts, Family Courts or CBI Courts etc.

Tribunals

The statutory law and procedures laid down. Composition, functions and powers of the tribunal. Type of pending cases. Mode of filing cases, forms and documents provided for – presentation of cases and arguments – orders and decisions – Appeals and revision process. System for circulation and dissemination of orders.

Media

The issues concerning registration and circulation, Press Council of India, Wage Board, defamation, intellectual property rights, secrecy and privacy matters, sting operations, paid news.

Law Publishing

The provisions relating to registration, Press Council of India, if applicable, defamation, intellectual property right aspects, copyright, royalty agreements.

Regulating Authority

The object and purpose, its jurisdiction, rules and procedure, statutory provisions, if any, system for redressal of grievances, powers to impose penalty or punishment, scope for appeal, right to seek information. Such authorities include National Disaster Management Authority, Telecom Regulatory Authority of India, Trade Fair Authority of India, Indian Council of Medical Research, New Okhla Industrial Development Authority, Lucknow Development Authority, Delhi Development Authority etc. Punjab Urban Planning and Development Authority.

National Authority

Jurisdiction, statutory provisions, rules, regulations and notifications, jurisdiction, organization, distribution of work, supervision and monitoring, power to impose penalty and punishment, appeals, etc. Examples of such authority would include Film Censor Board, Press Council of India, Insurance Regulatory and Development Authority, Port Trust Authorities, Airports Authority of India, Sports Authority of India etc.

High Court/Supreme Court

The internship could be with the judges, registry or with practicing advocates.

Supreme Court

The internship could be with the judge, registry, a practicing advocate or with advocate on record.

Legal Branches of Military or Para Military

Induction, grant of Commission, summary trial, statutory and non-statutory complaints, administrative action, courts martial, pay and allowances, induction of women, Armed Forces (Special Powers) Act, queries under the Right to Information Act.

List of some of the offices are shown below.

1.	Armed Forces Tribunal, Principal Bench, West Block VIII, Opp. Mohan Singh Market, Sector-1, R.K. Puram, New Delhi – 110 066. E-mail : aftdelhi@yahoo.in
2.	Judge Advocate General, Army HQ, Sena Bhawan, DHQ PO New Delhi – 110 011.
3.	Judge Advocate General, Air HQ, Vayu Bhawan, New Delhi – 110 011

4. Chief Law Officer,
Coast Guard HQ,
National Stadium Complex,
India Gate,
New Delhi – 110 011.
E-mail : pro@indiancoastguard.nic.in

Post-Graduate Law Teaching Institutions

The internship could be with a faculty or with the library. It would be useful to be associated with a research scholar with a view to acquire knowledge about research methodology.

Political Party

The constitution, agenda and the manifesto of the party. Its position with regard to law reforms and particular legislations it is a desirous of amending. The new laws it is committed to frame. The frame work of election of its office bearers. Its stand on electoral reforms. Organisation and role of its legal cell election symbol, funding and political alliance.

Trade Union

The particular industries or segments it represents. System of its membership and election of office bearers. The main demands and legal feasibility of their implementation. Trade Unions Act, 1926. The Industrial Disputes Act, 1947.

Child Labour

Documentation

Filling of following forms:

1. Vakalatnama
2. Application for deposit of rent
3. Acknowledgement of application in Form A under Right to Information Act
4. Address Form
5. Application for adjournment of a case in High Court
6. Form No. 45 (Sections 437, 437, 438 and 441 of Cr. P.C.)
7. Affidavit
8. Particulars and documents to be given on bail application
9. From CAI (rule)
10. Certified copy form
11. Application for issue of certified copy from Sub-Registrar
12. Treasury Challan
13. Supply of copy registered number from the Sub-Registrar
14. Application for inspection of documents (Central Administrative Tribunal)
15. From No. 22 under rule 117 of CAT Principal Bench
16. Application for execution of degree/order

17. Check list under section 138, Negotiable Instruments Act
18. Form of complaint to be lodged with Banking ombudsman
19. Application on behalf of the complainant for inspection of judicial file
20. Application for copies of documents
21. Form A under rule 5 of Delhi Stamp (Prevention of Undervaluation of Instrument) Rules, 2007
22. Application for Talaash Muaayana Aam
23. Application for grant of certified copy from Debt Recovery Tribunal
24. Application for inspection of documents records in DRT
25. Application for inspection of court record
26. Application for issue of entry pass (Supreme Court)
27. Acceptance of decision of Beema Lokpal
28. Acceptance of decision of confirmation for settlement of dispute
29. Application for Registration of marriage under section 8 of HMA, 1955
30. Registration under section 13 or 16 of Special Marriage Act
31. Application for inspection of file in High Court
32. List of documents under Order XIII, rule of CPC
33. Memorandum of Appearance
34. Notice of Motion
35. Process Fee Form
36. Summons to an accused person in a summon's case
37. Order sheet for civil appeals (Order 41, rule 1, CPC) in High Court
38. Opening sheet appeals in courts subordinate to High Court
39. Opening sheet for criminal revision under section 394/401, Cr .P.C.
40. Writ Petition (Payment of Fees Form)
41. Index (High Court)
42. Listing Proforma (High Court)
43. Application for office/certified copy of proceedings/signed order/stay in High Court
44. Application for issue of visitor's pass
45. Stamp Paper
46. Affidavit

DIARY OF THE INTERNSHIP

The rules framed by the Bar Council of India in the matters of legal education lay down internship in the courts, which is mandatory for the law students as part of the Clinical Legal Education. The students are expected to maintain a diary or register to chronicle their daily record. However, these are in guidelines or explanatory notes to educate the students in this regard.

1. The students should maintain diary regularly. It is a truthful narration in the handwriting of the student.

2. The primary objective is to keep a formal and progressive record of the daily output of the internee.
3. Where a student has been asked to research a topic, the entry should describe in brief the issue (subject-matter or question) of research and also the research material used (*e.g.*, SCC, AIR, SCC online, or a book containing commentary etc.). To illustrate, the entry could read:

Example 1

Researched whether lawyer of a party to the dispute can be appointed as an Arbitrator. Searched in SCC online and AIR ....SC ....(give citation)

Example 2

Researched on cause of action in the case of a cheque dishonoured. Searched in SCC and AIR (give citation).

4. If a student has attended the court, then the diary must show name of the court, court number and name of parties etc. If a hearing or cross-examination, etc., took place in the court, then its short gist must be written down. If it was merely an adjournment or pass over that was encountered, then this should also be recorded.

Example 3

Went to Delhi High Court in Court No. ....and .... kept a watch for coming up of following case(s):

(Name of party) v. (Name of party), Serial No. ....of cause list.

Example 4

Attended arguments or cross-examination in the matter of.................v. ....in Court No. ....of Karkardooma Court.

Example 5

Attended Consumer Forum, Saket. The matter of ....v. ....did not come up as the Judge was not present.

5. Similarly, if a student has gone for inspection of a file, then the diary must show the name of court, court official, case citation, and what was specifically to be checked/perused in the case file.

Example 6

Went to JR No. ....in Delhi High Court. Submitted an application. Examined the case file in case No. WP ....of 20 ....in the matter of ....v. ....

6. In the case of a client interview, a brief record of the name of the party, facts of the case and legal remedies anticipated may be written down.

Example 7

Attended the briefing of a case involving matrimonial dispute and custody of a minor daughter. The senior advised that a legal notice be first served.

7. Where the student was assigned the task to draft a legal document or to proof read or carry out due diligence, then the specific nature of document that was dealt with should be recorded. Further mistake, if any, pointed out by the senior or lessons learnt by the student must also be indicated.

Example 8

Was asked to draft a notice in the case of a cheque dishonoured by the supplier, or was asked to do the due diligence on an application.

8. Even if a very simple work has been assigned to the student this may be clearly indicated in the diary.

Example 9

Was asked to keep a watch when the matter relating to ....at Serial No. ....in Cause List of Court No. ....in Patiala High Court reaches its term.

INTERNSHIP REPORT

The record furnished by the student at the end of the internship should describe the period of internship, the name of the lawyer, law firm or judge etc. It should mention what were the timings and place of work. Similarly describe if the law office had a number of associates then under whom was the student assigned to work. What was the general nature of duties that were assigned and carried out by the student. What is the impression of the student about the lessons learnt or the benefit that accrued to the student must be shown in the reports.

Apart from the above, each student is also expected to obtain from the lawyer or the law firm concerned, etc., a report indicating his performance during the period of internship.

Viva Voce Questions

While the range of internship for law students is quite exhaustive giving wide option to them, the training with the courts at various stages is undoubtedly the most crucial. It is only in the courts the students get adequate exposure to litigation and in law as it is practiced.

It is therefore, desirable that the students are subjected to a *viva voce* test at the end of their internship phase. The test may be conducted by the faculty assisted by one or more legal practitioners. The students may be called upon to answer simple questions to check their familiarity with basic terms relating to law practice and procedures. A few illustrative questions together with their answers are given below.

While these questions have been framed in the setting of law schools based in Delhi, these could be suitably moderated for other locations as well.

To illustrate, sample of a few actual reports issued by senior advocates, eminent government offices, well-known corporate entities, leading law firms, law publishers and NGOs are compiled in this book.

Sample 1

NEERAJ KUMAR JAIN

SENIOR ADVOCATE

31-2-2009

To whomsoever it may concern

This is to certify that Mr., student of Vth year, in the Amity Law School Noida, Amity University remained attached with me as a trainee from 1st January, 2009 to 31st January,

2010. During the training period he regularly attended my office. He also accompanied me to Hon'ble Supreme Court of India and Hon'ble Delhi High Court. He prepared brief notes in the cases which came up before the Hon'ble Courts and also helped me in research relating to case law.

I have watched him very closely during the training period. He is a courteous and well-behaved student. He has been a hard working and sincere trainee. He has shown exemplary zeal to pursue the case allotted to him and take out relevant case laws on the issues involved therein. I have no doubt that he would make an excellent lawyer. I wish him the very best in life.

(Neeraj Kumar Jain)

Sample 2

HARVINDER SINGH PHOOLKA
SENIOR ADVOCATE

1-2-2011

To whomsoever it may concern

This is to certify that Mr. , known to me for the last two years, has interned in my Chambers from the 3rd to the 31st of January, 2011. He has assisted me in a large number of cases involving Constitutional Law, Commercial Law, Property Law, Law of Arbitration, etc., and in particular Human Rights. His contribution in the Save the Children's Foundation Cases, pertaining to Child Labour and Bonded Labour, has been of the highest quality.

He has not only displayed a deep insight into litigation practice and the law but also backed it up by tremendous amount of hard work. His research assignments and case notes in matters assigned to him have been very impressive. In matters which required an in-depth study of records and examination of facts, I was pleasantly surprised by his intellectual outputs and analysis of the issues involved. He has all the qualities which are necessary for a very able and competent lawyer.

Through his briefings and a perusal of his case notes, I can also say that he possesses a strong command over the English language, both written and oral.

Though he had joined my Chambers as an intern, he has contributed in no manner less than a Junior and in a short period of time had become a valuable part of my office. I have no hesitation in recommending him both for academic and professional purpose, as I am certain that he would be an asset to any organization he chooses to join.

I wish him all success in his future endeavours.

H.S. Phoolka
Senior Advocate

Sample 3

GOVERNMENT OF INDIA
PLANNING COMMISSION
YOJANA BHAWAN
NEW DELHI – 110 001

31st January, 2011

To whomsoever it may concern

This is to certify that Mr. , a student of the fifth year, B.A. LL.B. (Hons.), Amity Law School, Amity University, Noida has successfully completed his Internship Programme in the Secretariat for Infrastructure, Planning Commission of India for a period of one month between 3rd January, 2011 and 31st January, 2011. During the period of his internship, he was attached with the officers of the Secretariat for Infrastructure and was introduced to the mandates and activities of the Planning Commission of India. His tasks and responsibilities, inter alia, *included.*

- *Being part of the process of formulation of Schedules for the Model Concession Agreement for setting up schools through Public Private Partnership. After undertaking research into secondary education with special focus on the conditions and goals in India, he formulated the Key Performance Indicators for the Scheme and also suggested the minimum requirements that should be expected from the private players.*
- *Research work for developing Schedules for the Model Concession Agreement in the domain of Public Private Partnership in education by studying the roles that a school should fulfil, education systems of other countries, education of India, Performance Indicators in other sectors, etc.*
- *Studying the Scheme and Guidelines for formulation, appraisal and approval of Public Private Partnership Projects and the Model Concession Agreements for Public Private Partnership in Highways, Ports and Urban Rail Systems.*
- *Attending meetings, discussions and round table conferences on the need for Private Participation in the Distribution of Electricity. Open Access in the Distribution of Electricity, etc.*

He was diligent and sincere in his work. He was found to be a keen learner with an inquisitive mind.

I wish him success in all his future ventures.

(Namita Mehrotra)

Sample 4

COMPETITION COMMISSION OF INDIA

To whomsoever it may concern

This is to certify that Ms. , a student of Vth year B.A. LL.B. (Hons.) from Amity University, Noida has successfully undergone a one month internship training under my guidance during 3-1-2011 to 2-2-2011. Her topic of research was ***"Cartel Sanction against individuals, a comparative study with anti-trust law USA".***

I wish her every success in life.

(P.K. Singh)
Director (Law)

Sample 5

AIRTEL

To whomsoever it may concern

This is to certify that Ms. of Amity Law School, Noida has successfully completed her training and worked on ***"Net Neutrality and Legal Regulatory Scenario"*** *project.*

She worked at Bharti Airtel Ltd., Gurgaon from 3rd January, 2011 to 31st January, 2011 under the guidance of Ms. ....

She was sincere, hard working and honest during her training. We would like to appreciate her quality of work and the result orientation she displayed.

We wish her all the best for future endeavours.

Authorised Signatory

Bharti Airtel Ltd.

Sample 6

TATA TELESERVICES LIMITED, NOIDA

31st March, 2011

To whomsoever it may concern

*This is to certify that Mr. student of Amity Law School, Amity University has successfully completed the "Training" under the guidance of Mr. ...."**Legal & Secretarial & Corporate Regulatory Affairs**".*

A detailed evaluation of his work during his tenure with us i.e., *from March 1, 2011 till 31st March, 2011 shows his performance to be* **Excellent.**

We wish him success and luck in all his career endeavours.

For Tata Teleservices Limited

Arun Soorma

Manager – Human Resources

Sample 7

TRIVENI ENGINEERING & INDUSTRIES LTD.

March 29, 2011

To whomsoever it may concern

This is to certify that Ms. ...., student of Fifth Year, B.A. LL.B. (Hons.) of Amity Law School, Noida has worked with the Company at their Corporate Office at Noida as an Intern for a period of three months i.e., *from 15-12-2010 up till 17-3-2011 (both days inclusive) excluding holidays.*

During her Internship, she was involved in various legal matters such as Arbitration, Civil Laws, Criminal Law, Property Law and assisted the undersigned in legal matters handled at the Corporate Office.

She possesses excellent communication skills and is articulate with her thoughts and analysis. These qualities will definitely make her stand in good stead in her legal profession.

It was a pleasure having her here with us. I wish her all the best for the future.

For Triveni Engineering & Industries Ltd.

Lalit Sachdeva

General Manager (Legal)

Sample 8

KARANJAWALA & COMPANY ADVOCATE

28 February, 2011

To whomsoever it may concern

This is to certify that Mr. ...., 5th year B.A. LL.B. (Hons.) student of Amity Law School, Amity University, Noida has interned with my firm for a period from 1st February, 2011 to 28th February, 2011. During this period, he has assisted the juniors in the best possible way and learnt the skills of drafting generally used in a Lawyer's office and further handled legal matters under their guidance. His attitude towards work showed an inclination to accomplish the same without any hesitation and it is a general impression in my office that he can accomplish successfully whatever work that is assigned to him. I wish him all success in his career.

(R.N. Karanjawala)

Sample 9

AZB & PARTNERS
ADVOCATES & SOLICITORS

May 10, 2011

To whomsoever it may concern

This is to certify that Mr. , Vth Year, B.A. LL.B. (Hons.) student of Amity Law School, Noida has successfully completed the internship with our firm during the period January 3, 2010 to March 31, 2011.

During this period, he was exposed to diverse legal matters and worked in various areas involving corporate and commercial laws.

A brief description of the work that he has been involved in during the course of his internship is given below.

- *Assisted in a due diligence of a company proposing an 'Initial Public Offering' which involved the following:*
    - *i. Assisted in the drafting of certain sections of the Draft Red Herring Prospectus; and*
    - *ii. Conducting due diligence on approvals, loan and corporate filings for the same*
- *Assisted in a due diligence of a company proposing a "Qualified Institutional Placement' which involved the following:*
    - *i. Assisted in the preparing the summaries of the board minutes, outstanding litigations, insurance and trademark documents of the company and its subsidiaries; and*
    - *ii. Assisted in drafting of certain sections of the Preliminary Placement Document.*
- *Researched and prepared a note on joint and several liability and enforceability of specific performance in a contract.*

During the course of his internship, we found him to be sincere, disciplined and diligent. We wish him all the best for a bright and successful future.

Raman Sharma
Senior Partner
AZB & Partners

Sample 10

AMARCHAND MANGALDAS

March 7, 2011

To whomsoever it may concern

The Director,

Amity Law School,

Noida.

Dear Sir,

Mr. ...., 5th year B.A. LL.B. (Hons.) student from Amity Law School, Noida has interned with us at our Delhi Office, India from January 10, 2011 to January 21, 2011. He has assisted us in the following areas:—

- *Conducted research and prepared notes on various topics*
- *Researched on case laws and prepared summaries*
- *Proof read documents*
- *Submitted a research paper on the topic 'Practice by Party In-Person'*

During his training period, he worked under the overall guidance of Mr. Manu Nair, Partner.

Yours Sincerely,

For Amarchand & Mangaldas & Suresh A. Shroff & Co.

(Shardul S. Shroff)

Managing Partner

Sample 11

FOX MANDAL & CO.
Solicitors & Advocates

March 31, 2011

To whomsoever it may concern

This is to certify that Ms. ...., a student of 5th Year, Amity Law School, Noida has worked with **Fox Mandal Little, Noida** *as an intern for a period of one month from 1st March, 2011 to 31st March, 2011.*

During her internship, she was involved in various legal matters and did extensive research on issues related to Contract Act and whether private schools can be used as Corporate office of a private company. She has also researched upon custom duty on certain goods, limit of FDI investment by NBFCs, latest developments on the Ancient Monument and Archaeological Sites and Remains Act, 1958, case relating to setting aside of arbitral award in lieu of public policy and FDI in LLPs and she drafted various legal replies and notices.

She has also prepared research notes on jurisdiction of Indian courts in case of online shopping, Registration procedure for a new establishment under Labour and Industrial laws, concept of defaulter in relation to Telecommunication (Broadcasting and Cable Services) Interconnection Regulation, 2004, Section 27 of the Contract Act, down-linking of TV channels, sports laws and its implications on IPR and functioning of Law firms as LLPs.

She also made a presentation on "Comparative Advertisement and Trademarks" in the firm's weekly meeting, which was widely appreciated.

She possesses excellent communication skills and is articulate with her thoughts and analysis. These qualities will definitely make her stand in good stead in her legal profession. It was a pleasure having her herewith us. I wish her all the best for the future.

For **Fox Mandal & Co.**
(Swati Sinha)
Partner

Sample 12

TRILEGAL

28 February, 2011

To whomsoever it may concern

This is to certify that Ms. ...., student of Fifth year, B.A. LLB. (Hons.), Amity Law School, Noida has worked as an intern at Trilegal, New Delhi from 3 January, 2011 to 28 February, 2011.

During the period of internship, she carried out work/research on the following:—

- *Research relating to 'Anti-Dumping' as to what is the basis for calculating 25% domestic production as per rule 2(b) of Customs Tariff (Identification, Assessment and Collection of Anti-Dumping Duty on Dumped Articles and for Determination of Inquiry) Rules, 1995 and made a note on who is an Interested Shareholder.*
- *Research relating to the scope of operation of section 34 of the Arbitration and Conciliation Act, 1996 and found case laws on the same.*
- *Made a note on Right of Way under the Easements Act, 1882 and did a research relating to Civil Procedure under the IT Act, 2000 with special emphasis to sections 43 and 58 respectively.*
- *Research relating to whether the government can simply breach a Common Contract by saying that it has the right to do so under its eminent domain?*
- *Research relating to whether a party can sue another party to a contract for doing something which is not provided for in the contract but is not illegal under 'Production Sharing Contracts'.*
- *Research relating to Solar Payment Security Fund, case law research on section 73AB of Bombay Land Revenue Code, 1879 and research relating to the list of Oil Blocks that have been approved by the Government of India under Rig Moratorium Policy.*

- *Case law research relating to 'Arbitration clauses in Shareholder's Agreement' and 'Operational Mismanagement in the Companies Act, 1956' with reference to sections 397 and 398 of Companies Act, 1956.*
- *Research relating Stamp Duty by way of Deposit of Title Deeds in (Mortgage) and the Stamp duty payable in Maharashtra, New Delhi, Andhra Pradesh and Chhattisgarh.*
- *Research relating to incorporation procedure of a 'Small Company' under the Companies Bill, 2009.*
- *Case law research relating to 'Dishonest Abstraction of Electricity' and 'Theft of Electricity' and the requirement for issuing notice within the prescribed time frame.*

She has also prepared a research project on 'Introduction of GST in India'.

She carried out all tasks assigned to her in a diligent and conscientious manner.

We wish her the very best in her future endeavours.

Counsel

Sample 13

KHAITAN JAYAKAR SUD & VOHRA (K.J.S.V.)

To whomsoever it may concern

This is to certify that Ms. ...., a student of 5th year B.A. LL.B. (Hons.) of Amity Law School, AUUP has worked as an intern with our firm from 3rd March to 3rd April, 2011.

During her association with our firm, we found her very hardworking, sincere and devoted to the profession. She was very cordial in her behaviour with colleagues and staff members. Within this period, she has gained extensive work exposure from research work relating to Civil & Corporate litigation along with Corporate Department which involved extensive research, drafting and preparation of legal opinions.

She made significant contribution as a team member of the firm. We found her to be extremely diligent, painstaking and innovative with high degree of inherent legal and cognitive skills envisaging her early success as a legal professional.

We wish her success in her future ventures and assignments. We are sure that she will succeed in her career.

For *KHAITAN JAYAKAR SUD & VOHRA*

(Umesh Khaitan)

Partner

Sample 14

LINK LEGAL

ADVOCATES

April 19, 2011

To whomsoever it may concern

This is to certify that Mr. , a final year law student, studying at Amity Law School, Noida affiliated to Amity University, Noida has undergone internship at Link Legal from 10th January, 2011 to 13th April, 2011.

During the internship, he was involved in research, drafting, and assistance in forming legal opinions. He demonstrated proficiency in various areas of the law and conducted research on matters relating to various topics including Concession Agreements, Nuclear Liability Bill, Inland Container Depots, Duty Drawback, SEZs in India, Different Voting Rights in India, Mergers, Refund of Terminal Excise Duty. He also assisted lawyers of the firm in research in various aspects of the Code of Civil Procedure, Delhi Co-operative Societies Act, Consumer Protection Act, Arbitration and Conciliation Act, Limitation Act, Negotiable Instrument Act and the Indian Contract Act. He undertook substantive research on various aspects of the Industrial Disputes Act, Competition Act, Indian Evidence Act, SEBI Act and Rules and the Takeover Code and Regulations. He also assisted in a due diligence work conducted by our firm, which involved regular client visits and interaction with officials of our client company.

He has actively participated in various corporate team and litigation team assignments in relation to various cases of our firm listed before the Supreme Court of India, High Court of Delhi, the National Consumer Redressal Commission, District Courts and the Debit Recovery Tribunal in Delhi.

He has shown proactiveness in carrying out all tasks assigned to him. He is extremely attentive, hard working, bright and displays a sense of commitment to his work. He is of a pleasant deposition and exhibits the utmost promise requires out of a young lawyer.

We feel that he possesses an incisive mind which, complemented by his personal capabilities and personality will enable him to achieve success in the legal profession.

We wish him the very best for a most successful career.

Milanka Chaudhry

Partner

Sample 15

PRIMA CARTA
Law Offices

April 5, 2011

To whomsoever it may concern

This is to certify that Mr. , fifth year student at Amity Law School, Noida did his internship at my firm from February 1, 2011 to April 4, 2011.

During his internship he was involved in a variety of matters. He researched on various subjects such as Code of Civil Procedure, Indian Contract Act, Negotiable Instrument Act, Transfer of Property Act and Arbitration & Constitution.

He attended arbitration proceedings, and court proceedings at the Delhi High Court.

I found Mr. to be a very sincere and dedicated worker and he has the necessary talent to develop into a fine young lawyer. I wish him all the best in all his future endeavours.

(Arun Kumar Varma)

Advocate

Sample 16

THOMSON REUTERS

6 April, 2011

To whomsoever it may concern

Ms. has interned directly under me on a special project of significant strategic importance to the dissemination of legal knowledge in India.

I had tasked her with analyzing how our editorial products can be used by the millions of solo practitioners in India. She undertook this project over the period December 18 to March 31 in Delhi, Hyderabad and Aligarh.

In executing this assignment, she drew up different questionnaires for various advocates, judges and clerks. After this, she did the fieldwork and interviewed 217 current and potential users of legal information (in print or CD or online form). She then tabulated her findings, prepared detailed debriefs and presented them to our editorial and content development teams, and explained her logic and methodology in a very clear and cogent manner. After formulating hypotheses on how each of our relevant products could be used and/or needed to be modified. She shared these hypotheses, defended them and convinced the entire team.

She worked with deep passion. She is gifted in the law and loves it. She has very strong conceptual skills, tremendous energy and has a naturally methodical and organized mind. She is able to quickly arrive at the core of any problem and then she pursues the solution till she finds it.

Her integrity is unimpeachable. She will never do something convenient and easy, if it wrong. She will never take a short-cut, if it means leaving difficult but important work undone.

She is an exceptionally rare individual. Her presence will make any team successful.

(Devashish Sarkar)

Country Manager India

Sample 17

CENTRE FOR SOCIAL RESEARCH

8 March, 2011

To whomsoever it may concern

Mr. spent eleven days between January 3, 2011 and January 19, 2011 working on his thesis at the Gender Training Institute in the Centre for Social Research. During this time he learned about the work conducted in GTI and began to research his thesis.

Centre for Social Research is a non profit voluntary development organization based in New Delhi working for the empowerment of women, gender equality, elimination of violence against women and improving living conditions of the underprivileged section of society, especially adolescent girls and women. Currently our focus is on violence against women, gender justice, political empowerment of women and economic empowerment of rural women. Our activities include research, training, development and capacity building initiatives, advocacy, lobbying and networking.

We wish him all the success in his career and life.

(Dr. Ranjana Kumari)
Director
Centre for Social Research

PERFORMANCE APPRAISAL

The internees are expected to submit their own reports at the end of internship. The main purpose of seeking these reports is to make the students carry out a self-appraisal exercise to estimate their gain from such a practical exposure. The report in a concise and factual manner must reveal what were the benefits.

A few examples of the reports furnished by the students after conclusion of their internships are reproduced below.

Example No. 1

I did internship/training at three places for a period of three months.

1. *Competition Commission of India (CCI).*
2. *Amarchand & Mangaldas & Suresh A. Shroff & Co.*
3. *High Court of Delhi.*

The experience of working in all three reputed places was outstanding. I had an excellent exposure of the legal background and position of the legal system in India. I got an opportunity to face and experience the theoretical knowledge which we have studied in books into real practical world.

1. Internship under Competition Commission of India (CCI):

I had interned for a period of one month starting from January 3, 2011 – February 03, 2011 under the guidance of Mr. Pramod Kumar Singh, Director (Law). The exposure which I received under this commission was outstanding. I got an opportunity to study and learn in detail the various provisions of the Competition Act, 2002, the relevant case laws, judgments under the Act and also about the institution – Competition Commission of India (CCI) framed under it.

I saw in practical life the making and passing of the various sections and provisions of the Act, the effort and cooperation made in deciding and establishing the relevant provisions of an Act.

I also experienced field work which was undertaken by the Commission, I was a part of the enquiry and investigation process of the "Onion Cartel case" so got an excellent opportunity to attend it.

Also prepared a Report and Presentation on – 'Cartels-sanction against individuals – A comparative study with Anti Trust Law of USA.'

2. Internship under – Amarchand & Mangaldas & Suresh A. Shroff & Co.

I had interned from February 21, 2011 – March 18, 2011 under the overall guidance of Mr. Ciccu Mukhupadhya, Partner. The exposure of working in a Law Firm is of great significance and importance. The knowledge and experience which I gained by working over there helped me a lot in improving and shaping in my legal knowledge. I learned to prepare summaries/brief of case laws – how main points and facts are condensed and put forth in a brief manner.

Conducted research on various subjects like Arbitration, Company Law, and IPR etc. I learned how to make notes on the matter researched. Also submitted a Research paper on 'Development and Practice of Arbitration in India – Has it evolved as an effective legal institution.'

3. Internship under H.M.J.G.P. Mittal at the High Court of New Delhi.

I had interned under the guidance from February 7, 2011 – February 18, 2011 and March 19, 2011 – April 2, 2011.

Internship at High Court under the guidance of a Reputed Judge was an amazing experience. I got an opportunity to attend and hear the hearings of various cases. How counsels present their facts, defend their clients and the statements of Prosecution Witnesses (PW'S). I got an opportunity to study and go through the various Case Files, Compilations, and Lower Court Records (LCR's).

I learned how to make case briefs, notes of various cases such as writing down:—

- *Facts.*
- *Points contended in favour of Appellant.*
- *Points contended against the Appellant.*
- *Grounds of Bail.*
- *Judgment.*
- *Appeal.*

Thus my overall experience during the entire internship period has been very knowledgeable and enlightening. Internship in all three areas has helped me to understand and gain a lot of information which was much needed for improving my legal knowledge and exposure.

Example No. 2

The advocates (Ms. Mala Narayan and Rahul Narayan) practice in the High Court of Delhi and District Courts of Delhi. They deal with civil matters relating to property, marriage, Hindu laws, arbitration and corporate matters. I interned with for the month of January and February 2011. I was assigned various cases for research and perusal. I had a very learning experience with them. It was an opportunity to understand the practical aspects of the profession and application of law.

The learning at the office was diverse as I could gain knowledge about Civil Procedure in the courts, Family Laws, Arbitration and Corporate matters. I was also taken to courts many times to observe the court proceedings. The best part was that I was taken to arbitration proceedings as well. The Arbitration proceeding was relating to dispute relating to non-payment of dues by one party and the other claiming that they were not entitled to pay the same. The Arbitration proceeding was very interesting as a non legal person (the arbitrator) was analyzing the dispute and deciding on the same.

I also got the opportunity of reading the case files and meeting the clients. The interaction with the clients and understanding the client's needs and problems are one of the vital features of the practicing lawyers. I also learned that a lawyer is not only a counsel for the client but also has to function as a friend, guide, mentor, psychologist and counselor to the client. The clients break down into tears at times and they have to be consoled and motivated by the lawyer, especially in divorce cases.

I was also provided with the opportunity to draft various legal documents. I got the opportunity to learn the drafting of plant, written statements and written arguments. I was also assigned to draft legal notices and conveyances such as agreement and will. Though, I made mistakes in drafting but the drafts were liked by the advocates and they also made it a point that I learn them properly.

I also observed that the opponent lawyers highly respected each other. They also ensured professional conduct during the proceedings and in cases of divorce, the advocates ensured by all means that both the parties could reconcile.

I was treated with a lot of affection and care. The advocates are very competent in their profession and I learned a lot from their dedication and hard work. The most important lesson learnt from them is that a lawyer has to be a good human being before being a lawyer. They are very compassionate towards their client and work hard to ensure justice into the clients. They are an example of treating the law profession as a noble profession.

Example No. 3

As part of my five year requirement for the degree of B.A. LL.B. (Hons.) at Amity University, Noida, I have successfully completed my ninety days requirement of internship at High Court of Judicature at Allahabad, Lucknow Bench under Hon'ble Mr. Justice from January 10, 2011 to April 18, 2011.

During my stint with Mr. ...., I observed court proceedings and assisted the court by preparing notes on various questions of law in the cases dealt with at the court. These issues inter alia *include those relating to inconsistency in the exercise of statutory power exercised under equally valid existing laws by Centre and State; right of a grandson as coparcener in self-acquired property of grandfather; classification of the statutory power of creation, alteration or abolition of boundaries or jurisdiction of a district by the executive or legislative; necessity for the court to record a finding of title before granting temporary injunction.*

Since my attachment with the Hon'ble Senior Judge, I got an opportunity to do research in matters concerning Constitutional Law, Company Law, Corporate Governance, Service Writs, Environmental Law and Public Interest Litigations.

The details of work experience acquired during the aforesaid period of my internship at the High Court under the Hon'ble Senior Judge are as follows:—

1. *I prepared a concept note on Tenth Schedule to the Constitution.*
2. *I did research on the question as to whether relaxation of marks in appointment to public service in the matter of SC/STs could be sought as a matter of right.*
3. *I did research on the legality of town planning projects.*
4. *I worked on the issue if a writ petition is maintainable at the instance of an unregistered trade union of employees and the* locus *of such employees union.*
5. *Whether writ of* quo warranto *lies to challenge an appointment made until further orders on the ground that it is a not regular appointment?*
6. *I prepared a note on the role of Public Interest Litigation in the upliftment of the rural class.*
7. *I did research on the right of grandson as coparcener in self-acquired property of grandfather.*

8. *I did research on Centre-State relations.*
9. *I tried to explore the boundaries of Conditional and delegated Legislation.*
10. *I explored the issue of necessity of the court to record a finding on a title before granting temporary injunction.*
11. *I prepared brief in service writs.*
12. *I explored the scope of power of SEBI to regulate securities transactions of unlisted companies, as a matter of investor protection.*
13. *I did research on the meaning of marketable security and the test of marketability.*

I feel that the practical experience of the real life situations of the Court proceedings and legal work and my interaction with the court, lawyers and the litigants would immensely help me in facing the challenges of legal profession when I complete my degree and step out of the University to start my career in law.

Example No. 4

I hereby want to share my internship experience during my final semester of my law school.

I have done my internship in Calcutta, more specifically the first two months I completed my internship with Dr. . During this internship I was required to attend the chambers of Dr. and take notes on the daily clients who came with issues. I was also required to do intensive research on the issues that were given to me such as company matters, partition matters and tenancy matters.

During the internship which lasted from 5th January, 2011 to 28th February, 2011, I acquired skills in drafting affidavits, verifications and notices. I was asked to do minimal work and I do not believe I have contributed a lot to his practice, however, I have learnt a great deal about the pace of legal work and proceedings during my internship under Dr.

My second internship was with Victor Moses & Co., also situated in Kolkata. I enjoyed working for this firm more than the previous internship because there was more work and the seniors expected more work from us. We were not just treated as interns but as part of the firm. I was required to report in office at 10.00 every week day and leave by 18.30. I stayed till about 20.00 every day because I never liked to keep the work pending till the next day. This is how I received the nick name 'Workholic'.

I was asked to visit court proceedings mostly during the mornings and then report the same to my seniors later when we met. I was asked to do extensive research in company matters which included research on sections 397 and 398 of the Companies Act, 1956. I was also required to make list of dates for various cases such as the Victoria Jute Mill case and Biman Behari Sen case. I also worked on the Worldgate matter which is in the process of being drafted. I was also required to attend arbitration proceedings and take notes on them.

During both my internships, which were a mandate for the completion of my degree, I have learnt that what we have been taught in academia during the past five years in law school has minimal importance in the practical world of law. By this I mean that what we have learnt formed a basis for our actions in the practical world because we had the legal knowledge, but after the internship, I have learnt how to implement this legal knowledge acquired over the five years of law school.

I hope to have made contributions to the organizations I have worked with in, as they have helped me grown in a professional way. I believe that this internship has groomed me for the practical legal world. To understand the matter in which the courts and the legal system functions is crucial to any legal professional and that is that what I believe, I have learnt these past three months while interning.

Example No. 5

The experience of interning at a Government office was pretty enriching and altogether very different from the experience I have had at Corporate Law Firms or even at individual lawyers from 3rd January, 2011 to 31st January, 2011.

I was lucky enough to get an opportunity to attend meetings which was chaired by the Deputy Chairman of Planning Commission of India – Mr. , the experience of listening to the ideas and thoughts of some of the most talented brains of our country was absolutely great. I was attached under the Secretariat of Infrastructure and their basic work was to prepare agreements for Public Private Partnership Projects. When I joined work, I thought that the attitude of the seniors would be very indifferent and non-courteous, but all my presumptions turned wrong when I actually interacted with each one of them. They were very humble, understanding and polite and listened and answered to all my queries very patiently.

Though the timings were from 10.00 AM to 5.00 PM, but there were officers who even used to work till 8.30 PM. The whole experience of getting to interact with the top officials, understand and observe the working at the Planning Commission from the inside helped me change my perspective towards Government organizations as well as towards people who are working there.

I felt quite confident with myself when I was given the task of preparing the Schedules to the proposed PPP project for opening of Schools in India. It not only helped me to understand the way such important agreements are drafted but also expanded my knowledge relating to the Education sector in India a lot. I was able to complete the Schedules within time allotted to me with the help of my seniors as they were very co-operative, there were certain instances when to meet the senior I had to visit their room five to six times as they were very busy all the times. But when I finished the internship I realized that the amount of exposure I got interning at Planning Commission and the knowledge I gained was actually worth all the efforts I put in while interning there.

Example No. 6

I interned at C&C Associates, Karanjawala & Co. and A.B. Dial & Associates during the ninety days internship period.

During my internship at C&C Associates starting from 23rd December, 2010 to 23rd January, 2011, I was asked to research on various aspects of Corporate Law and Arbitration. Research on Arbitration gave me exposure to some international laws dealing in Arbitration. Research on Companies Act also helped me gain some additional knowledge on the topic. Overall the research was so extensive that I developed various researching skills.

Apart from research work I was asked to read and brief up case files. Briefing up helped me gain a hand on various applications filed in civil suits. It also brushed up my reading and briefing skills.

My second internship was at Karanjawala & Co. from 24th January, 2011 to 28th February, 2011, where I mostly researched on case laws on Indlaw, SCC, Westlaw etc., with a little bit research on provisions of IPC, Cr P.C. and Negotiable Instrument Act. During the case law research I learnt that methods of researching on case law websites which I was not exposed to before.

I was also given an opportunity to visit Supreme Court of India and attend proceedings in the Court of law from where by observing I learnt how arguments are made in court of law.

In all my experience at such a prestigious firm was great which helped me learn a lot.

My last internship was at A.B. Dial & Associates from 3rd March, 2011 to 31st March, 2011. On the first day itself I was sent to various district courts for inspection of documents. This was new to me as I had never visited the lower court.

I mainly visited Debt Recovery Tribunal and Debt Recovery Appellate Tribunal, where I heard and observed proceedings through which I learnt the process of proceedings in matters of debt recovery.

I was also asked to read and brief up files and explain the same to my senior. I also prepared rough cross-examination questions.

I attended and observed various proceeding in Hon'ble High Court and Joint Registrar, High Court.

The overall activity taught me one's conduct in court of law.

The internship made me grow as a professional and exposed me to various jobs of a law firm.

I also realized that there is a huge difference between academic knowledge and the practicality of it.

In all, my internship helped me grow as a person.

INTERNSHIP IN COURTS

Viva Voce Questions

While the range of internship for law students is quite exhaustive giving wide option to them, the training with the courts at various stages is undoubtedly the most crucial. It is only in the courts the students get adequate exposure to litigation and in law as it is practiced.

It is therefore, desirable that the students are subjected to a *viva voce* test at the end of their internship phase. The test may be conducted by the faculty assisted by one or more legal practitioners. The students may be called upon to answer simple questions to check their familiarity with basic terms relating to law practice and procedures. A few illustrative questions together with their answers are given below.

While these questions have been framed in the setting of law schools based in Delhi, these could be suitably moderated for other locations as well.

1. What is MACT and what is its role?

   MACT stands for Motor Accident Claims Tribunal. These have been provided to specifically deal with matters relating to claims for compensation to the victim of motor accidents.

2. What is difference between CAT and AFT?

   CAT stands for Central Administrative Tribunal. These are specially *quasi*-judicial bodies established to adjudicate matters relating to service division of Central Government employees. On the other hand, AFT stands for Armed Forces Tribunal which are meant to provide an opportunity for appeal to those aggrieved for the orders of court martial and also to settle disputes relating to service condition of the men in uniform and in some cases ex-service-men or NOK.

3. Name any five district courts in Delhi?

   Tis Hazari, Patiala House, Saket, Karkardooma and Rohini, etc.

4. What is meant by juvenile court?

   Juvenile Courts are the courts established to deal with juvenile offende. They derive their authority from Juvenile Justice Act and Probation of Offenders Act.

5. What are the judges called in Armed Forces Tribunal?

   There are two categories of judges in the Armed Forces Tribunal which are called judicial members and administrative members.

6. State the names of any three tribunals.

   Examples of various types of tribunals would include Central Administrative Tribunal, Armed Forces Tribunal, Debt Recovery Tribunal, Motor Accidents Claims Tribunal, Sales Tax Tribunal, Land Acquisition Tribunal and so on.

7. What type of courts deal with cases like divorce, etc.?

   Matters in the nature of matrimony, divorce and adoption, etc., are dealt by Family Courts.

8. What is a large bench in the context of Supreme Court?

   A large bench in the context of Supreme Court would be one consisting of three or more number of judges.

9. What is a vacation judge?

   A vacation judge refers to a judge sitting during vacation of the High Court or Supreme Court for the hearing of such applications as may require to be immediately or promptly heard.

10. What is the difference between a WP and LPA?

    A writ petition is a petition filed before the High Court or the Supreme Court relating to a denial of a fundamental rights. On the other hand LPA (Letter Patent Appeal) are the appeals filed in the High Court against the decision by way of appeal against decision of single Bench.

11. What is the difference between the scope of Articles 32 and 226 of the Constitution?

    Article 32 relates to a fundamental right provided to move to Supreme Court in the situations of denial of a fundamental right as provided for in Part III of the situation. On the other hand, Article 226 is a remedy to invoke a jurisdiction of the High Court for denial of fundamental right or constitutional right.

12. State the difference between a suit for possession and a suit for succession?

    A suit for possession would relate to an action initiated praying for possession of a property. On the other hand, a suit for succession would be applicable to claim the Right to Succeed under the laws of inheritance.

13. What is a rent notice?

    A rent notice is a demand initiated by or on behalf of landlord for the monetary amount due.

14. What is an eviction petition?

    An eviction petition is a legal process initiated with a view to evict a tenant or other person, who is in custody or possession of a property.

15. What is a curative petition?

    A curative petition is a legal process provided for in the Supreme Court to seek a final redressal in the matter with party stands decided by the Supreme Court.

16. What is a counter-claim?

    A counter-claim is a legal process set in motion based on claim or demand initiated by the opposition party?

17. What is a caveat?

    Caveat is a formal notice or caution given by the party interested to a court or judge against the performance of certain Judicial Act to stop the court or judge concerned from eviction or entertaining or guaranteeing in relief without the knowledge of the party that files a Caveat.

18. What is meant by clubbing of cases?

    Clubbing of cases refers to bunching of matters based on individual or similar facts where remedies prayed for also similar.

19. What is understood by mediation?

    Mediation is a process under the category of alternative disputes resolution by way of trying to reach a settlement between the parties by using conciliation.

20. What is meant by pleading?

    These are formal statements by which the parties bring forward the material facts, which constitute their respective claims and defences.

21. State any forms of pleadings.

    Plaint, written statement and replication.

22. What is a plaint?

    A plaint is a statement in writing, detailing with the facts constituting cause of action, on the basis of which a person (plaintiff) comes to court and claims the relief.

23. What is meant by question of fact?

    It is an issue of fact in which the truth or falsity (or a mix of the two) is to be determined by the court in order to reach decision in the case.

24. What is a question of law?

    An issue arising in a matter which only relates to determination of what is the law, how it is applied to the facts in the case, and other purely legal points in contention.

25. Differentiate between 'questions of fact' and 'question of law'?

    Question of fact is one where rival contentions as to fact are being considered by the court to determine which is a fact or not a fact.

    A question of law is actually in two parts (1) an interpretation of law and (2) application of law to the fact as found. Sometimes there is an element of discretion with the court as regards the extent to which question of law can extend. It is best to look at in the form (1) and (2) law and (3) application of law, the second and third being the questions of law.

26. What is a leading question?

    It is a question asked by an advocate during a trial that suggests the answer.

27. What is a suit for partition?

    A law suit filed by one of the co-owners of an immovable property to get a court order requiring the division of the property between the co-owners.

28. What is suit for specific performance?

    A legal action set in motion to enforce the right of a party to a contract to demand that the defendant (the party) who is claimed to have breached the contract be ordered in the judgment to perform the contract.

29. What is a notary public? What are his functions?

    A notary public or notary is a public officer constituted by law to serve the public in non-contentions matters like deeds, powers of attorney apart from administering oaths and affirmations, take affidavits and statutory declarations and authenticate execution of certain type of documents.

30. What is a written statement?

    It is the defendant's answer in response to what has been averred by the plaintiff in the plaint.

31. What is a denial?

    It is a traverse of the facts alleged in the pleading of the adverse party.

32. What is a replication?

    It is a pleading by the plaintiff in the shape of further answer to the written statement and pleas of defence.

33. What is meant by procedure?

    It is the mode by which successive steps are taken in litigation for enforcing a legal right.

34. What is a Deed?

    It is a written instrument signed and delivered by which one individual conveys title to real property to another individual.

35. What is meant by eviction proceedings?

    Legal action initiated for the act of expelling someone from a immovable property.

36. What is meant by substantive law?

    It is the law which creates, declares and regulates the rights and duties of the parties.

37. What is meant by interrogatories?

    These are a series of questions which procedural rules allow one party to administer to the other and compel the other to answer on oath before the case is taken up for framing of issues.

38. State the difference between a 'decree' and 'order'?

    A decree means formal expression of an adjudication which, so far as the Court expressing it, conclusively determines the rights of the parties with regard to all or any of the matters in controversy in the suit. It may be either preliminary or final. An order on the other hand, means the formal expression of any decision of a court which is not a decree. Thus an order need not conclusively determine the rights of parties on any matter in dispute.

39. What are custody orders?

    The orders relating to care, control, guardianship and maintenance of a child, usually awarded to one of the parents in a divorce or separation proceedings.

40. What is meant by pagation?

    It is the arrangement and number of pages in a book.

41. Who is a defendant?

    The party sued in a civil law suit. In some type of cases (such as divorce) a defendant may be called a respondent. Plaintiffs sue defendants in civil suits in trial courts. The government prosecutes defendants in criminal cases in trial courts.

42. What is informed consent?

    An agreement to do something or allow something to be done only after all the relevant facts are known.

43. What is meant by Necessary Party?

    A person who ought to have been joined as a party and in whose absence no effective decree could be passed at all by the Court.

44. What is a Proper Party?

    A proper party is a party, who though not a necessary party, is a party whose presence would enable the court to completely, effectively and adequately adjudicate upon all matters in dispute in the suit, though he need not be a person in favour of or against whom the decree is to be made.

45. What is Parole?

It is early release of a prisoner who is then subject to continued monitoring as well as compliance with certain terms and conditions for a specified period.

46. What is a complainant?

A person who begins a lawsuit by filing a complaint and is usually called the plaintiff or petitioner.

47. What is claim?

In civil cases it refers to statement of relief desired.

48. What is counter-claim?

It is a retaliatory claim by a defendant against a plaintiff in a lawsuit included in the defendant's reply and with a view to off set or reduce the plaintiff's original claim against the defendant.

49. What is a recovery suit?

It is a legal action initiated for restoration of a former right, to recover a thing or right.

50. What is a transfer petition?

A process initiated with a view to get a matter transferred from one court to another.

51. Point out major parts of a writ petition.

(a) Short synopsis and

(b) List of dates (maximum three pages)

(c) Memo of parties

(d) Notice of motion

(e) Main body of writ

(i) Cause title

(ii) Main text

(iii) Ground

(iv) Prayer

(v) Interlocutory orders

(f) Affidavit

(g) Annexures

(h) Application for stay

52. What is understood by service?

The official delivery of legal documents such as summons, complaint or order to show cause, etc.

53. What is the purpose of 'list of dates'?

To give a sequential and chronological narration of relevant facts to facilitate easy understanding.

54. What is a 'memo of parties'?

It is a sequential list of parties to a dispute.

55. What is meant by *ad valorem* fees?

    Fee charged which is determined on value

56. What is a paper book?

    A book or paper containing an abstract of all the facts and pleading necessary to the full understanding of a case.

57. Explain an interim order?

    A temporary order of the court pending a hearing, trial, a final order, or while awaiting an act by one of the parties.

58. What is NDA (Non Disclosure Agreement)?

    It is a legal contract between at least two parties that outlines confidential material, knowledge or information that the parties wish to share with one another for certain purposes but wish to restrict access to by third parties. It is also known as confidentiality agreement or confidentiality disclosure agreement.

59. What is RFP (Request For Proposal)?

    It is issued at an early stage in a procurement process where an invitation is presented for suppliers, often through a bidding process, to submit a proposal on a specific commodity or service.

60. What is meant by due diligence?

    It is a term used for a number of concepts involving either an investigation of business or person prior to signing a contract, or an act with standard of care.

61. What is MSA (Master Service Agreement)?

    A document that specifies generic terms such as payment terms, product warranties, intellectual property ownership, dispute resolution and the like.

62. What is a Necessary Party?

    A person or entity whose interests will be affected by the outcome of a litigation, whose absence as a party in a suit prevents a judgment on all issues.

63. What is a restoration application?

    The process to get a matter restored on the file of the court when it has been dismissed for default.

64. Differentiate between 'dismissed' and 'withdrawn'.

    Dismissed is on merit whereas withdrawal is no adjudication of the matter.

65. What is meant by 'dasti'?

    Process of service by hand and otherwise than the normal formal manner.

66. Differentiate between adjournment and pass over?

    In adjournment the matter is posted for a next date whereas in pass over it is taken up again the same day.

67. What is a file inspection?
To inspect the court records for various purposes to check pagination or whether the file is complete.
68. What is meant by a judge recusing himself from a case?
When he refuses to hear a particular case for any reason.
69. Explain the term 'issue notice.'
Where the respondent/defendant in a processing is given formal notice to answer any pending matter before that court.
70. What is the difference between the term 'plaintiff' and 'appellant'?
Plaintiff is the initiator in original proceedings, usually a suit, whereas an appellant prefers an appeal against the order of an original court. An appellant is also described as one who files a formal appeal seeking appellate review as a matter of right.
71. Who is a deponent?
A person who swears on affidavit.
72. What is the difference between an Advocate and a Senior Advocate?
A senior Advocate is one who has been designated as such by a High Court or the Supreme Court by virtue of experience, standing at the Bar and possesses particular knowledge in a branch of law.
73. What is *amicus curiae*?
A friend of the court for the purpose of assisting the court in a particular matter.
74. What is a *vakalatnama*?
A power of attorney given to an advocate by a client to appear act, plead and represent him in a court of law.
75. What is meant by Re-notify?
When a matter is posted to next date.
76. What is a 'watch only' case?
Where you are only to watch the proceedings without actually participating in the matter.
77. What are the different stages in the examination of a witness?
These are examination-in-chief, cross-examination and re-examination.
78. What is a hostile witness?
A witness at a trial whose evidence is found by the court to be adverse to the party who has called him.
79. What is meant by an expert witness?
One who by virtue of education, training, skill or experience is believed to have expertise and specialized knowledge in a particular subject, beyond an average person.
80. Name a few journals of reported cases?
(a) All India Reporter.
(b) Criminal Law Journal.
(c) Service Law Reporter.
(d) Judgment Today.

(e) Supreme Court Cases.

(f) Income Tax Reporter.

81. Name any two online search engines of reported cases?

    (a) SCC online.

    (b) Manupatra.

82. Bring out the difference between AIR and SCC Online.

    AIR is a journal of reported cases of the Supreme Court and High Courts whereas SCC online carries electronically the cases reported by the Supreme Court and few High Courts.

83. What is meant by citation of a case?

    Citation is the way a particular case is reported in a law journal or the manner in which a particular case can be located in a journal.

84. What is meant by persuasive value of a ruling?

    Where it is not binding but only meant to persuade a judge to follow a particular line of reasoning.

85. What is a seizure memo?

    A document that lists out material and items, often their state or condition recovered or seized from a place.

86. What is meant by a confidentiality clause?

    A clause in an agreement where the parties decide that a certain or entire portion of the subject-matter of an agreement would remain confidential to third parties.

87. What is a cause list?

    A cause list is the list which is published by a court in advance and list the matters that are to be taken up by the court on that particular date.

88. What is meant by an Advance List, Supplementary List, Regular List, Weekly List?

    Advance list means a list which is issued over one week or so in advance and lists those matters which are likely to appear in the regular list. Weekly list is also a kind of an advance list in which matters appear and from which the matters for a daily list are selected.

    Supplementary list is a list which is prepared usually in the late evening on the previous day (or on a few occasions in the morning to show the matters) which are going to be taken up on the next day and which are not included in the earlier list. Regular list is also called a daily list.

89. What are the various types of listings under the cause list?

    It depends on the type of the court but usually in subordinate courts it is miscellaneous matters or regular matters or evidence matters or hearing matters. In criminal side it can be bail matters or appearance matters or evidence matters and arguments matters.

90. What is a Miscellaneous Matter?

Miscellaneous matter is that which will aid in some step of the legal proceedings. It could be simply an issue of notice, or service of notice, or filing of some papers or replies, or doing some other task. It does not require any long hearing. Often it could well be a ministerial work.

91. Bring out the difference between an Order and a Judgment?

Any order, even one adjourning, is an order, except an order summoning or an order fixing a date or any expression by the court of what is to be done, is an order. A judgment is one which decides the rights and obligations of parties or has some important effect in the proceedings. The same is called a judgment and not simply an order.

92. What is the implication of 'Judgment being reserved'?

It means the court has heard the arguments and has reserved the judgment which it will consider and then pronounce on some date in the future. The implication is that the hearing is complete and the judgment is awaited. Maximum period permissible now to issue the judgment is 60 days.

93. What is meant by a Party in Person?

Party in person means a party representing himself and not through a lawyer. It can also refer where the court desires that along with a lawyer the party also appears.

94. What is a dissolution deed?

Whenever there is a partnership that is dissolved the written document dissolving a partnership under Chapter VI of the Indian Partnership Act, 1932 is called a dissolution deed.

95. What is an Office Report?

Office 'report' is prepared by the clerk (called ahlmad) after scruitinising the filings and the other service of processes gives a report as to what was expected to be done, what has been done and what are the likely short coming or missing part for the next hearing. The report on whether service has been effected or not, and papers have been filed or not are the more popular prevalent parts of office report.

96. What is meant by Replication?

Replication is a pleading which a plaintiff answers in reply to the differences raised in the written statement. The first in sequence is the plaint, the second is a written statement and third is a replication. It is not in every case that a replication has to be filed.

97. What is a delay report?

Delay report is a report made usually by some senior person in the office as to why there has been delay in handling of the matter and explanations about the delay.

98. Who is an Oath Commissioner?

Oath Commissioner is a person appointed under the Oath Act, 1969 to administer oath to parties for purposes of affidavits.

When should an Affidavit be affirmed on the basis of personal knowledge as distinguished from being affirmed on the basis of record?

If the person has personal knowledge he swears to the facts or the absence of facts in an affidavit. Where he has no personal knowledge but is referring to record or after having examined the record is making the affidavit it is called affirmed on the basis of record.

99. What is a Bail Bond?

This is a bond by which a person ties himself down to appear to be present in court on the date of hearing or on being summoned in the court usually on certain conditions which are laid down by the court before he is released on bail after arrest or a possible arrest. Form is given in number 45 in Schedule 2 of the Cr. P.C. with regard to section 437/436 Cr. P.C.

100. What is a suit for injunction?

A suit for injunction is a type of a suit (all suits are filed under section 9 CPC) where the relief prayed as a perpetual relief is an injunction requiring somebody to do or restrain from doing something. Injunctions are of various types and most of which are covered by the Specific Relief Act. Order 39 of the CPC refers to temporary injunctions. Interim injunctions, only till the pendency of the suit must be distinguished from perpetual injunctions.

101. What is meant by a tendering of witness?

It is the process when a party is not inclined to examine a witness to give evidence but is prepared to offer him to be cross-examined by the opposite party.

102. Differentiate between a suspect, accused, undertrial and convict?

A suspect is a person who is suspected of an offence by the police in the course of investigation *i.e.*, after registering an FIR and before submitting their final report [section 173(a)] to the court. It can also be loosely referred to somebody upon whom a suspicion was raised.

Accused refers to the person against whom some evidence of having committed a crime has been unearthed or is in the process of being charge sheeted or has been charged with the offence.

Undertrial actually refers in common parlance to a person who has been facing trial in a criminal case. He can be either in judicial custody or on a bail, denied bail and is in judicial custody to prevent him from fleeing or is unable to submit a bail.

A convict is a person who has been found guilty of an offence upon a judgment under section 264 in summary trial and section 353 of the Indian Penal Code in other trials. The sentencing process is subsequent.

103. What is the difference between the ratio of a judgment and *obiter dicta*?

The ratio of a judgment is that which the court has considered and laid down as a rule of law and principle of law and it is that alone which forms part of the doctrine of precedent. *Obiter dicta* are those observations in a judgment which have not been considered at any length. These could be even a passing reference and have no value as a precedent.

104. What is a letters patent appeal?

All the High Courts have (accept perhaps the newly formed ones) have a letters patent which were issued in the early part of the last century or even earlier and provide intra-court appeal from a single judge of the court to a division bench of that court.

105. Elaborate the abbreviations.

(a) BCI - Bar Council of India
(b) CAT - Central Administrative Tribunal
(c) CIC - Chief Information Commissioner
(d) DRT - Debt Recovery Tribunal
(e) FAO - First Appeal against Order
(f) HMA - Hindu Maintenance Act
(g) ITAT - Income Tax Appellate Tribunal
(h) LPA - Letters Patent Appeal
(i) MACT - Motor Accidents Claim Tribunal
(j) MLC - Medico Legal Case
(k) NCDRC - National Consumer Dispute Redressal Commission
(l) NDOH - Next date of hearing
(m) NHRC - National Human Rights Commission
(n) SLP - Special Leave Petition

Legal Latin Phrases

Meaning of a few common latin phrases

Ab initio	–	From the beginning
Ad hoc	–	For this purpose
Ad valorem	–	According to value
Alibi	–	At another place, elsewhere
Ante	–	Before
Amicus Curiae	–	Friend of the court
Audi alteram partem	–	Hear the other side
Bona fide	–	Sincere, in good faith
Caveat	–	May he beware
Certiorari	–	To be more fully informed
Contra	–	To the contrary
Corpus	–	Body
Corpus delicti	–	Body of the crime
De facto	–	In fact
De jure	–	Rightful, by right

De novo	–	Starting afresh
Dictum	–	Proverb
Ejusdem generis	–	Of the same class
Erratum	–	Having been made in error
Et cetera	–	Other things of that type
Ex facie	–	On the fact of it
Ex gratia	–	Out of kindness, voluntary
Ex officio	–	From the office
Ex parte	–	Proceedings brought by one person in the absence of another
Ex post facto	–	By reason of a subsequent act
Factum	–	An act or deed
Fiat	–	Let it be done
Gravamen	–	Things weighing down
Habeas corpus	–	May you have the body
Ibid	–	In the same place
Id est	–	That is
Idem	–	The same person or thing
In absentia	–	In absence
In camera	–	In private
In curia	–	In court
In extenso	–	At full length
In limine	–	At the outset, on the threshold
In pari materia	–	In the same matter
In personam	–	In full
In re	–	In the matter (of)
In situ	–	In its place in total
Inter alia	–	Amongst other things
Inter se	–	Amongst themselves
Interim	–	Temporary, in the meanwhile
Intra vires	–	Within the powers
Ipso facto	–	By that very fact
Jus	–	A right that is recognized in law
Lacunae	–	Void, gap
Locus standi	–	A place for standing
Mala fide	–	In bad faith
Mandamus	–	We command
Mens rea	–	Guilty state of mind

Modus operandi	–	Manner of operation
Mutatis mutandis	–	Having been changed that which needed to be changed
Nexus	–	Connection
Nisi	–	Unless
Non Sequitur	–	An inconsistent statement, it does not follow
Pari passu	–	On an equal footing
Pendent lite	–	While the litigation is pending
Per contra	–	By that against
Per curiam	–	In the opinion of the court
Per se	–	By itself
Persona non grata	–	Unwelcome person
Post mortem	–	After death
Prima facie	–	On the face of it
Pro forma	–	As a matter of form
Pro rata	–	In proportion
Qua	–	Which
Quantum	–	How much, an amount
Quasi	–	As if
Quid pro quo	–	Consideration, something for something
Quo warranto	–	By what warrant
Re	–	In the matter of
Res gestae	–	Things done
Res integra	–	A matter untouched (by decision)
Res judicata	–	A matter judged
Res nullis	–	Nobody's property
Respondeat superior	–	Let the principal answer
Seriatim	–	In series
Sine die	–	Adjournment without a day
Sine qua non	–	Without which nothing
Stare decisis	–	To stand by decision (precedent)
Status quo	–	Current or existing state of affairs
Sub judice	–	Under judgment
Sui generis	–	Unique, of its own kind
Suo moto	–	Of its own motion
Supra	–	Above

Ultra vires	–	Beyond the power
Terra firma	–	Solid ground
Verbatim	–	Word by word, exactly
Veto	–	I forbid
Vice Versa	–	The other way around

COMMON TERMS IN REFERENCE TO CASES DECIDED BY SUPREME COURT

1.	Applied	–	law applied on facts
2.	Followed	–	law applied on law
3.	Relied on	–	deduce new principal from the case relied on
4.	Approved	–	Apex court approving the law laid down by the High Court
5.	Referred	–	only passing reference
6.	Explained	–	case explained in detail
7.	Considered	–	discussed but treatment not clear
8.	Distinguished	–	not applicable either on facts or on law
9.	Explained & distinguished	–	explained in detail not applicable either on facts or on law
10.	Dissented	–	equal Bench disagreement
11.	Doubted	–	equal Bench disagreement
12.	Overruled	–	Supreme Court against Supreme Court or Privy Council or High Court
13.	Impliedly overruled	–	by implication not clearly stated
14.	Reversed	–	lower court case under appeal overruled or disapproved
15.	Held overruled	–	observation on matter not in issue *Obiter dictum*
16.	*Per in curiam*	–	in ignorance of law statute law or case law
17.	*Per curiam*	–	per court per whole court where many opinions or per majority essence of what is laid down by majority or all the judges

Reproduced before are a number of forms commonly used in courts of law, tribunals and authorities for various routine matters. These would help the students during their internship period to familiarize themselves with procedural aspects of law practice. The wide range of purposes for which these forms are used would be advantageous to the students to get accustomed to the procedural norms.

INTRODUCTION TO A FEW FORMS COMMONLY USED

The students are advised to seek help of practicing advocates under whom they intern to understand the purpose of these forms and the manner to make their use.

VAKALATNAMA

IN THE COURT OF *Chief Metropolitan Magistrate, New Delhi*

Suit/Appeal No. *123/2013* JURISDICTION of 200

In re:—

Ravi Mahajan Petitioner

Versus

O.P. Malhotra Accused

KNOW ALL to whom these present shall come that I *Ravi Mahajan, S/o Late Mr. Rakesh Mahajan*

The above named *Petitioner/Accused* do hereby appoint

(herein after called the advocate(s) to be my/our Advocate in the above noted case authorize him:—

To act, appear and plead in the above noted case in this court or in any other Court in which the same may be tried or heard and also in the appellate court including High Court subject to payment of fees separately for each court by me/us.

To sign file, verify and present pleadings, appeals, cross-objections or petitions for executions/review, revision, withdrawal, compromise or other petitions or affidavits or other documents as may be deemed necessary or proper for the prosecution of the said case in all its stages subjects to payment of fees for each stage.

To file and take back documents, to admit and/or deny the documents of opposite party.

To withdraw or compromise the said case or submit to arbitration any differences or disputes that may arise touching or in any manner relating to the said case.

To take execution proceedings.

To deposit, draw and receive money, cheques, cash and grant receipts hereof and to do all other acts and things which may be necessary to be done for the progress and in the course of the prosecution of the said case.

To appoint and instruct any other Legal Practitioner authorizing him to exercise the power and authority hereby conferred upon the Advocate whenever he may think fit to do so and to sign the power of attorney on our behalf.

And I/We the undersigned do hereby agree to ratify and confirm all acts done by the Advocate or his substitute in the matter as my/our own acts, as if done by me/us to all intents and purpose.

And I/We undertake that I/We or my/our duly authorized agent would appear in court on all hearings and will inform the Advocate for appearance when the case is called.

And I/We undersigned do hereby agree not to hold the advocate or his substitute responsible for the result of the said case. The adjournment costs whenever ordered by the court shall be of the Advocate which he shall receive and retain for himself.

And I/We undersigned do hereby agree that in the event of the whole or part of the fee agreed by me/us to be paid to the advocate remaining unpaid he shall be entitled to withdraw from the prosecution of the said case until the same is paid up. The fee settled is only for the above case and above Court. I/We hereby agree that once the fee is paid, I/We will not be entitled for the refund of the same in any case whatsoever and if the case prolongs for more than 3 years the original fee shall be paid again by me/us.

IN WITNESS WHEREOF I/We do hereunto set my/our hand to these presents the contents of which have been understood by me/us on this 4th day of February, 2013.

Accepted subject to the terms of the fees

Advocate *Client* *Client*

Smart Ali *Ravi Mahajan*

Acknowledgement of Application in Form A

DD No. .... *Dated :*

....

1. *Received an application in Form A from Shri Ravi Mahajan resident of 24 Tarlok Puri, Delhi under section 5(1) of the Delhi Right to Information Act, 2001.*
2. *The information is proposed to be given normally within 15 days and in any case within 30 days from the date of receipt of application and in case it is found that the information asked for cannot be supplied, the rejection letter shall be issued stating reason thereof.*
3. *The applicant is advised to contact the undersigned on.................between 11 AM to 1 PM.*
4. *In case the applicant fails to turn upon the schedule date(s), the Competent Authority shall not be responsible for delay, if any.*
5. *That applicant shall have to deposit the balance fee, if any, with the authorized person before collection of information.*
6. *The applicant may also consult website of the department from time-to-time to ascertain the status of his application.*

Signature and stamp of the Competent Authority

E-mail address :............................

Website :..

Tel. No. :.......................................

IN THE COURT OF *Addl. Civil Judge* DELHI

Suit No. 94/2013

Ravi Mahajan .... Petitioner

Versus

S.K. Mehra .... Respondent

N.D.O.H. ___________

APPLICATION FOR DEPOSIT OF RENT

MOST RESPECTFULLY SHOWETH :

Petitioner may kindly be allowed to deposit the rent in the court.

Name of the Depositor	:	*Ravi Mahajan*
Name of person entitled for withdrawal	:	*S.K. Mehra*
Period	:	*March, 2013*
Amount	:	*1800*
Under section	:	

Delhi :

Date : *February, 2013*

Ravi Mahajan
Applicant/Tenant

NEGOTIABLE INSTRUMENTS ACT, 1881

CHECK LIST UNDER SECTION 138

POLICE STATION *Tilak Marg* — *INDEX WITH PAGING*

DISTRICT *New Delhi* — *FILE COVER*

1. *Name and Address of complainant*	*Smt. Raveena Ghai* *23/98, Bengali Market* *New Delhi*
2. *Name & Address of Accused (s)*	*United Tyre Store* *Karol Bagh Lane No. 422* *Delhi*
3. *Name of the Police Station*	*Tilak Marg New Delhi*
4. *Total cheque amount*	*Rs. 29,500*
5. *Details regarding any other cases under section 138 N.I. Act pending against same accused(s)*	*Nil*
5(A) *Name of the courts where such case is pending*	*Not Applicable*
5 (B) *Complaint case number*	*Not Applicable*
5 (C) *Next date of hearing before such courts*	*Not Applicable*
6. *Any other information (example agreement of loan etc.) with date and other particulars*	*Delivery Note No. 1234 dated 26 October, 2012 for supply of 72 car tyres*

PARTICULARS & DOCUMENTS TO BE GIVEN WITH A BAIL APPLICATION BY AN APPLICANT/I.O.

1.	*Whether the application is under section 438 or 439, Cr. P.C. :*		
2.	*F.I.R. Number and Date (with true copy)*	:	*903 of 2013*
3.	*Offence mentioned in FIR & Added subsequently (if any)*	:	*section 420 read with 34 IPC*
4.	*Police Station & the Police District*	:	*Chanakyapuri*
5.	*Date of arrest of each applicant*	:	*3 January, 2013* *4 January, 2013*
6.	*Interim bail availed of (if any) to each applicant*	:	*Nil*
7.	*Particular (i.e., Data & Nature) of orders made earlier in this aforesaid FIR by Session Court & High Court whether before or after filing of chargesheet on bail application 482 Cr. P.C. application of each applicant and each co-accused (please attach true copies of all such orders)*	:	*Not Applicable*
8.	*Particulars of other cases against each applicant and the present status of each cases*	:	*Nil*
9.	*Photocopies of authorities relied upon (relevant judgments)*	:	
10.	*Particulars of other co-accused who are yet to be arrested and properties yet to be recovered (to be furnished by I.O.)*	:	*Younger brother of accused No. 1*
11.	*Any other relevant information/ documentation*	:	*Accused No. 1 is a patient of acute hypertension*

Form No. 45

Bond and Bail Bond for Attendance before Office Incharge of Police Station of Court

[Cr. P.C., section 436, 438, 438(3) and 441]

In the court of Shri M.K. Jindal, CMM, 9, South Delhi

Police Station	:	*Parliament Street, Next date of hearing 13 February, 2013*
Under section	:	*326 IPC Sent to Jail on 16 January, 2013*
F.I.R. No.	:	*221 of 2013*

Bail Bond

I M.K. Johnson son of Shri John Wayne Residence 3/80 Lado Sarai having been arrested or detained without warrant by the Officer Incharge of Parliament Street Police Station for having been brought before his Hon'ble Court charged with the offence of IPC section 326 and required to give surety for my attendance before such Officer or Court on condition that I shall attend such officer or Court on every day on which any investigation or trial is held with regard to such charge and in case of my making default here in myself to forfeit to Government the sum of Rs. 20,000.

DELHI

DATED *Signature*

I O.K. George son of Shri M.P. George, Residence of 13/80, Lado Sarai hereby declare myself for the above said Shri M.K. John that he shall attend the Officer-in-charge of Parliament Street Police Station or the Court of Shri CMM-4, New Delhi every day or which any investigation in the charge is made or any trial on such charge is held that he shall be and re-appear before such officer or court for the purpose of such investigation to answer the charge against him (as the case may be) and in the case of his making default herein I bind myself to forfeit to Government the sum of Rs. 20,000.

Dated this *Day of* 20

Witness *Signature*

1. *P.K. Saxena*
2. *Raj Bahadur*

AFFIDAVIT

I *Dhan Bahadur* son of *R.B. Thapa*, R/o *23-A, Kingsway Camp, Delhi* do hereby solemnly affirm and declare as under:

1. That deponent is the resident of above said address and his/her Ration Card No. is *208916* and Election Card No. *10096*.
2. The accused is *nephew* of the deponent and deponent has full control over him/her.
3. That deponent is working as *Store Manager* at *Royal Café, M.G. Road, Ghaziabad, U.P.* and earns Rs. *16450* per month.
4. That deponent is owner of household articles valued about of Rs. *1,06,000*.
5. That deponent is the owner of the immovable property bearing No. *23-A, Kingsway Camp* measuring *110* sq. yards situated at *Kingsway Camp* valued do and about Rs. *24,00,000*.
6. That deponent undertakes to produce the accused before this honourable court on every date or hearing.

DEPONENT

Dhan Bahadur

VERIFICATION

Verified at Delhi on this *9th* day of *March,* 2013 that the contents of this Affidavit are true and correct to the best of my knowledge and nothing material has been concealed therefrom.

DEPONENT

Dhan Bahadur

Note:—

1. *This affidavit is meant for address, identity and solvency of surety.*
2. *In some States, this document may require court fee.*

FORM C.A.I.

(RULE)

Application copy of Urgent/Ordinary

To the District Officer *Competent Authority Delhi*

Name of the Applicant *Suraj Pandey* S/o *M.K. Pandey,* R/o *94, Darya Ganj, Lane No.1, Delhi*

Post Office and District *Darya Ganj, Delhi*

Description and number of the case from the record of which the copy is required *Eviction Proceedings*

Mauza

P.S. Goswara No.

District *Delhi*

Name of Parties *Suraj Pandey v. Ram Lal*

Nature of case *Eviction of Tenant*

Order *No. 2401* Next date fixed if pending *April, 2013*

Name of the court deciding the case of where pending *Tees Hazari, Delhi*

Date of order, etc. whether it is private use some court	Name of description of the papers of which copy is required	Purpose for which copy is required for or for filling in, etc.

Note:—

1. *CAI refers to documents in criminal matters.*
2. *Mauza is sub-division.*
3. *Goswara is the number assigned in Record Room.*

SPACE FOR COURT FEE STAMP

Court fee stamp filed with the application ....

Number *2401* Value *1,08,000*

One copy to be sent by post or
will applicant attend in
Person *Suraj Pandey*

Signature ....
Date ....

Order on application ....
Signature of the copying agent with...
Date ....

ADDRESS FORM

In the Court of : *AJM-9, Tees Hazari*

Case *Lala Ram*

Versus

Tarlok Singh

Suit *442 of 2013* Date of Hearing

The address of Plaintiff is as under:—

Name with Father's Name	Caste	Resident of	Post Office	Tehsil	Distt.	Remarks
1. *Kanhaiya Lal S/o Mathura Din*	*Bhumi-hary*	*3, Majnu Teela, Mathura*	*Civil Lines*	*Civil Lines*	*Mat-hura U.P.*	
2. *P.K. Joshi S/o P.P. Joshi*	*Brah-min*	*Lake Colony Nainital*	*Lake*	*Naini-tal*	*Naini-tal*	
3. *Ms. Nilofer*	*Chris-tian*	*38 Bandra Mumbai*	*Bandra*	*Band-ra*	*Mum-bai*	
4. *Mr. JFJ Jacob*	*Jew*	*99, Som Vihar, Tigris Road, Delhi Cantt.*	*Raj Rif Centre*	*Delhi Cantt.*	*Delhi-10*	*Presen-tly in Israel*

Sir,

All the summons, notices orders, etc., in connection with the above suit be sent to me at the address given above.

In case of any change in address, the same shall be communicated to you with full particulars and details.

Note"—

This document is used in Civil Suits. Service is effected on above addresses.

NOTICE OF MOTION

IN THE COURT OF DELHI AT NEW DELHI
No. *9894 of 2013*

SHRI *RKL Anand*

Advocate

IN THE MATTER OF :

Plaintiff/Petitioner

Lala Din Plaintiff

Versus

Sardar Jeet Singh Defendent

The enclosed application in the aforesaid matter as being filed on behalf of the *Plaintiff* and is likely to be listed on *June, 2013* or any date, thereafter. Please take notice accordingly.

NEW DELHI

THROUGH

DATE

(ADVOCATE)
RKL Anand
Lawyers Chamber Building
Delhi High Court, New Delhi

ENCLOSED COPY OF APPLICATION

Note:—

This document is used in High Courts for showing service of advance copy and informing the opposite party about tentative date of hearing.

MEMORANDUM OF APPEARANCE

of

R.L. Rana

M.A., LL.B., ADVOCATE

In the Court of *CMM-26, New Delhi*

In..

Versus

Delhi University

The undersigned is appearing in the above case on behalf of *Registrar, Delhi University*

He has been authorized to appear by *Registrar, Delhi University*

Date *May, 2013*

Advocate

Note :

This document is used to indicate the authority under which an Advocate is appearing without Vakalatnama.

PLAINTIFF

DEFENDANT

LIST OF DOCUMENT PRODUCED BY

Order XIII, Rule of the order of Civil Procedure form prescribed by the High Court in the Court of

Suit No. ....201...

....Plaintiff

Versus

....Defendant.

List of documents produced with the plaint (or the first Hearing on behalf of the Plaintiff or Defendant)

Date of hearing This list as filed by This day of 200

1	2	3	4	5	6
Serial No.	Descriptions and date if any of this document	That the document is intended to prove	What became of the document brought the record the exhibit mark put on the document	If rejected date of return to Party & Signature of Party or Pleader to whom the document was returned	Remark

through Advocate

Signature of Party or Pleader date of processing

CERTIFIED COPY FORM

1	2	3	4	5	6	7	8	9	10	11
No. of suit civil, criminal or revenue	Plaintiff or complainant with parentage	Defendant or accused with parentage	Nature of suit or offence amount of suit or detail of offence	Name of place where the suit property is situated or where dispute arose or offence was committed	Name of the first court and of the appellate court if any	Date of order in court	Next date of hearing, if any	For what purpose the certified copy is intended to be used	Details of documents of which copies are applied for with particulars of date or mark, if any	Signature of applicant & date of filing for copies

COMPLETE PERMANENT ADDRESS

12	13	14	15	16	17	18	19	20
Name of Applicant	Parentage	Residence with particulars Post Office & District	Signature of person through whom the petition is filed	Whether ordinary	Or Urgent	Who will take the delivery and with full address and his signature	Who will pay copying fee and other charges with full address and signature	REMARK

FORM

In the Court of *Addl. District Judge, III, Saket*

Anil Srivastava

Versus

Surinder Chandra

Dated 24 February, 2013

The Decree Holder prays for the **execution of the Decree/Order** the particulars where of are stated in the column hereunder.

1.	No. of Suit	*8634 of 2010*
2.	Name of Parties	*Dr. Anil Srivastava, 22, Long Road, Model Town, Delhi v. Surinder Chandra, Smart Tailoring Company, Sadar Bazar*
3.	Date of Degree/Order of which execution is sought	*04 July, 2012*
4.	Whether an appeal was filed against the decree/order under execution	*Yes*
5.	Whether any payment has been received towards satisfaction of decree/order	*No*
6.	Whether any application was made previous to this and if so their date and results	*1. 9 October, 2012* *2. 10 December, 2012*
7.	Amount of suit along with interest as per decree or any other relief granted by the decree	*Rs. 1,98,941* *Interest - Rs. 14,002* *Damage to Car Rs. 4300*
8.	Amount of costs if allowed by Court	*Rs. 4300*
9.	Against whom execution is sought	*Narinder Chandra, F/o Surinder Chandra*
10.	In what manner courts assistance is sought	*Possession of car (MARUTI ALTO) One motor cycle (Hero Honda)*

The D.H. humbly prays that

Since the decree has not been implemented so far and two chances have already been given to the opposite party, the final order may now be implemented.

Dr. Anil Srivastava

Signature of Decree Holder

Through

Advocate

Delhi

Dated

Verification

I *Dr. Anil Srivastava* verify that the contents of the application are true to my knowledge or behalf.

Verified at on this day of 20

Order Signature of Decree Holder

Dr. Anil Srivastava

Note: This document is meant for execution

BEFORE THE COURT OF Shri *R.K. Dhingra,* M.M., NEW DELHI

IN THE MATTER OF:

Punjab & National Bank, New Friends Colony ...... Complainant

Versus

Ram Behari Dahiya, 26, Sarai Kale Ali, Delhi ...... Accused

APPLICATION ON BEHALF OF THE COMPLAINANT FOR INSPECTION OF JUDICIAL FILE.

Kindly allow inspection of above file, I am authorizing Sh. *Lalit Mohan* Advocate to conduct inspection.

New Delhi :

Dated : *February, 2013*

(J.K. Jain)
Advocate

PROCESS FEE FORM

In the Court of *ADJ-V, Saket*

Case *Pranab Chatterjee*

Versus

Pratibha Reddy

Suit No. *33 of 2004* Date of Hearing *24 February, 2013*

Date of filing	Filed by whom	Purpose of filing	Number	Amount of P. fees	Court fee affixed
23 September, 2004	*Pranab Chatterjee*	*Specific performance*	*33 of 2004*	*1,88,410*	*9800*

In the Court of Shri *Mohan Rakesh, ADJ-vii*

In Re *Pranab Chatterjee* v. *Pratibha Reddy*

Date of Hearing ....

RECEIVED PROCESS FEE FORM

Date ....

OP

Ahlmad/Asstt. Ahlmad

Note: This document is necessary for issuing summons/NBW, etc.

IN THE COURT OF *Addl. DJ-III*

SUIT No. *4081 of 2010*

In the matter of :

Rahul Advani .... Plaintiff

Versus

Vinod Mahajan .... Defendant/Respondent

D.O.H. ....

Application for Inspection of Court Record

MOST RESPECTFULLY SHOWETH:

Please allow me to carry out inspection of the court record in the above captioned matter.

Plaintiff/Defendant

Through

I hereby authorize
Mr. *R.M. Johri*, Advocate
for inspection of the court record
in the captioned matter

(Ved Prakash Sharma) Advocate
Chamber No. 81, Civil Wing,
Tis Hazari Courts,
Delhi – 110 054.

Delhi :
Dated :

Note : DOH is date of hearing

ORDINARY/URGENT/DASTI

AHLMAD CIVIL NAZIR/S.H.O.

DATE OF ORDER DATE OF FILING OF P.F. DATE OF ISSUE	*22 November 2012*	NAME OF PROCESS SERVER
NO. OF DOCUMENTS ANNEXED		
NEXT DATE OF HEARING		NUMBER OF PROCESS
		DATE OF RETURN

SUMMONS TO AN ACCUSED PERSON IN A SUMMON'S CASE

In the court of Ms. Priya Mahendra, M.M., Special Court, Room No. 213, Dwarka Courts, New Delhi.

Punjab & National Bank .... Complainant

Versus

Ravi Shankar Das .... Accused

Whereas your attendance is necessary to answer to a charge under section 138 of Negotiable Instruments Act. You are hereby informed through this notice that you are required to appear in person before the court on ....at 10 AM (in accordance with section 65, Cr. P.C. and section 144 of N.I. Act, it is directed that a copy of summons shall be affixed at the premises in case accused cannot be served as per sections 62 to 64 of Cr. P.C.).

Dated................day of ....2010.

Checked by Ahlmad/Asstt. Ahlmad
Metropolitan Magistrate, New Delhi

Note :

1. *PF is Process Fee*
2. *This document is required to give notice to other party if he cannot be found.*

To.

The Sub-Registrar,
Sub District No. II,
New Delhi – 110 058.

SUBJECT: **Application for the issue of certified copy of ....**

Sir.

Kindly issue the certified copy of ....on urgent basis *i.e.*, on the day of application and I am ready to deposit the necessary fee as provided under provision of Article-III of TABLE OF REGISTRATION FEES IN DELHI, the particulars of the said Deed/Documents are given below:—

Registered as Document No.. : ....
In additional Book No. : ....
Volume No. : ....
On pages : ....
On dated : ....
Executed by : ....
....

In favour of : ....
....
....

Details of property : ....
....
....

It is therefore, requested to supply the said certified copy today and oblige.

Thanking you,
Yours Faithfully

Dated : ....

Note:

This is meant to obtain certified copies of will, sale deed or other document.

Subject : SUPPLY OF COPY REGISTERED NO.

ADDL BOOK NO. ....VOLUME NO. ....

PAGE ....TO PAGE ....DATE ....

EXECUTED BY ....

IN FAVOUR OF ....

PROPERTY NO. ....

DEAR SIR

KINDLY SUPPLY ME COPY OF DOCUMENT, PARTICULARS OF WHICH ARE GIVEN ABOVE ON THE PRESCRIBED FORM.

YOURS FAITHFULLY,

Name ....

Address ....
....
....

CHECK LIST

1. VALUATION OF SUIT/ JURISDICTION
2. NAME & ADDRESS OF ADVOCATE
3. NATURE OF SUIT
4. WHETHER ANY EARMARKED COURT
5. CAVEAT
6. COURT FEE AFFIXED
7. CONNECTED CASES IF ANY & NAME OF THE COURT WHERE PENDING

COURT FEE

1	2	3	4	5	6	7	8	9	10	11
Whether Civil Criminal or Revenue	Plaintiff or complainant with particulars	Defendant or accused with particulars	Nature or suit or offence amount of suit or detail of offence	Name of place where the suit property is situated or where dispute arose or offence was committed	Name of first court and of the appeal court, if any	Date of order in first court	Next date of hearing, if any	For what purpose the certified copy is intended to be used	Details of documents of which copies are wanted with particulars about the date of hearing, if any	Signature of applicant & date of filing application for copies

COMPLETE PERMANENT ADDRESS

12	13	14	15	16	17	18	19	20
Name of Applicant	Father's name of applicant	Residence with particulars Post Office & District	Person through whom the petition is filed, address particulars	Whether ordinary	Or Urgent	Who will take the delivery and with full address and his signature	Who will pay copying fee and other charges with full address and signature	REMARK

FORM A

[*See* Rule 5 of the Delhi Stamp (Prevention of Undervaluation of Instruments) Rules, 2007]

1. Name of office of Registrar/Sub-Registrar : ....
2. Name & Father's name of the transferor : ....
3. Address of the transferor : ....
4. Name & Father's name of the transferee : ....
5. Address of the transferee : ....
6. If the property was transferred earlier (Yes/No) : ....

   (a) If yes, amount of consideration thereof : ....
7. Amount of consideration of the present transfer : ....
8. Other information:—

A. In case of agricultural land

(i) Name of Revenue Estate : ....

(ii) Khasra Number (s) : ....

(iii) Area of land under transfer (in hect/sq.mtrs.) : 1. Acre = ...sq. mtr.
2. Bigha = ...sq. mtr.
3. Biswa = ...sq. mtr.

B. In case of non-agricultural land:—

(i) Location to the property:—

(a) Name of the colony/locality : ....

(b) Sl. No. of the colony/in the list : ....
colonies/localities : ....

(c) Category of the colony/locality : ....

(If the name of colony/locality is not included in the list of colonies/localities, the category of the nearest colony/locality may be mentioned).

(ii) Area in sq. yds. : ....

(iii) Land use:—
(Fill the corresponding value of the following land use as applicable in your case) : (a) Residential
(b)
(c)

9. In case of built-up property other than flats

(i) Total area of the plot :

(ii) Land Use : ....

(Fill the corresponding value of the following land uses as applicable in your case) :
(a) Residential - 1
(b) Govt. Public purpose 1
(c) Private public purpose (*e.g.*, private schools, colleges, hospitals)
(d) Industrial - 2
(e) Commercial - 3

(iii) Total plinth area of the property (in sq. mtr) : ....

(iv) Plinth area under transfer (in sq. mtr.) : ....

(v) Year of construction : ....

(vi) Nature of construction : ....
(in case of colonies falling in categories 'G and H' please mention the corresponding value of the following types of structure applicable in your case)
Pucca - 1.0
Semi pucca - 0.75
Katcha - 0.5

In case of Flats	:	
(i) Constructed by DDA/Co-operative Group Housing Society (CGHS)/Private Builder	:	....
(ii) Plinth area of the flat (in sq. mtr.)	:	....
(iii) Whether number of storey in the building of your flat exceeds four or not (Yes/No)	:	....

Name & Signature of Treasurer

VERIFICATION

I ....do hereby solemnly declare that what to the best of my knowledge and belief.

Note: This document is needed at the time of registration of any document particularly sale deed.

BEFORE THE DEBTS RECOVERY TRIBUNAL NO....., NEW DELHI

O.A./M.A./R.C./APL NO.........OF.......

.... APPELLANT

VERSUS

.... DEFENDANTS

APPLICATION FOR GRANT OF CERTIFIED COPY

1. Name & Address of Applicant
2. Whether the Applicant is a party to the case Advocate for
3. Whether the case is pending/disposed off
4. Description with date of documents of which copy is applied for
5. No. of copies required and nature of Application
6. Amount of fee deposited
7. Details of I.P.O./D.D. Deposited

Dated : .... Advocate for.........................

FOR OFFICE USE

1. No. of pages photocopies ____x Rs. 5.00	Rs.
2. Whether the Applicant is entitled for copies	
3. Whether the Application is in order	
4. Date on which copy is ready	
5. Date of delivery	

GRANTED/REJECTED

REGISTRAR/SECTION OFFICER

DRT No.	:	Date of receipt of Application	:
Q.A./M.A./R.C./APL. NO.	:	Date of delivery	:
In the matter of	:		
Documents applied for	:		
Amount of fee deposit	:		
I.P.O./D.D. No.	:		

IN THE DEBTS RECOVERY TRIBUNAL No...., DELHI

O.A. No. N.D.H.

L.D.H.

APPLICANTS ....

Versus

RESPONDENTS ....

APPLICATION FOR INSPECTION OF DOCUMENTS RECORDS

I hereby apply for grant of permission to inspect the documents/records to office a case. The details are on follows:—

1. Name & address of the person seeking inspection :
2. Whether he is party to the case of this legal practitioner :
3. Details of the papers/documents sought to be inspected :
4. Reason for seeking the inspection :
5. The date and the duration of the inspection sought :
6. Details of DD or IPO if any furnished :

Place :

Date : Applicant(s)

For Office use

....

Registrar Debts Recovery Tribunal

APPLICATION FOR REGISTRATION OF MARRIAGE UNDER SECTION 8 OF HINDU MARRIAGE ACT, 1995

(25 of 1955)

Note: Please read the instructions (overleaf) carefully before filling up the form

1. NAME & PARENTAGE OF THE PARTIES (IN CAPITALS) : HUSBAND ....
FATHER'S NAME ....
WIFE ....
FATHER'S NAME ....
2. DATE OF BIRTH AND AGE (IN YEARS) AT THE TIME OF MARRIAGE : HUSBAND ....
WIFE ....
3. PERMANENT DWELLING PLACE (IN CAPITALS) : HUSBAND ....
WIFE ....
4. PRESENT DWELLING PLACE (IN CAPITALS) HUSBAND ....
WIFE ....
5. RELATION OF PARTIES BEFORE MARRIAGE : ....
6. A HINDU Marriage was solemnized between (Name of Husband) .... And (Name of Wife) .... on (Date) .... at (Place) .... according to our customary rites and environment and we declare that we have been living together as Husband and Wife ever since the date noted above.
7. We hereby declare that:
   (i) Neither of us had a spouse living at the time of Marriage.
   (ii) Neither of us an idiot or lunatic at the time of Marriage.
   (iii) The husband had completed the age of Twenty-one Years and the wife had Completed the age of Eighteen years at the time of Marriage and the consent of the guardians of the wife *viz.* .... (here enter the name of the parentage and relationship of the guardian) had been obtained for the marriage.
   (iv) We are not within the degree of prohibited relationship (OR) according to the custom or usage;/having the force of law governing each of us marriage between us is permitted though we are within the degree of prohibited relationship.

   NOTE: Score out whichever is not applicable
8. Martial status at the time of marriage of the parties HUSBAND ....WIFE ....
9. We also declare that the above particulars are true to the best of our knowledge and belief.

Station .... Signature .... (Husband)

Dated ....Signature ....(Wife)

INSTRUCTIONS FOR REGISTRATION UNDER SECTION 8 OF THE HINDU MARRIAGE ACT, 1955

1. Application form can be collected from the Personal Branch of ADM (East) on any working day.
2. Application form should be duly filled in and signed by Husband and Wife. Both of them should appear before the Registrar of Marriage, at the time of submitting the application.
3. Documents to be attached: All the photocopies of documents and photographs should be attested by a Gazetted Officer.
   (a) Documentary evidence of date of birth of both the parties (Matriculation Certificate/Birth Certificate/Passport). The husband should have completed 21 years of age and the wife 18 years of age at the time of marriage.
   (b) The party should be domicil of East Delhi District and he/she will submit his/her residential proof in the form of Ration Card/Election Identity Card/Passport. The other party should also submit residence proof in the form of Ration Card/Election I. Card/Passport.
   (c) Separate affidavits from husband and wife on Rs. 10 non-judicial stamp paper duly attested by Notary Public or Oath Commissioner in the following format.

NOTE: AFFIDAVIT SHOULD BE IN PRESCRIBED FORMAT AND PLEASE CHECK IT BEFORE SIGNATURE

I, ...S/o, D/o, W/o ....with present address at ....and permanent address ....do hereby take oath and solemnly affirm and declare as under:—

(i) That I got married to ....S/o, D/o ....R/o ....on ....at ....

(ii) That my date of birth is ....and I have completed ....years of age at the time of marriage.

(iii) That I was ....(unmarried/widow/widower/divorce) till the time of marriage on ....and I did not have a spouse living at the time of marriage.

(iv) That the marriage was conducted as per....................................(Hindu/Buddhist/Jain/ Sikh) rites.

(v) That I belong to ....religion.

(vi) That at the time of marriage, I was capable of giving valid consent and of sound mind, not suffering from any mental disorder/insanity.

(vii) That until the time of marriage, I was not related to ....S/o, D/o ....within the prohibited degree of relationship and not sapindas as per Hindu Marriage Act.

(viii) That I am a/an ....citizen.

DEPONENT

Verification

Verified that the above contents are true and correct to the best of my knowledge and belief and nothing has been concealed therein.

(d) Passport size photographs of both parties (3 copies each) and one marriage ceremony photograph all of which should be affixed on plain paper and duly attested by Gazetted Officer on front of each photograph.

(e) Legally valid divorce decree/order in case of a divorce (certified copy) and death certificate of spouse in case of widow/widower.

(f) Marriage Invitation Card in original.

(g) In case of Foreign National, a certificate from the Embassy/High Commission concerned regarding his/her present marital status. Valid visa documents should also be submitted.

(h) In case of one of the parties belonged to other than Hindu, Buddhist, Jain and Sikh religions and converted to any of these religions before marriage, a conversion certificate from the priest who solemnized the marriage.

(i) Where marriage has been solemnized at a religious place, a certificate from priest is required.

4. Incomplete application forms not supported by required documentary evidence and forms or applicants not within the jurisdiction of the Registrar of Marriage, East District, will not be accepted.
5. Fee of Rs. 100 is to be deposited at the time of submission with Marriage Clerk in Room No. 9 *i.e.*, Personal Branch of ADM (East) and the Receipt is to be appended with form.
6. Completed documents should be submitted in Room No. 9 in the Personal Branch of ADM (East) by 1.00 PM on any working day. Registration will be done between 11.00 AM and 1.00 PM on the date given. Both the parties will be present along with persons/officer (who attended the marriage of the party) of the following categories, (A) Any person having Pan of Income Tax with original and copy of Pan Card or (B) Any officer/official of Central or State Government or Union Territory Administration of P.S.U./ Autonomous bodies whose identity can be established with official Identity Card, on the day of Registration, as witness of their marriage.
7. Please bring all your original documents while submitting the application form as well as at the time of Registration.
8. Any one, who procures a marriage of him or herself in contravention of the conditions specified in the Hindu Marriage Act shall be punishable with simple imprisonment or fine or both as per the Act.
9. A separate affidavit is required if the surname of the wife is intended to be changed, by virtue of marriage.

Requirements for registration under section 13 or 16 of Special Marriage Act, 1954

(a) Application duly filled and signed by the Boy & Girl.

(b) Fee of Rs. 50 is to be submitted with the Marriage Clerk in Room No. 8 and the receipt is to be appended with the form.

(c) Documentary evidence of date of birth of the Boy & Girl (Matriculation certificate/School leaving certificate/Birth certificate).

(d) Copy of the ration card of one of the parties pertaining to the district North-West.

(e) Two passport size photograph of Boy & Girl duly pasted on the application.

(f) ....The applicant is a Foreign National, a No Objection Certificate in original from the concerned High Commission be submitted with the application form.

(g) Separate affidavits from the Boy & Girl giving details of

1. Date of birth
2. Citizenship
3. Marital status at the time of marriage
4. Affirmation that the parties __________ related to each other within the prohibited degree of relationship as per Special Marriage Act.
5. Affirmation of intention of marriage between the applicants.

Note:

Section c, d, e, is to be duly attested by the Gazetted Officer.

Section g (1-5) to be prepared on Rs. 0 stamp paper and duly attested by Notary Public or Oath Commissioner.

The completed application form can be submitted in Room No. 8 at 10.00 AM on any working day except Saturday, Sunday and gazetted holiday.

The applicants should come in person to deposit the application form along with their original documents on the specified day and time.

CHALLAN NO.

T.R.G.

(Treasury rule 92) Treasury/Sub-Treasury

Challan of cash paid into the State Bank of India

Reserve at...........................

To be filled in by the Remitter			To be filled in by the Department Officer of the Treasury			
By whom tendered	Name (or designation) and address of the person on whose behalf money is paid	Full particulars of the remittance and to Authority if any	Amount	Head of Account	Accounts Officer by whom adjustable	Order to the Bank
			Rs. P.			

Annexure 'A'

FORM OF COMPLAINT (TO BE LODGED) WITH THE BANKING OMBUDSMAN

(TO BE FILLED UP BY THE COMPLAINANT)

To :

The Banking Ombudsman

Place of BO's office ....

Dear Sir,

Sub: Complaint against...(Name of the bank's branch) of ....(Name of the Bank)

Details of the complaint are as under:—

1. Name of the Complainant : ....
2. Full address of the Complainant : ....

   ....

   Pin Code : ....

   Phone : ....

   No./Fax No. ....

   E-mail
3. Complaint against (name and full address of the branch/bank) : ....

   Pin Code : ....

   Phone : ....

   No./Fax No. ....

   E-mail:
4. Particulars of Bank or Credit Card Account (if any) : ....
5. (a) Date of representation already made by the complainant to the Bank (please enclose a copy of the representation)

   ....

   ....

   Substituted by Notification Ref CSD.BOS.No. 4736/13.01.01/2008-09 dated February 3, 2009.

   (b) Whether any reminder was sent by the complainant? YES/NO

   (Please enclose a copy of the reminder)
6. Subject-matter of the complaint (Please refer to clause 8 of the Scheme)
7. Details of the complaint:

   (If space is not sufficient, please enclose separate sheet)
8. Whether any reply (within a period of one month after the Bank concerned received the representation) has been received from the Bank?

Yes/No

(if yes, please enclose a copy of the reply)

9. Nature of Relief sought from the Banking Ombudsman (please enclose a copy of documentary proof, if any, in support of your claim)
10. Nature and extent of monetary loss, if any, claimed by the complainant by way of compensation [please refer to clauses 12(5) & 12 (6) of the Scheme] Rs. ....
11. List of documents enclosed:

    (Please enclose a copy of all the documents)
12. Declaration

    (i) I/We, the complainant/s herein declare that:

    (a) the information furnished herein above is true and correct; and

    (b) I/We have not concealed or misrepresented any fact stated in the above columns and in the documents submitted herewith.

    (ii) The complaint is filed before expiry of period of one year reckoned in accordance with the provisions of clause 9(3)(a) and (b) of the Scheme.

    (iii) The subject-matter of the present complaint has never been brought before the Office of the Banking Ombudsman by me/us or by any of the parties concerned with the subject-matter to the best of my/our knowledge.

    (iv) The subject-matter of the present complaint has not been decided by/ pending with any forum/court/arbitrator.

    (v) I/We authorize the Bank to disclose any such information/documents furnished by us to the Banking Ombudsman and disclosure whereof in the opinion of the Banking Ombudsman is necessary and is required for redressal of our complaint.

    (vi) I/We have noted the contents of the Banking Ombudsman Scheme, 2006.

Yours faithfully,

(Signature of Complainant)

NOMINATION – (If the complainant wants to nominate his representative to appear and make submissions on his behalf before the Banking Ombudsman or to the Office of the Banking Ombudsman, the following declaration should be submitted).

I/We, the above named complainant/s hereby nominate Shri/Smt. ....who is not an Advocate and whose address is..

As my/our REPRESENTATIVE in all proceedings of this complaint and confirm that any statement, acceptance or rejection made by him/her shall be binding on me/us. He/she has signed below in my presence.

ACCEPTED

(Signature of Representative)

(Signature of Complainant)

Note: If submitted online, the complaint need not be signed.

FORM NO. 14

Pending/Disposal of

CENTRAL ADMINISTRATIVE TRIBUNAL

PRINCIPAL BENCH

DA/RA/CP/NO. OF

....Applicant/s

....Respondent/s

Application for Inspection of Documents/Records

I hereby apply for grant of permission to inspect the documents/records in the above case. The details are as follows:—

---

1. Name and address of the person seeking inspection :
2. Whether he is a party to the case/his Legal Practitioner and if so, his rank therein :
3. Details of the papers/documents sought to be inspected :
4. Reasons for seeking the inspection :
5. The date and duration of the inspection sought :
6. Whether any fee is payable and if so, the mode of payment :

Place :

Date :

APPLICANT

....

FOR OFFICE USE :

Granted inspection for..........................hours on ..../rejected

REGISTRAR

C.A.T., P.B.

FORM NO. 22

(*See* rule 117)

CENTRAL ADMINISTRATIVE TRIBUNAL

PRINCIPAL BENCH

NEW DELHI

OA NO. ....

OA/TA/PT/CP/MA NO. ....

....APPLICANT(s)

VERSUS

....RESPONDENT(s)

APPLICATION FOR GRANT OF CERTIFIED COPY

1. NAME & ADDRESS OF THE APPLICANT WHO IS APPLYING FOR CERTIFIED COPY ....
2. WHETHER THE APPLICANT IS A PARTY TO THE CASES, IF NOT WHETHER THE APPLICATION UNDER RULE 119 (RULE OF PRACTICE, 1993 IS FILED?) ....
3. WHETHER THE CASE IS PENDING OR DISPOSED OFF? ....
4. DESCRIPTION WITH DATE OF THE DOCUMENTS OF WHICH APPLIED FOR ....
5. NO. OF COPIES REQUIRED AND NATURE OF APPLICATION (WHETHER URGENT OR ORDINARY) ....
6. DETAILS OF THE FEE REMITTED ALSO WITH APPLICATION ....

SIGNATURE OF THE APPLICANT
OR COUNSEL OF THE APPLICANT

DATED : THIS .... DAY OF ..../
FOR OFFICE USE GRANTED/REJECTED
ADDITIONAL COPYING FEE PAYABLE/PAID AND DETAILS THEREOF.
(INITIALS OF THE OFFICE-IN-CHARGE)

ENGLISH CIVIL FORM No. 252

OPENING SHEET APPEALS IN COURT

Subordinate to the HIGH COURT

In The Court of ....

Civil Appeal No. ....of

Number & Date of the original Suit

No. & Date of Institution in first Court	Date of decision in first Court	Date of institution of Appeal	Value of sum and appeal for purpose of Jurisdiction	Value of appeal for purpose Court fees	Amount of fees on Appeal

Suit _____
Appeal ___

Against

Appeal filed by   Name of party, Agent

Or pleader filing the appeal
Appeal from the order of
Dated ....day of ....
Claim in appeal

Before the Hon'ble High Court of Delhi at New Delhi
W.P. (C) No. 7835 of 2010

Span Diagnostic Ltd. – Petitioner

Versus

Union of India & Ors. – Respondent

For the purpose of having my fee allowed on taxation against the Party or Parties, who may be liable for costs under the judgment or order of the Court, I G.S. Chaturvedi, Advocate, in accordance with rule 20 of rules/regulation, the counsel for Respondent No. 3 in the above case hereby certify that in the above case the following fees were paid to me as my exclusive fee on the dates and by the person or persons specified below and that such fees were paid before the final hearing of the appeal/suit or before the commencement of the argument or the conclusion of the evidence.

And that no portion of such fees has been, or has been agreed to be, returned or remitted or appropriated to the use of any other person by me or by any one acting in my behalf.

MATTER	FEES	DATE OF PAYMENT	BY WHOM PAID	ADDRESS OF PERSON WHO ACTUALLY MADE SUCH PAYMENTS

................................200

Advocate

H.C.D. Cr. I.

OPENING SHEET FOR CRIMINAL REVISION UNDER SECTION 397/401 CRIMINAL PROCEDURE CODE.

IN THE **HIGH COURT OF DELHI** AT NEW DELHI.

JUDICIAL DEPARTMENT

CRIMINAL REVISION PETITION No. ....OF 2007

DIVISIONAL REGISTER No. ....

DISTRICT	DATE OF FILING THE PETITION	WHETHER FILED BY APPELLANT IN PERSON OR BY COUNSEL OR AGENT	STAMP ON PETITION OF APPEAL

....PETITIONER

VERSUS

....RESPONDENT

Revision from the order of ....

Date ....

Charge under Section ....

SENTENCE

....

....

OPENING SHEET FOR CIVIL APPEALS

(Order XLI, Rule 1, Civil Procedure Code, 1908)

IN THE **HIGH COURT OF DELHI**

JUDICIAL DEPARTMENT

(Civil Appellant Side)

ORIGINAL SUIT				FIRST APPEAL				Date of filing appeal in High Court	Value for the purpose of jurisdiction	Value for the purpose of Court fee	Amount of Court-fee on petition
Instituted		Decided		Instituted		Decided					
Court	Date	Court	Date	Court	Date	Court	Date				

Presented by ....(name of party Advocate or agent filing Appeal).

Appeal (Plaintiff or defendant) ....

Respondent (Plaintiff or defendant) ....

Appellate Court and Date (Plaintiff or defendant) ....

Confirming, reversing or modifying ....

Original claim as given in the plaint ....

Claim in appeal (stating whether appeal is from a decree/order) ....

Enactment and section under which the appeal lies ....

IN THE **HIGH COURT OF DELHI** AT NEW DELHI

To,

The Deputy Registrar,

Delhi High Court,

New Delhi

Case No. ....of 20...

....Plaintiff/Appellant/Petitioner

Versus

....Defendant/Respondent

Date of hearing or decision if any ________________________________

Decided on ....

Sir,

The Counsel of the ....Request that he may kindly be allowed for **inspection of the file** of the case noted above on payment of usual Court fee which is affixed on this application. The required record be made available on ....

Yours faithfully

NEW DELHI　　　　Advocate

Dated :　　　　For the Petitioner/Respondent

Address :

IN THE **HIGH COURT OF DELHI** AT NEW DELHI
Civil Appeal/Civil Revision/Criminal Appellate Jurisdiction
Original Civil Writ/Suit No.

VERSUS

INDEX

....Petitioner

....Appellant

VERSUS

....Respondent

S. No.	Particulars	Court Fees	Pages
1.	....		
2.	....		
3.	....		
4.	....		
5.	....		
6.	....		
7.	....		
8.	....		
9.	....		
10.	....		

Dated this day 20

Advocate

IN THE HIGH COURT OF DELHI AT NEW DELHI
APPLICATION FOR ADJOURNMENT

To,

The Deputy Registrar (Judt.),
High Court of Delhi
New Delhi

Sir,

Kindly postpone the hearing of the case/s particulars whereof are given below:—

1. Case No.
2. Is it admission or after notice/Misc. Matter
3. Name of the petitioner/applicant
4. Name of the respondent
5. Names of the advocates for both the parties in proper sequence with their signature in token of consent for adjournment.

6. Name of the Court with date with details of the matter on the last hearing.
7. Next date of hearing
8. No. of adjournments already taken
9. Is there interim stay in the matter
10. Date of which the matter is sought to be postponed
11. Order of the Joint Registrar (Judt.) Re : Postponement of the matter

Signature of the applicant
Advocate with address

APPLICATION FOR ISSUE OF VISITOR'S PASS

1. Name (s) ....
2. Age ....
3. Father's Name ....
4. Permanent Address ....
5. Present Address ....
6. Recommended by : (a) .... Senior Advocate
   (b)...Advocate
   (c)...Officer of the Court
7. Pass required for entry to Court No. ....
   Item No. ....
8. Purpose of visit ....
9. Date ....

Signature of the person ....
Recommending the application

Signature of Applicant (s)
with Seal/Stamp

IN THE HIGH COURT OF DELHI AT NEW DELHI

Case Type Number Year

IN THE MATTER OF :

NAME :...PLAINTIFF/PETITIONER

VERSUS

NAME : .... DEFENDANT/RESPONDENT

1. (a) Case Category
   (b) Case Category

2. (a) Date of impugned order :
2 (b) Case Type/Number :
3. Similar Matter
   Case Type/Number :
4. Statute involved :
   Criminal Matters – Code 100 to 105
   FIR No. :
   FIR date :
   Police Station :
   Service Matters – Code 500 to 505
   Department/Authority :
   Organization etc. :
   Motors Accident Claim Matters – Code 600
   Insurance Company :

Lawyers Code :

Court No. ....

Item No. ....

Section No. ....

IN THE **SUPREME COURT** OF INDIA

CIVIL/CRIMINAL/ORIGINAL APPELLATE JURISDICTION

S.L.P./C.A./W.P./T.P. (CRIMINAL/CIVIL) NO. ....OF 200

IN THE MATTER OF :

.... PETITIONER(S)

VERSUS

.... RESPONDENT(S)

The Registrar,
Supreme Court of India,
New Delhi – 110 001.

Sir,

Kindly issue me a copy of the Proceedings/Signed Order/Stay Bail Order/ Judgment dated ....in the above matter.

Dated this the .... day of 200

Date : (DR. SUSHIL BALWADA)

Advocate Petitioner (s)/
Appellant(s)/Respondent(s)

....

Regn. No. .... Dated :

Court No. ....

Item No. ....Court Fee ....

Date ....

CHAPTER 3

Legal Writing

Legal writing is a type of technical writing used by lawyers, judges and other law professionals to express legal analysis and legal rights and duties.

For the purpose of this book and to sensitize the students in Clinical Legal Education, legal writing would include papers or articles, reviews and comments.

Papers or articles may be prepared for presentation at a meet or for inclusion in its proceedings (or in a journal) or for both.

Legal writing is different than other types of articles or papers in that the former places great reliance on authority (statutory provisions and case law). The assertions and statements about the existing practice or a policy is always backed up by quoting legal provisions or the binding decisions of judicial forums. Legal writings would at times be also based on the findings of empirical data or flow from doctrinal analysis.

How to Develop

1. **Title** – The title or the theme of the article must be in tune with the main portion of the text. The title must give a clear indication of the scope of the paper.
2. **Text** – Facts of the cases discussed, legal issues raised and the law laid down must be clearly shown. The text should be divided in proper paragraphs and progress in a logical and systematic manner.
3. **Language** – The text must be in easy and simple language. It should be easy to understand.

Legal writing is to be distinguished from other forms of writing because of its reliance on authority, precedents and technical vocabulary. It is also characterized by its formality.

Ways to Improve Legal Writing

1. Remember your audience.
2. Organise your writing.
3. Write short sentences and use simple English.
4. Avoid the legalese.
5. Use action words.
6. Avoid passive voice.

7. Avoid adjectives.
8. Edit ruthlessly.

Remember your Audience

Any legal writing must focus on the audience. A suit for specific performance would be quite different from a legal notice, from a house owner to his tenant or from a paper presented at a law seminar.

Organise your Writing

The subject-matter should be arranged in a chronological and sequential manner. The text should develop in a progressive manner. The ideas should not appear disjointed. There should be no repetitions.

Write short Sentences and use simple English

The text must be simple and easy to understand. Eliminate all unnecessary words. If a text is to be read many times to understand what it conveys, it is not simple.

Avoid the Legalese

Specialised legal phrases and jargon must be avoided.

Use Action Words

To make the text more powerful and vivid.

Avoid Passive Voice

This would clearly bring out responsibility or culpability.

Avoid Adjectives

Adjectives such as very, most, fully totality, greatly, etc., must be avoided.

Edit Ruthlessly

The text must be carefully read and re-read to cut down unnecessary words.

A few illustrations of impressionable and powerful writing are given below.

From the Pen of Mohandas K. Gandhi

1. *I cannot be too plain in saying that no one in our position should go to South Africa with a view to pile (up) money. You should go there with a spirit of self sacrifice. You should keep riches at an arm's length. They may then woo you. If you bestow your glances on them, they are such a coquette that you are sure to be sighted. This is my experience in South Africa.*[1]
2. *No client would be fool enough to engage me.*[2]
3. *There was not any immediate work for me.*[3]
4. *....one, whom God wishes to save, cannot fall even if he will.*[4] .

1. 'Letter to FS Taleyarkhan' October 18, 1896, CWMG 2, pp. 67, 68 (1976 Edn.).
2. An Autobiography: The Story of My Experiments with Truth (Boston Press, Bencon, 1957), p. 92.
3. *Ibid.*, p. 121.
4. Satyagraha in South Africa (Standord: Academic Reprints, 1928) p. 58.

5. *I am doing nothing for the community for the sake of reward or fame. Everything I do is as a matter of duty, and I shall continue to do so in the future. If anyone wants legal advice, my office is always open. And I shall give the best advice I can.*[5]
6. *I was afraid that my main business might become merely money-making.*[6]
7. *What, then, is to be attitude of the British Indians amid such a crisis? To our mind, it is quite clear what it should be. The Indians must keep themselves absolutely cool and remain patient, still relying upon justice being ultimately done. They must make respectful representations to the Government, but they should also firmly decline to give proof to the Receivers of Revenue, offering to do so before the Commission that is to be appointed.*[7]

The Writings of Nani Palkhivala

8. *The acceptance of indiscipline is even more disastrous than indiscipline itself.*[8]
9. *The preamble to a Constitution is its identity card.*[9]
10. *Legal redress is time-consuming enough to make infinity intelligible. A law suit once started in India is the nearest thing to eternal life ever seen on this earth.*[10]
11. *When the hour struck, the man was found – Mahatma Gandhi – the greatest of our leaders. He lit the imagination of the entire nation. He created men out of dust. He taught the unforgettable lesson that cynicism corrupts absolutely.*[11]
12. *Animals can be trained; but only human beings can be educated. Education requires personal participation and transformation. It cannot be given to anyone; it must be inwardly appropriated. It involves cultivation of the mind, not merely with a view to equipping you to earn a living or to possess it as a commodity for sale in the market place.*[12]
13. *The national sport of the Americans is no longer football, baseball or basketball. It is law and litigation.*[13]

From the works of H.M. Seervai[14]

Having read the 1959 edition of Azad's India Wins Freedom countless times, and having read and re-read the 1988 edition, I believe that the title of this Post Script, "Shattered Dreams" expresses accurately the effect on the reader of the 1988 edition. For in my view, the thirty pages suppressed in the 1959 edition and restored in the 1988

5. Speech at Meeting of British Indian Association, February 2, 1908, CWMG 8 (55) (December 1962 Edn.).
6. Gandhi, An Autobiography, p. 219.
7. A New Year's Gift, Indian Opinion, January 14, 1904.
8. My Experiences as an Ambassador.
9. Truth and Services Above All.
10. Forty-three years of Independence.
11. *Ibid.*
12. Education and the Art of Reading.
13. My Experiences as an Ambassador.
14. H.M. Seervai, 'Partition of India; Legend and Reality', Universal Law Publishing Co. Pvt. Ltd., 2nd Edn., 2012, pp. 252-53.

edition have altered the tone of the whole book. A note of sadness runs through the 1988 edition, which was absent in the 1959 edition. Azad's narrative in the 1988 edition shows how everything which he had cared for, and worked for and suffered for, lay broken at his feet, largely because his wise advice was rejected.

From 1920 Azad was a staunch nationalist Muslim who supported the various programmes which Gandhi launched to secure the freedom of India; and Azad stood by Gandhi through times good and times evil. Azad worked and suffered for the cause of the Congress because he believed, and proudly proclaimed, that the Congress was a National organization working to secure freedom for the whole Nation and not for any particular community. He lived to admit that, in effect, the Congress was predominantly a Hindu body working to secure power and freedom for Hindus since eminent Congress leaders proclaimed that real democracy meant "one man, one vote". Azad had believed that Nationalist Muslims had an important part to play not only in the Congress, but in a free and united India. He lived to see Nationalist Muslims quietly put away in 1945 when freedom and power were near. And even more, he lived to write the Vallabhbhai Patel was the real flag-bearer of the two nation theory.

A passage from Justice H.R. Khanna[15]

I am in receipt of your letter which I saw after return from Bangalore, having been away there for more than three weeks. The question as to whether one should join the profession or pursue further studies by joining LL.M can best be answered by a person himself, because he knows best his own circumstances and aptitude. As regards, the place for starting practice, I personally prefer one's own State. It is only after a person has made headway in the profession in his own State that he should think of shifting to Delhi. Starting practice in Delhi is also a costly proposition because of the high cost of securing residential accommodation and also the cost of transport. Calcutta is a big place and if you join the Bar there it may not cost you much because you would be living with your father. Personally I do not think it very desirable for a lawyer to frequently shift from one place to the other. I am not sure as to how long would your father remain posted in Calcutta.

Prose of D.D. Basu

As regards Tagore Law Lectures,[16] *it has long been exhausted and I can at best given you a mutilated copy. No fresh edition of that book has been brought out because the matter has been rewritten and published as my Comparative Constitutional Law. I intend to give you complimentary copies of all my books which you do not so far possess. For that purpose, I am enclosing herewith a list of my books so that you may indicate which of them you do not so far possess in your personal library. One of my latest works is to "Constitutional Remedies and Writs", a copy of which you will receive from Kamal Law House of Calcutta very soon. They did not so far dispatch it.*

The real problem is how to send so many books to you. The best thing for you would be to come here during the Puja vacation and collect these books apart from holding a

15. V. Sudhish Pai 'Legends in Law, Our Great Forebears', Universal Law Publishing Co. Pvt. Ltd., Ist Edn., 2012, p. 473.

16. *Ibid.*, p. 491.

discussion with me. If that is not possible, please nominate any relative or friend to collect the books from me.

Please also remember the difference of outlook between the Shorter Constitution and the Commentary.[17] *The Shorter is in the nature of a digest of all relevant cases. The object of the Commentary, on the other hand, is to explain the principle underlying the various cases, so that you may yourself add captions which deal new principle evolved in the latest cases. In writing anything you should place yourself in the position of an ordinary reader and then you will realize what to write and how much.*

From the Pen of Fali S. Nariman

14. *At the Bar, a young lawyer learns much – simply by osmosis. Scientifically, osmosis is the diffusion of a liquid through a porus barrier. But learn the law by osmosis is simply being with other lawyers (senior to you) and imbibing what they say and do.*[18]
15. *Chief Justice M.C. Chagla was the brightest and the best of judges in my time. He had a fine mix of the qualities of an ideal judge. He was highly intellectual and very judicial. And his treatment of juniors was exemplary.*[19]
16. *When you argue a case in court, be clear and precise, not confused. Your mental output must flow. And for it to flow you must be well-equipped and well-prepared.... Don't be messy. Present a cogent and logical argument. Think like a lawyer and not like a philosopher. Your head must not be up in the clouds. And, respond to the court's questions promptly even when the question puts you off the track of your argument.*[20]
17. *Never exaggerate in court about the facts of your case or the applicable law. Avoid rhetoric, and don't be too smart. And for heaven's sake avoid being funny. You will be stigmatized either as impertinent or flippant.*[21]
18. *The essence of good lawyering is acquainting oneself with the relevant law, including case law, on the subject at hand. The essence of good advocacy is to know the facts of your case, and then apply the law to those facts.*[22]

Justice Vivian Bose

Then again, what does equality mean? All men are not alike. Some are rich and some are poor. Some by the very accident of birth inherit riches, others are born to poverty. There are differences in social standing and economic status. High sounding phrases cannot alter such fundamental facts. It is, therefore, impossible to apply rules of abstract equality to conditions which predicate inequality from the start.[23]

17. *Ibid.*, p. 500.
18. Before Memory Fades (Hay House India, 2010) p. 51.
19. p. 64.
20. p. 93
21. p. 99.
22. p. 93.
23. *State of West Bengal* v. *Anwar Ali Sarkar*, AIR 1952 SC 75.

Justice K.K. Mathew

In determining the constitutionality of the Act we would construe it in such a manner as to sustain it and every possible presumption will be indulged for that purpose. Our attempt should be to preserve and not to destroy. Respect for a co-ordinate branch of government demands it.[24]

Justice P.N. Bhagwati

In this day and age, most judges would confess to technical activism. Indeed, they would be embarrassed to admit to not being activist in this sense. Thus, most judges of the Supreme Court of India have been anxious to declare the width of their power. They have declared that they are free to depart from their previous decisions. They have refused to put any constraints on the jurisdiction of the Supreme Court to hear appeals from any court or tribunal in the country.[25]

Author Guidelines

While different journals or publishing houses have set their own rules and style, a few common guidelines are given below.

- Contribution may be sent in MS word format only and preferably by e-mail.
- Word length should not exceed 5000 including footnote, for articles, 2500 words for book reviews and 1500 words for case comments. At times contributions exceeding this limit may be included at the discretion of the editorial board.
- Contributions should have one inch margins on each side with double spacing and should be justified.
- Main text should be in font size 12, style Times New Roman and footnotes should be in font size 10.
- Oxford Standard for Citation of Legal Authorities (OSCOLA) must be used for citing legal authorities. Some institutions follow "The Blue Book: A Uniform System of Citation, Harvard Law Review (19th edn)."

Except for renegotiated secondary publications, manuscript submitted must be previously unpublished and not be under consideration for publication elsewhere.

Manuscript should be accompanied by a cover sheet that provide (1) the full title of the article, (2) author's full name, (3) author's contact information, including mailing address, telephone, e-mail, and fax, and (4) the author's biographical note including academic affiliation, (5) and the author's area of specialization.

Articles should be accompanied by an abstract (in about 300 words) that briefly describes the purpose, methods and arguments of the study, and a list of key words (upto 10 words) to be used as index terms.

Law Publishers

Given below are the particulars of a few publishing houses and law journals for information of law students.

---

24. Dissenting judgment in *State of Punjab* v. *Khan Chand*, (1974) 1 SCC 549.
25. My Tryst with Justice (Universal Law Publishing Co. Pvt. Ltd., 2013 Edn.), p. 60

1. *Universal Law Publishing Co. Pvt. Ltd.*
   C-FF-1A, Dilkhush Industrial Estate,
   (Near Azadpur Metro Station)
   G.T. Karnal Road,
   Delhi-110 033
   Tel : 011-27438103, 27215334, 42381334
   Fax : 011-27458529
   E-mail : edit@unilawbooks.com
   Website : www.unilawbooks.com

---

2. *Lexis Nexis Butterworths Wadhwa,*
   14th Floor, Building No. 10, Tower B,
   DLF Cyber City, Phase-II,
   Gurgaon – 122 002
   Tel : 0124-4774444

---

3. *Thomson Reuters*
   10th Floor, Birla Towers
   East Tower 25, Barakhamba Road
   New Delhi – 110001
   Tel: 011-51781000

---

4. *Wolter Kluwer India*
   10th Floor, Tower C
   Building 10, Phase II
   DLF Cyber City
   Gurgaon, Haryana (India)
   Ph: 91-124-4960999
   Fax: 91-124-4960-888

---

5. *Eastern Law House Pvt. Ltd.,*
   54, Ganesh Chander Avenue,
   Kolkata – 700 013.

---

6. *Taxmann Publications*
   59/32, New Rohtak Road,
   New Delhi-110005
   Ph: 011-28711181

---

7. *Eastern Book Company,*
   34, Lalbagh,
   Lucknow – 226 001

LIST OF LAW MAGAZINES AND JOURNALS

S. No.	*Name, Address & E-mail*	*Periodicity*	*Website*
1.	*LAWYERS UPDATE* *Universal Book Traders,* *80, Gokhale Market,* *Opp. Teez Hazari Courts,* *Delhi – 110 054* *E-mail : unilaw@vsnl.com*	*Monthly*	*www.lawyersupdate.co.in*
2.	*WITNESS* *B-1/6 Khan Market,* *New Delhi – 110 016* *E-mail : pba@WitnessLive.in*	*Monthly*	
3.	*The PRACTICAL LAWYER* *Eastern Book Company* *34, Lalbagh,* *Lucknow – 226 001*	*Monthly*	*www.ebcwebstore.com*
4.	*LAW PROFILES* *Law Profiles Publications,* *14-15 (GF),* *Pushpa Complex,* *City Palwal,* *Haryana – 121 102*	*Monthly*	*www.lawprofiles.com*
5.	*LAWZ* *207 Essel House,* *10, Asaf Ali Road,* *New Delhi – 110 002.* *E-mail: lawz@lawmagazine.com*	*Monthly*	*www.lawmagazine.com*
6.	*ICA Quarterly* *Indian Council of Arbitration,* *Federation House,* *Tansen Marg,* *New Delhi – 110 001* *E-mail : ica@ficci.com*	*Quarterly*	
7.	*Jindal Global Law Review* *Jindal Global Law School,* *Sonipat Narela Road,* *Near Jagdishpur Village,* *Sonipat,* *Haryana – 131 001* *E-mail: jglr.jgls@gmail.com*	*Annually*	*www.jgls.org*

S. No.	Name, Address & E-mail	Periodicity	Website
8.	The Indian Journal of Public Administration, Indian Institute of Public Administration, Indraprastha Estate, Ring Road, New Delhi – 110 002	Quarterly	
9.	Competition Law Reports, Manupatra Publishing Pvt. Ltd., B-37, Sector-1, Noida – 201 301 E-mail : print@manupatra.com	Bimonthly	www.manupatra.com
10.	Indian Journal of International Law, Indian Society of International Law, V.K. Krishna Menon Bhawan, 9, Bhagwan Das Road, New Delhi – 110 001. E-mail : isil@giasdlol.vsnl.net.in	Quarterly	www.isil-aca.org
11.	NLIU Law Review, The National Law Institute University, Kerwa Dam Road, Bhopal – 462 224 (M.P.)	Quarterly	
12.	Mewar Journal of Law, Mewar Institute of Management, Sector-4C, Vasundhara, Delhi-Ghaziabad Link Road, Ghaziabad – 201 012 E-mail : mim@mimcs.com	Yearly	www.mimics.com
13.	GNLU Journal of Law, Development and Politics, GNLU, E4-GIDC, Electronics Estate, Sector-26, Gandhi Nagar, Gujarat – 382 028 E-mail : gildp@gnlu.ac.in	Annually	
14.	Arbitration & Works Contract Law Journal, Suvidha Law House, 28, Malviya Nagar, Roshanpura, Bhopal – 462 003	Bimonthly	www.suvidhalawhouse .com
15.	Vitasta Journal of Law, Vitasta School of Law & Humanities, Vitasta Campus, Pohru Crossing, Nowgam, Bye Pass NH-1A, Srinagar (J&K) E-mail : contact@vitastacollege.in	Yearly	www.vitastacollege.in

S. No.	Name, Address & E-mail	Periodicity	Website
16.	Corporate Law, Adviser, 613, Metro View Appts., Pocket B, Sector 13, Dwarka, Delhi – 110 075. E-mail : info@claonline.in	Fortnightly	www.claonline.in
17.	Indian Bar Review, Bar Council of India Trust, 21, Rouse Avenue, Institutional Area, New Delhi – 110 002 E-mail : trustbci@gmail.com	Quarterly	
18.	Nyay Deep, National Legal Services Authority, 12/11, Jamnagar House, Shahjahan Road, New Delhi – 110 001	Monthly	www.nalsa.gov.in
19.	Dehradun Law Review, Law College Dehradun, Arcadia Grant, Post Chandanwari, Prem Nagar, Dehradun E-mail : rajesh-bahuguna @yahoo.co.in	Quarterly	
20.	Chanakya National Law University Law Journal, CNLU, Nyaya Nagar, Mithapur, Patna – 800 001 E-mail : registrarcnlu@gmail.com	Annually	
21.	Christ University Law Journal, Christ University, Hosur Road, Bangalore – 560 029 E-mail : mail@christuniversity.in	Biannually	ISSN : 2278 4332
22.	Lingaya LALITA Devi Journal of Professional Studies, LLDIMS, 847-848, Mandi Road, New Delhi – 110 047.		www.ildims.org.in ISSS-2230-987X
23.	CPJ Law Journal, Chandraprabha Jain College of Higher Studies and School of Law, Plot No. OCF, Sector-A8, Narela, Delhi – 110 040.		ISSN : 0976-3562

Book Critique Assignments

Law students may be assigned to undertake review of a book by the process of describing and reacting to an author's complete work in a book. For these assignments, they may either select a book out of approved readings decided by the law school or may be allowed to select their own book. The length of the review should be around 600 words.

A Guide for the Writing of a Critique

This form of legal writing is a critical evaluation of a book to keep the reader by an objective assessment. A few guidelines are given below.

- Is the information factually correct.
- Is the book going to be an addition to the existing knowledge on the subject.
- How is the presentation? What impact does it make.
- What is the main theme of the book and what is the overall purpose of the study.
- The findings. What are conclusions or recommendations.
- Author's qualification.
- The Reviewer's Discussion. Whether interpretations or explanations are reasonable, do the inferences appear logical, were the specific hypothesis confirmed or not,

Bibliographic information, place of publication, name of publisher, year, pages, price, ISBN No.

A few samples of book reviews are given below.

Sample 1

Nani Palkhivala: A Role Model. Edited by Maj. Gen. Nilendra Kumar, Universal Law Publishing Co. Pvt. Ltd., New Delhi, India, 4th Edn., 2012, pp. 490, Rs. 595, ISBN: 978-93-5035-197-0.

Two illustrative book reviews are extracted below. Each book has been separately reviewed by two experts to indicate different approaches taken by the reviewers.

Festschrift to a 'lawyer extraordinary'

Nani Palkhivala carved out a niche for himself among distinguished Indians of the post Independence era not only by his distinctive contribution to constitutional law and governance but also by living a life of a responsible citizen committed to democracy and human values.

A festschrift in his memory reflecting the views of eminent persons from all walks of life is indeed a magnificent tribute coming as it does from a soldier of the status of the Judge Advocate General of the Indian Army.

As the editor of the volume emphasizes, Palkhivala's life and writings have a special appeal to the youth of the country who constitute, incidentally, the majority of citizens of the world's largest democracy.

Dynamic advocacy

Sorabjee thinks his clarity of thought, precision and elegance of expression, ability to think on his legs, innate humility and phenomenal memory have been part of the armoury of Palkhivala, the lawyer.

P.P. Rao quotes Justice Khanna's remark on Palkhivala's performance before the 13 Judges in the Keshavananda Bharati case (1973 Supp SCR 1) *to the effect that "The height of eloquence to which Palkhivala rose on that day has seldom been challenged and never surpassed in the history of the Supreme Court." There can be no better testimony of professional excellence of the man than what is said in this quote from one of India's greatest judges.*

Tributes

This book brings a large number of contributions of people from all walks of life who had interacted with him and found in him "integrated consciousness", "disillusionment with Indian brand of socialism", "disenchantment with too much of government and too little of governance", "compassionate reaction to human suffering", "a total commitment to the concept of Dharma", "an astute corporate vision" and "living the life of a real Karmayogi".

His understanding of economics, taxation and public finance has been of a very high order which found expression in his annual speeches immediately after the presentation of the Central budget.

The volume inspires one to know more about Palkhivala and his life and the secret of his success.

N.R. Madhava Menon
The Hindu

Sample 2

PALKHIVALA : THE GIFT OF GOD

When Finance Minister P. Chidambaram made his annual Budget speech, literally thousands in Mumbai and elsewhere in the country must have fondly remembered one name, that of Nani Palkhivala. For years, till a couple of years before he passed away, it was Nani's incisive analysis of the annual Budget that was so eagerly looked forward to by Mumbai's intelligentsia. And Nani never disappointed them. They came to hear him not in the hundreds but in thousands and they never returned disappointed.

Nani's analysis of the Budget would be though, grueling and unparallel. Nani was an institution by himself. There was never anyone like him before and one suspect that there never will be another like him in the foreseeable future. In that sense Nani was unique. Let the world forget the reminiscences of many who personally know Nani or always were his fans and admirers and no greater tribute could ever have been paid to Nani than this beautifully produced work.

It is eulogistic but none will possibly question either its relevance or authenticity. Solicitor General Goolam E. Vahanvati stated the dilemma he faced in writing about Nani in proper perspective when he said. "What do you say about a man who has been avowed with every conceivable form of praise? What do you say about a man whose multifaceted personality and diverse achievements have been chronicled in so many different ways? How do you put in prose a tribute to a man whose mastery over the written and spoken word was legendary? How do you encapsulate in an obituary a tribute, which would run into various chapters?"

It is admittedly a tough job. But the good soldier and Judge Advocate General of the Indian Army that Maj. Gen. Nilendra Kumar is, he has succeeded by any imagination in getting some 75 distinguished citizens from various walks of life including judges, fellow lawyers, bureaucrats, journalists and politicians to write about Nani as they knew him and the fact that so many willingly and happily obliged itself is a tribute to the high regard and affection in which Nani was universally hold.

Among those whose contributions are recorded are President A.P.J. Abdul Kalam, M.C. Chagla, Speaker Somnath Chatterjee, Prime Minister Manmohan Singh, Karan Singh, P.C. Alexander, Justices P.N. Bhagwati, R.S. Pathak, V.R. Krishna Iyer and Sujatha Manohar, corporate leaders like Ratan Tata and Ajay Piramal, fellow lawyers like Soli J. Sorabjee, Fali S. Nariman and Iqbal Wagla, politicians like Atal Bihari Vajpayee and academicians like P.R. Brahmananda. Interestingly, four Army officers all over the ranks of Lt. General also have made their contributions.

The contributions make the reading most touching. To quote some of the statements made by leading contributors should be enough to convey the high regard and even awe in which Nani was held. "Nani Palkhivala was the greater advocate that I had ever known." "For sheer advocacy Nani was unsurpassable". "Above all, Nani was a human being par excellence. Fame and fortune did not increase the hat size of the legendary Nani Palkhivala." "He could hold the Supreme Court of India and the High Courts spellbound by his masterful advocacy and his persuasive oratory. No judge could resist the magnetic pull of his arguments." "The breadth of his scholarship was astonishing." "He went to become the country's foremost constitutional lawyer." "His memory was breath talking", etc. He excelled even as a human being.

Of all the tributes that one could pay his is one that said that Nani never spoke ill of people, even these who were particularly upset with him. Nani would never retaliate. Anybody familiar with constitutional law would be familiar with the famous Keshavananda Bharati case, which has been universally claimed as Nani's greatest success. It was to prevent tampering with the basic structure of the Indian Constitution for all time to come.

When an effort was made to get the case reconsidered, Nani's memorable contribution needs to be written in letters of gold. In his book, Neither Roses Nor Thorns, Justice H.R. Khanna was to write. "The height of eloquence to which Palkhivala rose on that day had seldom been challenged and never surpassed in the history of the Supreme Court." What greater tribute, may one ask, can one possibly give to Nani? But to the end of his he remained what he always was humble. No man was more approachable.

Even at the height of his professional popularity, his doors were always open to anyone who wanted to see him or seek his counsels. Countless numbers of people, young and old, rich and poor, celebrities and unknown passed through the doors of his elegant office in Bombay House day after day, week after week. He was, as one friend of his has noted, "Just as comfortable in the company of Dukes as he was in the company of dustmen."

Nani's generosity matched his humility. Born in an ordinary middle class family, he gave away in crores of rupees without any fuse. He hated publicity. What he gave away was between him and the receiver – and God. His intellectual integrity scared those in power. He would never flinch from doing what was right and he could not care less who was offended by his total honesty. He had accepted a brief from Indira Gandhi, but when he failed to persuade her that she had committed a monumental injustice by declaring a state of Emergency under which civil liberties were suppressed he had the courage to quietly but firmly return the brief. That was Nani. The tributes so richly paid to him in this back still remain inadequate. As C. Rajagopalachari said of him. "He was God's gift to India."

Such a collection of tributes needed to get published, lest we forget so noble a soul. These who would want to know about his legal work would be happy to note that included as an appendix is a list of some 140 cases in which Nani appeared in court, which would illustrate the range and catholicity of his career as a lawyer. But an even more welcome offer is a free CD of one of Nani's speeches which is thoughtfully presented with the text. For which praise be. Nani thus lives as much in words as in his imperishable voice. It is an unforgettable gift to the reader for which there cannot be enough praise for the editor and publisher. To be able just to listen to Nani is to hear him alive.

M.V. Kamath

Sample 3

COURTS MARTIAL UNDER SCRUTINY

Through this book, the author has attempted, successfully, to discuss and highlight various complex issues pertaining to current topics of international law, inter-alia, *human rights, its interface with terrorism, and military law* vis-à-vis *torture. Having made out a case for an apparatus of assess "disciplinary health" of our Army in the opening Chapter, the author, in the following 13 Chapters, has discussed the legal implications and inadequacies of the UN peacekeeping operations; pragmatic measures and humanitarian approach for these operations to be smooth and successful, the role of the International Committee of the Red Cross (ICRC) with particular reference to the Kargil conflict and their motivation and reasons, valid or otherwise, to act or not to act in a manner desired by the affected and concerned country.*

The treatment, at length, of the topic, which has recently shocked and horrified the world at large, i.e. *"torture" in Chapter 10 in the light of the related and well-known International Conventions, would furnish, equally a reader and a critic, the requisite information and knowledge on the subject, including the legal refrains.*

The topic of terrorism, a major challenge to the world, has been aptly dealt with in Chapters six to nine, including the difficulties encountered in bringing the terrorists to law and, certain measures and the methodology to overcome these problems. The need to follow the law even in the prosecution of a "terrorist" has been brought out with the help of relevant judicial pronouncements on the subject.

The reader is likely to find the discussion on "Natural Justice in Procurement Process", Chapter 12, interesting, illuminating and innovative.

The book makes an interesting reading and furnishes sufficient and useful information on the topics therein. The text read with the bibliography would, indeed, serve as a useful and handy reference material to a discerning reader.

Maj. Gen. S.K. Sanan
AVSM, VSM (Retd.)
U.S.I. Journal

Sample 4

MILITARY JURISPRUDENCE

MILITARY LAW is a subject least understood outside the defence services largely because of the absence of teaching and research in mainstream legal education.

Of late, there has been a spate of constitutional challenges against standards and procedures of court martial and of service matters, which compelled a revision of colonial statutes on the subject. Adoption of a series of international conventions in respect of armed conflict is also added to an otherwise limited area of military jurisprudence.

Given the size of the army and the complexity of tasks in which it is involved in the defence of the country, it is natural that military discipline and operations will increasingly become the subject of legal scrutiny for perfecting standards of adjudication and justice. However, the statutes of adjudication and justice. However, the statutes and occasional decisions by the superior courts are inadequate material to do academic research of any value.

In this context, scholarly writings by officers of the Judge Advocate General's office who give legal advice to the Army Chief and administer justice to the army personnel are an important source of instructive information both to the officers and men of the army as well as the concerned citizens outside.

The author has made a significant contribution in this regard by publishing a series of books on different aspects of military law of which, the one under review is the latest. The book is a compilation of 14 articles, apparently written on different occasions to critically examine emerging issues and challenges like prosecuting terrorists, enhancing disciplinary, health and professional competence, proxy war and national security, U.N. peace keeping operations, military conflict and international humanitarian law, protection of basic human rights of army personnel and legal accountability mechanisms of defence procurements.

A great deal of research on law and comparative study of practices elsewhere has gone into the writings and they are presented in a style understandable to both the lawmen and the laymen. A widespread concern for rule of law and fairness in procedures is evident in the analysis, which displays a judicial approach comparable to those of the judiciary outside.

If this is indicative of the level of knowledge and approaches of the Judge Advocate Generals in the three Defence Services, one fails to understand why are not being considered for elevation to the higher courts of the land where there is need for multiple talents and of persons with higher levels of integrity and discipline.

Reading the book one gets the impression that it will be mutually beneficial for the country's judiciary as well as Defence Services, if Judge Advocate Generals, with legal training and experience, are made eligible for positions in high courts, tribunals and even the apex court.

Taking a cue from the judgment in Vineet Narain case (AIR 1998 SC 889) *on fighting corruption, the author pleads for an office of Inspector General at the Army Headquarters to assume the role that the Central Vigilance Commission plays in the government. According to him it will help prevent corruption and economic offences in the Armed Forces and help evolve checks and balances fair to all concerned.*

The court of inquiry is found to be inadequate to deal with rising incidents of mala fide *exercise of discretion on the part of commanders and their supporting staff.*

Discussing about the protection of human rights in conflicts involving national and international security, the author makes an expert analysis of application of human rights treaties and constitutional guarantees in certain situations in the Punjab and the North-East.

He pleads for a mechanism to prevent malicious actions intended to harass ex-servicemen for an act done by him in the discharge of his official duties. He argues that human rights violations are military offences under the Army Act (sections 54 to 68) and can be dealt with by military courts as well as by the ordinary courts.

However, the author, from experience, contends that the military law approach is better suited to deal with human rights violation for a variety of practical reasons like speed, efficiency and fairness consistent with discipline and accountability.

If a Court Martial Appellate Tribunal as in the U.K. can be instituted in the Indian Armed Forces it will satisfy needs of justice in case of human rights violations.

Given the fact that information warfare in modern times has war winning potential, the author wants a pro-active and transparent approach in dealing with human rights in situations involving national security. The most interesting part of the book is the four chapters dealing with the prosecution of terrorists for which the author emphatically advocates a "military justice apparatus."

He is impressed by the model presented by the U.S. administration after the September strike. The evidentiary modifications are welcome and military commissions are more appropriate for trial of terrorist acts. The trial procedures are so designed to render a balance between the rights of the accused, justice to victims and the need for protection of witness.

If terrorism remains a menace to life and security despite the normal provisions of law, the society might consider the author's proposal for POTA like legislations to deal with militant groups resorting to large-scale violence causing suffering of innocent people.

The scope of right to freedom of expression of men of the defence services is dealt with by the author in the final chapter of the book. Acting under the authority of Article 33 of the Constitution, the Central Government, under section 21 of the Army Act, has restricted the exercise of fundamental rights by army persons.

There is prohibition in communicating to the media on "service information" and "service subject". According to the author such rigorous restrictions have discouraged the creative ability of service personnel. He argues for a review of the wide restriction imposed upon freedom of expression to enable them to enjoy fundamental rights in a meaningful manner.

The book is a welcome addition to legal literature and will generate thinking on the legal framework, surrounding the defence services.

N.R. MADHAVA MENON

Rapporteur

A rapporteur is a person who is appointed by an organization to report on the proceedings of its meeting. It is common for any major seminar or a conference to have a set of rapporteur to attend and report on the deliberations. If the seminar has a number of sessions or parallel technical sessions, then a panel of rapporteurs is assigned to cover each session. Rapporteur is a person who gives report.

People assisting or helping the rapporteur are called 'shadow rapporteurs'. They may vary in number depending on the issue.

It would be useful for the law students to undertake an assignment of a rapporteur at a professional meeting on a legal subject.

Rapporteurs are charged with coordinating the essential task of objectively recording the proceedings and major presentations.

A student who is asked to cover a session must first make himself familiar with the theme and main purpose of the seminar and then also the particular session that he has been asked to cover. If possible, he may try to obtain a copy of the papers being presented at the session. These would require a careful and thorough study to assimilate the main points. The rapporteur would then attentively attend the presentation. He should prepare a brief resume of the basic thrust and the questions that are put to the speaker or the comments made by other delegates. If the chairperson at the session proceeds to make his impression then the same may also warrant a mention in the report of the rapporteur.

Advantages

Exposure to the role of a rapporteur during studies in a law school helps the student in developing confidence and the ability to grasp the main issue of a presentation. He also acquires the capacity to compile a brief report using minimum essential text. He is using minimum essential text. He is introduced to eminent experts on the theme of the seminar apart from the organizers. The contacts made by him would later be useful in his profession.

Those who develop a liking for the role of a rapporteur may be trained to be specially selected for taking up the key assignments *e.g.*,

1. United Nations Special Rapporteur.
2. Special Rapporteur of the International Law Commission.
3. Special Rapporteur for Freedom of Expression.
4. Special Rapporteur on Trafficking.
5. Special Rapporteur on Counter Terrorism and Human Rights.
6. Special Rapporteur on the Human Rights on Migrants.
7. Special Rapporteur on Violence Against Women.
8. Special Rapporteur on the Right to Education.
9. Special Rapporteur on Contemporary Forms of Slavery.
10. Special Rapporteur on Disability.
11. Special Rapporteur on extra judicial summary or arbitrary executions.

12. Special Rapporteur on Freedom of Religion or Belief.
13. Special Rapporteur on the Independence of Judges and Lawyers.
14. Special Rapporteur on Extreme Poverty and Human Rights.
15. Special Rapporteur on the Rights to Freedom of Peaceful Assembly.

Coverage of a conference that was spread over seven sessions is given below as an illustration.

11TH ALL INDIA LOKAYUKTAS CONFERENCE, 2012

3rd Nov 2012 – Technical Session

REPORT

SESSION 1

THEME: *Strengthening of institutions for eradication of corruption, bringing probity, transparency in governance and role of various stake-holders.*

CHAIRED BY: *Hon'ble Mr. Justice T.S. Thakur, Judge, Supreme Court of India.*

CO-CHAIRED BY: *Hon'ble Mr. Justice Kailash Gambhir, Judge High Court of Delhi.*

SUBJECT: *Role of Lokayukta*

SPEAKERS: *Lokayüktas from different States*

The 11th All India Lokayukta started with Justice Mr. Manmohan Sarin giving a brief description about the office of Lokayukta's and the program of the conference.

First session was chaired by Hon'ble Mr. Justice Kailash Gambhir with Hon'ble Mr. Justice T.S. Thakur as Chief Guest referred to the current scenario of corruption in our country presenting statistics that placed India at a considerable high level on the corruption index. Enumerating how corruption both petty and large scale has quantified with time with severe consequence.

Justice Subhash Chandra Reddy (Lokayukta of Andhra Pradesh, Former Judge of Andhra Pradesh High Court) began his disclosure by differentiating corruption into two types that perpetrated by necessity and by habit.

Proposals:

(1) Redefining "public servant".

He made a proposal for redefining the word "Public Servant" suggesting it to read "any person involved in Public works". He was in favour of the definition to be all inclusive. He cited section 18 of Andhra Pradesh Lokayukta Act which empowers the High Court to delegate the superintendence of vigilance agencies to the Lokayuktas only in exceptional circumstances. He proposed that Lokayukta's be given the power of superintendence of vigilance agencies at all times, enacted in the legislation.

(2) With respect to power to intervene

He drew an interesting analogy by explaining section 12 of the Human Rights Protection Act, 1993, which defines functions of the Commission. Section 12(b) specifically gives the Commission the power to intervene in any proceedings relating to human rights violations pending in any court. He suggested the same to be done for Lokayukta to have intervention powers incase of any existence or apprehension of any partiality or inefficiency in investigation, or in any case of delay or any flaw in the ongoing investigation by the means of a petition by the Lokayukta.

(3) With respect to power of search and seizure.

He added that even though the Andhra Pradesh Lokayukta Act has a lot of positive features but it still lacks any provision for search and seizure power to the Lokayuktas. He advocated the police authorities to be brought under the supervision and guidance of Lokayukta's.

Comments of the chair

Justice T.S. Thakur commented on the recommendations of the speaker and expressed his disagreements over classifying corruption according to cause as it was impractical. Complete eradication of corruption by necessity by eliminating the causes is an utopian idea. While dealing with corruption we cannot depend on whether or not equal opportunity has been provided by the system or not. He also raised questions to the Lokayukta's asking them to reassess their role in punishing the corrupt, preventing corruption and creating public awareness.

Finally, he suggested enabling the Lokayukta's to have a say in recommending amendments in the existing Lokayukta Acts.

SESSION 2

***SUBJECT:** Role of Vigilance and Investigative Agencies*

***SPEAKER:** Mr. Sri Kumar, Commissioner Vigilance*

He focused upon how to control the menace of corruption while also discussing the road map that needs to be laid out. He discussed why the vigilance and anti corruption agencies have not taken a lead in this regard. Various measures need to be taken providing examples of agencies in Hong Kong and Singapore which have proposed necessary measures for zero tolerance of corruption should be made. Steps which are both punitive and preventive should be adopted. He emphasized the role of citizen participation and discussed CVC's participative Vigilance.

Disposal of cases took approximately seven years which is a very long period during which the judge changes, witnesses turn hostile and holders of the office also change. He proposed a new and reformed model "watch them, catch them and shame them."

Though police are the first law keepers of the society but the Police Act of 1861 presents the police as an agent of the Government and not of law. Only a dozen out of 30 States have changed their law but majority have not taken into consideration the Supreme Court guidelines. Pointing out the problems faced by Vigilance Commission he highlighted the absence of the CBI Act. The CVC Act is also in the draft stage. Vigilance Commission has three members and most of the time there is no uniformity and unanimity. There is a need for skilled man power, technology, capacity building, mechanism for investigation and record keeping etc.

PROPOSALS:

(1) Paper Networking

(2) Grants to Vigilance Commission referring to Vijay Programme launched by CVC which professionalizes the officer in charge and collection evidence becomes foolproof.

(3) *Multi-jurisdictional investigative platform for well co-ordinated investigation.*

(4) *Formation of the Indian Association of Anti-corruption agencies.*

Comments of the chair

On a scale of 0 to 10 of corruption, where '0' means extremely corrupted and '10' means honest, in 2010 the rate of corruption was 3.5 but it had gone down to 3.1 in 2011.

SESSION 3

Chaired By – Hon'ble Mr. Justice T.S. Thakur, Judge, Supreme Court of India

Co-Chaired – Hon'ble Mr. Justice Kailash Gambhir, Judge, High Court of Delhi

Subject – Role of Orti Mechanism and Whistle Blowers

SPEAKERS – Mr. Satyananda Mishra, Chief Information Commissioner

Ms. Aruna Roy, National Campaign for People's Right to Information

Quoting "Corruption is the flavor of the day". Mr. Satyananda Mishra pointed out that corruption not only exists among public officials but is equally seen among the common man. Corruption is manifestation of poor governance. He strongly emphasized that the society is governed by a ruling government is responsible for everything. It should not be taken for granted as in certain situations even it may lack competence. Praising the usefulness and accessibility of RTI he noted that it has created a climate of transparency. He regretted the fact that the public officials usually did not fully comply to the mandatory provisions call for disposing off a complaint within three days.

The second speaker Ms. Aruna Roy appealed to everyone to join in with eradication of corruption. Quoting "if we lose hope thing is left with us" she urged everyone to work together against this evil. She conceded that one cannot work without a system or an institution. Yet the system should be transparent and must be accountable to the public. To this end, RTI has become a fulcrum.

According to Ms. Aruna Roy, democracy is facing many challenges but for the first time ordinary man is interested in issues of governance, mechanisms and corruption. She wanted the Lokayukta and Lokpal to function on parallel lines as both are equally important.

Being a social activist, Ms. Aruna Roy formulated the RTI Act in five critical points:—

- *that the public need information;*
- *need to be heard;*
- *need relevant action;*
- *need participation; and*
- *need protection.*

She proposed the

- *Need for a strong Lokpal at the Center to tackle high level corruption.*
- *Establishment of an independent Lokayukta at the State level.*
- *Bringing in an independent as well as multiple mechanism.*

- *Enacting legislations for grievance redressal and whistleblower.*
- *Law should be allowed to operate freely and properly.*

Comments of the Chair

Justice Manmohan Sarin pointed out that whistleblowers normally encounter a problem after a complaint has been lodged. He favoured the legislation to be sensitive to provide an adequate protection to the whistleblower.

SESSION 4

Subject : Role of Judiciary and Legal Fraternity

Chaired By : Hon'ble Mr. Justice Dipak Mishra, Judge, Supreme Court of India.

Co-Chaired : Justice Hima Kohli, Judge, High Court of Delhi.

SPEAKERS : *Mr. Parag Tripathi, Sr. Advocate and Former Additional Solicitor General of India.*

Mr. P.H. Parekh, President, Supreme Court Bar Association.

Mr. P.P. Rao, Senior Advocate, Supreme Court of India.

Justice Dipak Mishra in his opening remarks to the session said that democracy in India is fundamental and a basic feature of the Constitution of India. Thus, eradication of corruption becomes a constitutional facet and judiciary plays an important role in this field.

Mr. Parag Tripathi started his presentation by stressing that "we are a society in transition. All societies in transition have big issues of corruption." He said that institution today is showing a "trust deficit". Thus, the approach from the institutional and rights deficit has been shifted to trust deficit. There is a need for introspection. The role of judiciary comes into play. He urged to exhibit faith and hope and work together for eradication of corruption. He called for an appropriate scheme for appointment of lokpals. The basic idea was to have the involvement of higher judiciary which would be impartial in its nature. It would then be helpful in having an independent and impartial body to monitor the public servants.

Mr. P.H. Parekh commented that the Constitution of India has within itself many provisions against corruption. Article 14 is an-anticorruption law, extended by Article 19(1)(a). By virtue of Article 12, a State is made accountable to Article 14. Mr. Parekh suggested that though a lot has been done to fight against corruption under the 'Prevention of Corruption Act' but this is not sufficient.

Mr. P.P. Rao submitted that even after the passage of Prevention of Corruption Act in 1988, corruption in its true sense has not been prevented or reduced. Strangely it has escalated. The underlying reason, as pointed out by him, was the deficiency in the existing law.

Proposals and comments of the chair

Commenting to the various views raised by the speakers, Justice Hima Kohli concluded the session by pointing out the need for a channelized network to function in a beneficial way and not in a destructive manner. She felt that the judicial intervention at the instance of NGO/ Panchayat is an effective mechanism against corruption. She pointed out that getting rid of 'blacksheep' at all levels is another measure to fight against corruption.

SESSION 5

SUBJECT: *Role and Significance of Media in building public opinion for institutions, of Lokayukta, Disciplinary and Vigilance Agencies.*

Chaired by : *Hon'ble Ms. Justice Ranjana Prakash Desai, Judge, Supreme Court of India.*

Hon'ble Ms. Justice Geeta Mittal, Judge, High Court for Delhi

Speakers

1. *Mr. Arun Shourie, Former Union Minister and eminent Journalist.*
2. *Mr. Aroon Purie, Editor-in-Chief, India Today.*
3. *Mr. Soli Sorabjee, Sr. Advocate and former Attorney-General for India.*

Mr. Arun Shourie observed that corruption is a cancer and not a mere scandal. Lokayukta would exhibit its importance only if it was allowed to function. Keeping all the exceptions apart this institution has not been allowed to function. The Administrative Reports are published periodically but are not relied upon by the executive. He referred to the 12th Report of the Administrative Reforms Commission submitted by the Justice Manmohan Sarin (Lokayukta NCT) in this regard and pointed out that the recommendations of 11th Report had also been ignored. Lokayuktas are not allowed to be effective as the applications filed before them are forwarded to those departments by the government which are already corrupt. The reports which are sent in reply by those departments are erroneous. The government finally acts on the basis of these reports. The speaker quoted the remarks of Justice R.M. Lodha while observing that the power of search and seizure should be given to all Lokayuktas as provided for in Madhya Pradesh and Karnataka. He said that the question of Jurisdiction is raised in every State to hamper further investigations. It was not just the provisions of this Act that are powerless but even the lawyers play a crucial role in delaying court proceedings.

Mr. Aroon Purie highlighted the definition of 'Power' and remarked it was used to mean "How much wrong doing you can do and yet get away with it". Government is accountable to the citizens for the use of resources but sadly it still works under a cloak of secrecy. He noted that progress is maximum when there is a transparency in public sphere. Media's conscious efforts have given meaning to the word 'SCAM'.

SCAM (wrong doing) can be categorized into three stages:—

1. *Exposure by means of RTI, media, agency or a social activist.*
2. *Investigation, search and seizure and arrest by the executive.*
3. *Trial and conviction by judiciary.*

The major problem in India is that everybody wants to interfere with the other person's job. According to him, one organ should not usurp the power of others. The amplification of issues by media has enhanced knowledge of the public and therefore the officials cannot maintain secrecy any more. Political class has come to know the power of media and has begun to use it for its own advantage.

Mr. Soli Sorabjee, the third speaker opined that a question before him was that if the existing legislations have many lacunas then how can the Lokayuktas be made effective? He highlighted that at present Lokayukta has only recommendary power. It should be made mandatory under the law to make Lokayukta effective. The following are the drawbacks of Lokayukta system.

1. *They do not have the power to order and direct.*
2. *They lack the power of search and seizure.*
3. *They cannot take* suo moto *action.*

Media can place emphasis on the eradication of these drawbacks. The media should maintain the momentum of public opinion. The press has the duty to be accurate about its facts while exercising its powers to express. Otherwise it can also be said to violate Article 21 of the Constitution.

The gist of the proposals

1. *The people of India should rise to build a culture against corruption. Public should exhibit a zero tolerance policy towards corruption. Media should expose the faces of the culprits indulged in corrupt practices after completion of their trial.*
2. *Lokayuktas created by government should be given the power to act independently. While media is active the system of enforcement and judicial process is weak. Hence communication between the media and Lokayukta must be increased.*
3. *Press should be given the power to monitor the report submitted to the Government by various agencies and launch campaign to make the public aware of the loopholes in the legislations.*
4. *Public pressure have to be maintained to make the system of Lokayuktas effective. However, the same cannot be done till the time they are given effective powers. If Lokayuktas want to achieve success in their efforts then they should not look for any kind of favour from government but they should consider government as their adversary.*
5. *No more need for institutionalization but what is required is due implementation and effectiveness.*

Comments of the chair

In her concluding speech Hon'ble Justice Ranjana Prasad Desai recommended that one of the major roles of media is to educate people. People should be sensitized to respect Lokayuktas and its decisions. Section 12 of the Delhi Lokayukta Act, 1995 is an enabling provision to make the office of Lokayukta become more accountable. Commenting on the role of media, she explained that exposure of corrupt practices is not the major role of media. Instead their job is to build public opinion. A pro-active media will ensure respect for citizen, protect their rights and improve the quality of administration.

Justice Manmohan Sarin summed up the entire session while observing that all the orders given by the Lokayuktas are available on the internet giving unhindered accessibility to the media persons and also the public.

SESSION 6

Subject : Eradicating and containing corruption in public life.

Speakers : *Dr. R.K. Raghvan, former Director, CBI*

Mr. Vinod Rai, Comproller and Auditor General of India

Dr. S.Y. Quraishi, former Chief Election Commissioner

Chaired by : *Hon'ble Mr. Justice (Dr.) B.S. Chauhan, Judge, Supreme Court of India*

Dr. R.K. Raghavan, former Director, CBI raised the issues related to problems of combating corruption. He quoted Mahatma Gandhi's line that "Justice does not help those who slumber but only those who are vigilant." He raised the issue that why one should pay bribe? The traditional method of combating any crime was for the State to enhance the punishment for the said crime. The studies conducted by various criminologist have proved that deterrent action is not effective in reducing the crime. According to him instead of adopting mechanism of harsher punishment the State should adopt hardening of its approach to check siphoning of public wealth by the public servants. He recalled the words of Plato that 'Good people do not need laws to make them responsible and bad people will always find a way to go around them." He said that there were no police station where a report can be filed without paying bribe. Hence there is a necessity to bring transparency in the present system and to enhance the integrity at IPS officer level. He wanted an increase on inputs on adoption of ethics. He also emphasized the creation of a police complaint authority.

Mr. Vinod Rai, Comptroller and Auditor General of India remarked that issue of corruption is not new. It was deep rooted in the Indian society. He quoted the midnight speech of S. Radhakrishnan, first Vice-President of India delivered on 15th August, 1947 that "Opportunities are great but when power outstrips ability the nation will fall on evil days". When the power outstrips ability then there arises corruption. Now we cannot blame the British for corruption and nepotism in public life. He mentioned that citizens have taken the centre stage and civil societies are raising their voice. We live in a glass house and all our activities can be seen, adjudged. The officials are accountable for their decisions. Only then economic growth will be sustainable at a desired pace.

Dr. S.Y. Quraishi, former Chief Election Commissioner started with a statement that corruption is in everyone's mind and is deep rooted also. It has become so common that one often laughs on it. In recent times due to Anna Hazare, the public has again started showing anger and frustrations at being cheated. Last word of corruption is yet to be heard. Present 162 members of Parliament are those who have criminal cases pending against them. This number was increase to 124 last five years. Statements like "all politicians are thief is a dangerous statement" since all are not involved in the corrupt practices. The elections are the root cause of corruption. He raised a question that from where has election money come to the politicians? He mentioned that this money comes from corporates and public etc. Earlier when the election became competitive, the ministers started taking help of the muscle men. Now muscle men instead of providing support to others have started using their money power for themselves and in this way they are now contesting elections.

He proposed

1. *A need to educate voters that they should practice ethical voting and avoid voting corrupt candidates.*

2. *Check expenditure to ensure transparency in donations to the political parties.*
3. *Audit report to be put on the website. It is more important to catch a corrupt person at the gate* i.e. *at initial stage, rather than apprehending him at a point by demanding a Lokpal. It is very important to enhance the power and position of Central Vigilance Commission as it was a statutory authority.*

SESSION 7 :

Subject : Rationalizing Jurisdiction of Lokayuktas over Public Functionaries and Civil Servants, including the head of the statutory Corporations.

Chaired by : *Hon'ble Mr. Justice A.P. Shah, Former Chief Justice High Court of Delhi.*

Speakers:

Lokayukta of Kerala

He remarked that Lokayukta cannot proceed suo motu *and hence applicable laws should be amended. Lokayukta in his statement has entertained and admitted complaints against tehsildars and other petitions. He said corruption is cancerous growth and highlighted that there are lacunas in the Act and it needs reforms.*

Lokayukta of Jharkhand

He pleaded for adequate jurisdictional powers and Lokayukta to be kept beyond the ambit of RTI. However, the chair added that in a case which was still pending, furnishing of information was not necessary and the same has been enacted in the provisions of RTI.

Lokayukta of Odisha

Being the senior most Lokayukta, he recommended various steps to combat corruption.

Lokayukta of Bihar

He emphasized on morality and quote Vivekananda "we are high on principles but low on practice" directing towards the lacunas in the Act and misconduct of people leading to increased corruption.

Lokayukta of Haryana

He proposed the idea of moral education to be introduced in schools and colleges and quoted Dr. Rajendra Prasad "Let there be hundreds of defects in the Constitution. Unless the elected are men of integrity and honour nothing wrong can last for long." He also added that the Act of Lokayukta is a paper tiger and needs amendments and implementation.

Lokayukta of Uttar Pradesh

He observed that uniformity is not attainable and that the Act needs to be interpreted in each one's own way.

Legal Drafting

Legal drafting creates binding legal text. This form of writing is used by lawyers, judges, law corporates, legislators and other law professionals to express narration of facts and legal analysis.

Legal Memorandum

Purpose

The object of a legal memorandum is to study and analyze a legal problem and to present an objective legal opinion on that issue. It is used to examine available options and to formulate arguments.

Addressee

A legal memorandum is meant for generally another lawyer like a briefing counsel or a law corporate or the client. It is usually not conveyed to the judges or opposite counsels.

How to prepare

(a) Carefully read the entire record including the pleadings and annexures.

(b) Outline the substance of the record and key elements of the case.

(c) Outline the facts in a chronological order. Link up with page or file numbers.

(d) Familiarize yourself with the overview of the applicable law.

(e) Legal research on applicable substantive and procedural law.

(f) Substantive research to be carried out in a top down manner, starting with Supreme Court decisions.

(g) List out favourable and unfavourable case law.

(h) Chart the law against facts. To check and record that all necessary ingredients of law have been matched.

(i) Formulation of legal issues raised that are either in conformity with favourable rulings or distinguish from unfavourable case law. All such issues should be clearly identified and analyzed.

(j) Outline or final opinion – Based on the elements of the law, this indicates a legal plan as to how each legal issue is connected to the facts and in what manner should it be addressed.

(k) Conclusion – Based on the salient summary of facts and the law reviewed, it demonstrates a brief about the approach or outcome of the discussion.

Motions

This is a legal writing common in United States and a few other countries.

A motion is a legal writing executed in the form of a procedural device to present a limited issue for decision by a court. Usually it is likely to be contested. In the context of judicial practice in India, these are more commonly referred as a 'miscellaneous application'. These may be moved at any stage of a civil, criminal, revenue or taxation proceedings or litigation.

Motions may be moved in the form of an oral request in an open court followed by presentation or filing of a written document in the court.

Case Brief or Case Summary

It is a short and concise summary of a judicial decision.

Purpose

A case brief is generally prepared for discussion in a class but can also be needed to prepare a reference while conducting research on a legal topic or while working out a brief to go in for an appeal or revision.

Components

A case brief would usually consist of:

(i) Title and citation.
(ii) Facts of the case.
(iii) Statutory and procedural law involved.
(iv) Legal issues.
(v) Decision or ruling.
(vi) Reasons or justification.
(vii) Concurring and/or dissenting views.
(viii) Followed, relied, dissented or over ruled, etc.
(ix) Significance of decision.

E-Journals

Electronic journals or e-journals are scholarly journals or intellectual magazines that can be accessed *via* electronic transmission. In other words, they are usually published on the web. Their purpose is to provide material for academic research and study. They are formatted like journal articles in traditional printed journals.

A large number of electronic journals are online and only journals. An increasing number of journals are now available as online open access journals, requiring no subscription and offering free full text articles and reviews to all.

Most electronic journals are published in HTML and/or PDF formats, but some are available in only one of the two formats.

It would be advisable for the students to start e-journals for their law schools. It offers following distinct advantages over printed journals.

1. E-journals are less expensive to produce. Consequently, the challenges of marketing it or to find sponsors is avoided.
2. These carry advantage of continuous inclusion of data as opposed to annual or bi-annual publications.
3. These offer scope for continuous proof reading and improvement of the included text.
4. The problems of unsold or unsubscribed copies of the printed journals are not faced.
5. Plagiarism or theft is easier to detect.
6. The mode is more environment friendly.

CHAPTER 4
Moots

What it is?

Clinical Legal Education prepares law students to practice and attain proficiency in what they have learnt in class rooms. Actual application is difficult to learn from mere classroom lectures. Law Schools ought to place great reliance on Clinical Legal Education. Moots, mock trials, legal aid clinics, law reforms competitions, legal writings and highly competing quizzes help law students attain proficiency in actual application of law to real life situations.

Conflict resolution is one of the foremost tasks for the lawyers to perform. Amongst divergent claims, disputed facts and challenging interests, a deep study of applicable legal regime and their clear enunciation is a prime requisite to prosecute the client's brief. Scope for interpretation in the legal provisions provides a scope for sharp lawyering skills. This is systematically put to practice in a moot by the law students in a competitive spirit.

A moot is a simulated court proceeding in which two teams argue points of law before a court. Mooting is a legal hearing modelled on an appeal from a trial. By this stage, all the facts have been agreed upon. However, within the boundary of given facts there is freedom to present them in different perspectives. There are no witnesses. What is to be judged is the way in which the law is applied to the facts and this is argued out before a judge or a panel of judges. Moot is heard by a panel drawn from a list of experienced lawyers, judges or law teachers. A moot court is therefore, viewed as an extra-curricular activity where participants take part in simulated court proceedings. The entire exercise usually involves first drafting briefs or memorials and thereafter participating in oral arguments. It is therefore, obvious that the practice of mooting was devised to equip law students to make a persuasive presentation in a court of law and to expose them to advocacy skills.

The underlying concept of a moot is to present a place of meeting to the law students for discussion of a hypothetical question. The aim is to equip a student on an undisputed facts situation and to introduce them to the rules and etiquettes of the court.

Use of moots, as one of the modes of law learning is meant to develop advocacy skills, reasoning ability, sharp legal perspective, and application of law amongst the future law professionals. Mooting provides opportunities to develop instinctive legal reasoning which can aid in future legal studies. It provides a chance to learn advocacy techniques and become more confident with the law.

To derive optimum benefits, moots need to be specially formulated legal exercises. The setting should not be stereotyped. They should be drafted with requisite innovation to fathom expertise of law students in different branches of law. Well-designed events organized with total transparency and fairness in a stimulated atmosphere of tough competition are the hallmarks of different competitions conducted by the law schools.

The clear and uniform rules of the competition help to generate a high standard of performance. The panel of judges drawn from a wide sphere of relevant subject experts by their penetrating questions is helpful in an objective assessment of winners. The keenly contested rounds between the teams representing Law Schools within the country or abroad judged by a galaxy of expert judges show case most prestigious law moots in the region. It also prepares them to enhance their communication skills, advocacy competence and sharp legal perspective.

Moot court competitions are an innovative mode to familiarize legal students to the practical facets of the legal profession. Mooting becomes a critical element of legal education because it provides the training skills essential for a prospective lawyer wishing to practice in appellate courts. The activity takes shape of a match where legal minds battle in a challenging time frame under complex conditions. It enhances their ability to articulate their thoughts and arguments.

The competition tests advocacy competence of the students. The event serves as a definitive test for the legal proficiency and dexterity of competing teams as appraised by the scholarly and eminent judges. It is beneficial to the participants to make them think out of the box, come up with sharp replies, develop confidence in public speaking and improve the ability to think on their feet.

Mooting aims at imparting excellence in legal education by preparing high grade law professionals capable of facing future legal challenges with confidence. It is in the moots that tomorrow's star litigators are moulded. An individual howsoever brilliant cannot win an event by himself. The event also stimulates team work and participation in it which is regarded as a great achievement. The event is designed with a view to provide an opportunity to the law students to exhibit their communication skills. The wonderful experience of a friendly and keen competition is long remembered by the participants.

It is an innovative and challenging test designed to provide a canvas for interaction and networking not only within the participants but also amongst esteemed jurists and legal experts. Even the student volunteers stand to benefit. The freshers who only get to witness an event get valuable lessons. It provides a unique opportunity for the learners to develop their research, writing and oral advocacy skills as they endeavour to come to grip with issues of relevance to international arena. It witnesses meaningful discussions. Mooters are judged individually in three board areas. A winner is assessed based on the moot performance, irrespective of the final outcome and an evaluation of who was better on the law. The general areas include:

- Legal research and content of argument
- Presentation: including court etiquette
- Question answering skills

This event bears testimony to the total enthusiasm, motivation and hard work of those who provide guidance for administrative support, faculty, staff and volunteer students.

Moot court competitions may be designed on diverse themes. These could be of domestic nature that focus on municipal law. The applicable law may be based on taxation, contract, human rights, family law, criminal law, competition law or environmental law etc. On the other hand, international moot competitions take up subjects such as public international law, international human rights law, international humanitarian law and international commercial arbitration.

It is necessary for the mooter to identify all the legal issues arising from the question, taking care to identify which of the issues is relevant. A few aspects may be included in the problem merely to distract or confuse. Thereafter, it is determined as to which issues would fall under the assigned responsibility (depending upon which of the positions – junior or senior counsel – has been allocated to the mooter).

How to Address the Court

The mooters would do well to practice how to address the judges appropriately.

A single male judge is to be referred to as 'My Lord' or as 'Your Lordship'. A male or mixed panel of judges are to be called as 'My Lords' or 'Your Lordships'.

A situation involving judges in an international tribunal/court may be addressed as 'Your Excellencies'. The use of the word 'you' or 'your' should be avoided'. Any occasion to address or interact with a particular judge is to be avoided as far as possible. Hence, if it is intended to say 'you may wish to see this document', it would be desirable to say 'My Lord (or My Lords/Lordships) may wish to peruse this document.'

Use of following words is recommended and is illustrative

1. 'My lords. I submit that'
2. 'With your lordship's permission I would like now'
3. 'I am deeply obliged. My lords'
4. 'My lords. I most humbly submit'

Judges should always be addressed as 'Your Honour' or 'Your Lordships'. When there is more than one judge sitting on the bench, they are referred to collectively as 'the Court', unless one judge has asked a question and the mooter is answering her/his question. Generally use the term 'your honour' instead of 'you'.

With due practice, the students would form a habit where this mode of address becomes a habit.

In the unfortunate event that a mooter has no idea about a particular case or question raised then it would be advisable to say :

1. "Your Honour, I am afraid I cannot assist the Court on that point" – but then link this to something the mooter knows; or

2. "Your Honour, I am afraid I cannot assist the Court on that point" (It would be preferable for the mooter to shift to a point about which he knows something about).

Questions from the Bench are one of the most important aspects of mooting and are to be welcomed. These are not to be regarded as impediments or interruptions. They test the strength of argument, familiarity with the facts and with the law. They provide a chance for mooters to show how confident they really are.

It would be prudent to make a note of the following.

1. To seek judge's permission at various stages of the presentation.
2. To keep a careful watch on the judges to see if they are following the arguments. In case they are busy finding a citation or in discussion amongst them to give a suitable pause. Do proceed only when they so indicate.

How to prepare

1. Read the facts of the case very carefully.
2. The facts should be assimilated in a chronological order and in proper sequence. Discard those that are irrelevant.
3. Make a note of points relevant to the legal issues involved in the memorial and those that have a bearing on the material aspects of the problem.
4. Identify the main problem; and then the applicable legal provisions both for and against.
5. The connected case law should then be applied to build up the arguments in favour, while also coming up with a reasonable and convincing explanation for rulings that are unfavourable.
6. The ruling should be catalogued in a manner to first bring out the binding precedents and followed by persuasive case law.

Remember the facts stated in the moot problem are sacrosanct. The mooter cannot discard or deviate from the facts. The mooting is on the law and not on the validity or reliability of any factual data. Do not comment on the truthfulness of the facts. Do not doubt the facts. Begin with the facts. Where required prepare a list of dates. Decide how all the facts relate together. It may be helpful to plan a chronology or flow chart by way of a diagram or map to assimilate the facts of the moot question. Understand how one event has influenced the other. Once the pertinent facts are known, think about which facts are more persuasive for each side and how these facts might be used in a legal argument.

The oral argument to be persuasive must be clear. To clarify, the mooter must add force. The proposition to be proved should be stated at the beginning, because the hearing of the facts adduced as evidence can then be more easily appreciated.

Try out different approaches and thrash out every point with the team. Answer the questions that occur to another mind. Prepare for any awkward query. See what sequence of facts are most effective. Accustom yourself to place your material in different arrangements. See what plan is most effective. Argue the case to oneself, friends and use every available anvil on which to hammer out own arguments.

Carry out a careful reconnaissance of whole ground not leaving any nook or corner unsurveyed. Undertake a preliminary survey of the whole ground of action and a careful forecast of all the contingencies that are likely to arise. Be prepared for the pitfalls or the stumbling blocks that one may encounter. Come up with a convincing mental preparation to meet theses contingencies. Do not ever give up easily. Remember that even a hopeless case can be argued in a persuasive manner.

It would be disastrous for a mooter to greater mistake than to ignore or attempt to conceal the weak points in his case. On the other hand it may be an effective strategy at an early stage of the argument to invite attention to one's weakest point. This should be done even before the court has discovered it. Then proceed to meet it with the best answer at one's disposal, to deal with all the remaining points and to end with as powerful a presentation of one's strongest point as one is capable of making within the time available.

The mooters path is generally not smooth and straight. When you know that your case is confronted with a serious difficulty in the shape of an awkward passage, in the evidence or an embarrassing precedent, do not shirk from it. Read the awkward passage with all emphasis or quote the authority without flinching. Be honest and truthful. Point out the difficulty which it creates for you. You will almost invariably find that the first instinct of the Judge is to assist you by pointing out that the evidence is less damaging to you than you represented or that the precedent is, on examination, distinguishable.[1]

Research and Role of a Researcher

Indepth research involves several key steps. This is one of the most significant part of the moot. The time and effort required at each stage will vary according to the particular nuances of the moot question. The research may proceed in the following manner.

Step 1

The starting point of research would involve identifying what law is to be applied. This is a crucial aspect. However, it may become obvious in one moot while not so obvious in another.

Step 2

Having identified what field of law the problem is based on, the next effort is to formulate one's response to the legal issues which have been identified. Take help of your friends and teachers. Discuss with them at length. This hypothesis or the 'hunch' would guide further research. Text books, journals or other literature may be consulted to help narrow detailed research. This is a critical matter. Don't be obstinate and rigid on your initial response. Don't be afraid to change or refine the hypothesis as the research developes.

1. Making of a Good Lawyer by Jagdish Swarup, Universal Law Publishing Co. Pvt. Ltd., Delhi, 2nd Edn., 2005, 115 pages, Rs. 125, ISBN 81-7534-447-4.

Step 3

Internal moots may not allow much preparation time but the key to success is in making the research comprehensive. This should be done in an efficient and effective manner. Some useful tips are:

- Let the problem guide the research. Usually the moot problem would be based on a recent and controversial problem. Often in internal moots there will be references to case law or statutes in the problem question. These may be starting point for the research work.
- Be aware of the status of the authorities to be relied on. Better to consult work of renowned and prestigious authors and experts.
- Statutes and decisions of superior are of courts binding value whereas decisions of other courts are persuasive in nature. Secondary sources (articles and texts) are merely illustrative. They accord persuasive guidance and no more. Further, it is important to note that the status of authorities will also depend on the 'jurisdiction'.
- Do follow up footnotes in cases/texts/articles. Always make it a point to read the original cases and not to rely on someone else's assessment or summary of them. However, in some cases the authoritative rulings may not be available. This will provide in-depth information.
- Don't let the trivials distract you from the big picture. These may have been inserted only to test depth of your study and understanding. Be familiar with the general principles of the area of law at issue – *e.g.*, don't fail to have authorities on duty of care to hand, just because the only question in dispute relates to breach of duty, since a Judge may still want to ask a question on duty of care.

The student assigned the role of a researcher plays a pivotal part. He is not to carry out his role individually or in isolation. He is a very important member of the team. He is to be actively associated and assisted by his other colleagues. Where possible, take help from other students, faculty and even senior practitioners.

It would be more appropriate to consider researching as an integral part of the mooting. It is not to be seen merely as the responsibility or the role of a researcher. Researching involves an extensive study and assimilation of the facts of the case. It requires due perusal of the relevant law issues together with examination of applicable legal regime. All connected case law or rulings must be carefully perused. A detailed estimation and assessment of the opponent's arguments is also vital. The process of researching would demand hard work over many hours carrying out legal analytical research and practical writing exercise.

Role of a Mooter

Role of a mooter is to present its case before the judges by use of logical and persuasive arguments. These are to be expressed in front of the judges, which is an essential skill for a counsel. This would demand a highly practiced and developed public speaking capacity.

Distribution of the task at hand could be shared by the mooters as indicated below. Here appellant may be read as mooter.

1. Appellant 1: presents all five parts – give appearances, introduces the case, gives an outline submissions of both appellants, presents their own submissions concludes their own submissions and then hands over to the second appellant.
2. Appellant 2: Needs to cover Parts 3, 4 and 5 only. In closing stage, the second speaker will need to deal with relief sought.
3. Respondent 1: Presents all five parts – gives appearances, introduces the respondent case, outlines the respondents submissions, presents their own submissions. He/she must also respond to the perspective to the respondent case, by being responsive to the appellants arguments; and then hand over to second respondent.
4. Respondent 2: Parts 3,.4 and 5 only. The second respondent must also be responsive, and highlight the relief sought.

Time Management

A very crucial part of mooting, time management must not be lost sight of. This aspect has many dimensions. To begin with, the time a student should give to mooting. It should be carefully decided and firmly struck to. Rehearsals should be carried out to see viability of time allotted. Time allocation is also applicable with regard to preparation of memorial. Participation in moots must not be at the expense of other studies. *Secondly,* at the actual moot the time allocated for discussion of various issues should also be pre-decided.

Each participant is required to present his submission clearly within a set time. They may further get time for a rebuttal at the end of the moot in case they wish to make further submissions.

Developing a Case Theory

The mooter should ask himself 'what do I need to provide to get the relief my client seeks?" The case theory is one's own stand or response to the problem.

To have a case theory, it is essential to understand one's complete case. It involves full comprehension how all the puzzles in the pieces of one's case fit together to make the winning picture. In other words, it is a work out of the complete case.

To develop a case theory it is essential that the mooter carefully consider questions such as:

- Must I prove all four (or necessary) elements of the test to succeed?
- Do I have a partial or complete defence?
- Do the second counsel's submissions rely on the success of the first counsel or would it be advisable for the second counsel to submit his case in the alternative?
- What is necessary? What is sufficient? Is it a convincing case?

It is essential that the mooters look out for any traps, that is, any inconsistencies or reverse burdens that may arise on the facts. These are to be guarded against. To navigate these traps ensure that he is aware of his co-counsel's arguments. Further, always consider what the standard of proof is and who bears the burden of proof. Is it in merely *prima facie* measure or in the way of beyond all reasonable doubt. Having a case theory also involves understanding the reason why his reasoning is the better argument.

Thinking Holistically

When preparing your submissions, don't close your mind to what everyone else in the moot is researching. Respond to most obvious theories or responses. It is important you think holistically in preparation for any moot. Do not overlook any versions lightly. Appreciating all angles of the case will make the mooter better on his allocated issues. Awareness of the opponent's case will (a) encourage the mooter to acquire penetrating knowledge about the relevant area of law; (b) enable one to improve one's case to combat the key points of the opponent's version; and (c) make the mooter better at researching (both with regard to their own submissions and also to questions from the bench).

Written Submissions

Written submissions may be used as an aid for the Court during oral submissions.

Written submissions in internal competitions are intended to give the judge a concise and precise overview of one's case. Often they are read only briefly by the Judge. As such it is important to make them clear and succinct. Written submissions should essentialise one's case, and help orient the judge if they get lost in the middle of your submissions. They may also assist the judges to carry out relative valuation of competing teams.

Written submissions may be read by the mooters only briefly. A tendency to rely on their extensive reading be avoided. This however, does not reduce their importance. The submissions constitute a work of substantive legal research and reasoning. It is essential that they are correct, wholesome address the issues; cite authorities; and, progress in a logical and reasoned order.

For any kind of written submissions adhere to the rules of writing *e.g.*, as to length and formatting etc. Exceeding word limits or failing to cite authorities correctly may invite an avoidable deduction of marks. Handing over additional material to the judge is often disallowed.

When planning one's submissions it is important to consider the order (sequence) of own submissions and to make sure they are arranged in the most persuasive way. In general, strongest submissions should be argued first. Start with a bang. This shows one is putting one's best foot forward, both in the law and as an advocate. Create the best impression right at the start. In certain circumstances, however, this rule can be discarded. For example, if it may be more logical to put forward a weaker submission X (say, on jurisdiction or standing) before a stronger submission Y (merits), then the mooter may decide to do so. Consider also whether to lead complete defences before partial defences.

The start of submissions may follow under mentioned broad principles.

- A mooter should always outline his submissions before he makes them.

- An outline is a quick summary of what he intends to submit before he actually submits them.
- It has five components as enumerated below.
    1. Signal what your submissions will address ("in relation to the second ground of appeal....");
    2. Say how many submissions you will make (“..... we have two submissions");
    3. State the proposition ("We submit that there is no duty of care involved with regard to opening fire");
    4. State the first submission (".....because, first, XXX);
    5. State the second submission ("Secondly, and in the alternative, we submit there was no duty of care because XXX")
- This method is nicknamed and also popularly known as "across before down", because you cover at a surface level everything you are going to say (*i.e.,* go 'across') before diving into the depths of individual arguments (*i.e.,* go 'down').

A submission is made by way of a "because sentence". It always seeks to achieve a desired outcome by reference to (or "because" of) a definite argument. The use of 'because' guards against any irrelevant reasoning. This is an apt answer to 'so what' question. One can conceptualize it as having three parts; (1) the proposition; (2) the "because"; and (3) the argument. For example, a submission in a criminal law moot might be: "The appellant is not guilty of the offence of homicide because in shooting the deceased, she acted in self-defence". Or in another situation, "the removal of property did not constitute because it was taken with the consent of the owner."

When citing authorities in support of a submission it is important to use reported citations where possible. Unreported judgments should only be stated when absolutely unavoidable and when reported ones are not available. Further, exact citations should be used where appropriate (do double check you give the correct pinpoint).

Submissions should not overlap one another (as that imply there is some redundancy in at least one of the submissions), nor should they leave any gaps. They should comprehensively address all the permutations of one's case theory.

What to do after receiving the opponent's written submissions? Adequate time be spent to peruse them.

Upon receipt of the opponent's written submissions, it would be advantageous to read them carefully. Make sure one understands the arguments/authorities on which the other party purport to rely. If the submissions raise cases or principles that own side had not anticipated, research them thoroughly and incorporate into your submissions where you think this is necessary.

Re-cast your submissions to take account of and rebut any points in the written submissions which may be detrimental to your case. Do not evade a good argument (leaving it unchallenged may lead to adverse results) rather expose its flaws and put the best case you can against it. In internal moots, you only get your opponent's written submissions shortly before the moot starts. In such situations, the document is more of an overview or aid, so don't panic too much about what is in them.

It is important to note that in inter-varsity competitions, where there is a considerable gap in time between written and oral rounds, mooters may not be generally bound by their written submissions. While one may not travel much beyond them but make use of them to build further arguments.

Oral Submissions

The mooters should learn how to structure oral submissions.

In broad terms, oral submissions have five parts (not all of which are required in all circumstances): (1) appearances; (2) introduction; (3) outline of submissions; (4) submissions; (5) conclusion.

Giving Appearances

This is the way a mooter introduces herewith to the Court at the start of the moot. This is an opportunity to make a good first impression. Be confident.

Appearances should cover three elements:

1. Names of counsel
2. Names of party that the counsel is representing
3. Time allocated to each speaker

For example:

> "May it please the Court, my name is Aakriti Mathur and I am joined by Mr. Avinash on behalf of the appellant in this matter, Mr. Fazal Guru. I will be speaking for the first 20 minutes and my co-counsel for a further 20 minutes."

Introducing the Case

Some mooters like to give a brief thematic overview at the start of their oral submissions. Such an introduction is used to enable the judges to see the case from their perspective. It is a broad outline of their version rather than just a jumble of facts and law. If one chooses to use such an introduction (though it is not necessary and may take up valuable minutes) it is important that it is both brief and persuasive (but not unduly emotional).

An example of such an introduction is:

"This case concerns the conflict between a State's right to protect itself against armed attacks and its obligations towards others on the international plane." Or that, "this case is based on the limitations upon command responsibility."

Signposting

When delivering one's submissions it is important that the mooter uses appropriate signposting. Generally, for this purpose when delivering a submission the following order should be followed:

1. **Restate your Submission**
   - Signal that the mooter is now turning to address his first submission, and restate it succinctly,

- The mooter may not need to restate it all – if he can develop a short hand way of referring to the submission by pointing out that: *e.g.* "I turn now to our first submission, which is that no duty of care exists".

2. Outline any 'Sub-submissions'

- It may at times be necessary that each submission the mooter makes will need to be broken down into several parts. For example, a submission that says *A* hitting *B* did not "cause" *B's* death might be broken down into two sub-submissions dealing with (i) intervening acts which break the chain of causation and (ii) remoteness of damage.
- If the mooter wishes to make sub-submissions, he should take care to outline them before making them. Use the same formula as above.

3. Make the Submission

- You are only now ready to start making your prepared substantive submissions. The stage when actual speaking session is to begin. This is where a mooter will need to exercise his legal reasoning skills. Every proposition he makes, should be supported by authority. That would give a legal base to the submission. He is not to leave out a single step in the reasoning process. This is so no matter what argument he is putting across to the judge. The key to good submissions is high persuasive quality. It gives a convincing force.
- The process demands continuous flagging to the court what the mooter is saying, and what kind of point he is making:
  - *The authorities are divided, your honour. If we look to the case of* X *we see that .... By contrast, your honour, the reasoning in....*
  - *The respondent submits that the approach of Sharma J is to be preferred for two reasons....*
    - *Contrary to what the applicant submitted, there is no right of self defence against non-state actors....*
    - *We differ from the plaintiff in one crucial respect: whether the duty of care was in fact owed....*
  - *The threshold issue, your honour, is whether the applicant has a legal standing to bring this claim.....*

In this manner, the court is taken through one's case. Such phrases flag for the judge why it is that the mooter is submitting what he is submitting.

It is important that the mooter structures his submissions so that they are compact or 'tight'. That is, each sentence should lead seamlessly into his next sentence, so there are no gaps in his argument – there are no questions left begging. An experienced mooter is able to structure his submissions in such way that a judge will only ask the questions which the mooter wants to be asked, those two only at the point in the submissions when the mooter want to be asked.

Conclusion

At the end of the submissions, the mooter should conclude appropriately. One way to do so may be simply by handing over to the co-counsel, saying "May it please the Court, those are my submissions, I defer to my junior counsel to continue the case for the appellant". On the other hand in the case of a junior counsel by saying "May it please the Court, those are the submissions of the appellant". A third option would be by stating what relief the side seek. The moot should always be concluded in one of these ways even if time is scarce. Stopping and sitting down mid-sentence would not leave a good impression.

Rebuttal and Sub-rebuttal

Rebuttal is the stage at which the appellant exercises his right to respond to the submissions made by the respondent. The counter to the same is sub-rebuttal. Sub-rebuttal is thus the right of the respondent to respond to only those submissions made by the appellant during rebuttal. Usually internal mooting competitions do not provide for the scope of rebuttal and sub-rebuttal. However, a few inter-varsity competitions do.

Answering Questions

The judges may put any question to a mooter at any stage. The interaction between a judge and a mooter is one of the most challenging but most enjoyable aspects of mooting.

This is one aspect that would invariably carry great impact on the final outcome of a team. The judges assess the performance mainly how their questions were tackled. How to prepare for it? Thorough preparation and adequate knowledge about the case would enable the participants develop requisite confidence to handle queries from the judges. Do not be in haste. The mooters should carefully listen to the question before coming up with their response.

Aim of the Judge in asking the question	Aim of the Mooter in answering the question
To test the strength of the argument	To engage in a conversation with the Bench
To test the knowledge of the mooter	To demonstrate the depth and breadth of research and argumentation
To test the mooter's resolve and style under pressure	To clarify the argument or correct a misconception
	To show one's personality

Different types of questions and how to deal with them

The questions from the judges may fall in different categories.

Type of Question	How to deal with the question
This may take the form of clarifications about the facts, mooter's submissions or the law	Clarification questions seek the quick response. This would involve giving information to the judge. This could be to supplement what the judge already knows The mooter should deal with these as quickly as he can (while giving a full answer).

Developing Good Advocacy Technique

Good advocacy requires not only that the mooter follows the structure outlined above, but also he masters several other aspects of the advocacy so that he delivers his case systematically. There is no 'one type' of advocacy but here are some useful pointers:

- Focus on the critical differences between the parties: it is essential that the mooter is aware of the central disputes in the case. This is what for majority of his time and efforts should be allocated to. Everything he says should either explicitly or at least by implication refute the other side's arguments. One exception to this rule is during question-answering. The mooter should address whatever the judge asks for, but he must make sure he returns to the central differences between him and the other side. To illustrate a common error for new mooters is to re-state the legal proposition already stated by their opponent. To explain further, if the appellant and respondent do not disagree on the law, but merely on the application of the law to the particular facts, then the mooter should so state and say "Your Honour, my learned friend has already stated the legal test as expounded in case X, with which we agree. The crucial difference between the parties in this case is how to apply that test to these facts. We submit, contrary to the appellants, that the rule in case X means... [the crucial point!]"
- Place submissions logically – this will help the mooter and also the Judge. For example, address any issue of jurisdiction or standing before tackling the merits of the matter.
- Argue persuasively both on the law and on the facts. A good advocate goes beyond stating the law or the facts and positive arguments as to why those laws or facts support his arguments.
- Be clear and concise. Indicate by pointing out in a subtle manner.
- Avoid words that are a 'red flag' to the judge. For example "The circumstances *might* indicate that the plaintiff was intoxicated..." as compared to "The respondent submits that the *reasonable inference* is that the plaintiff was intoxicated". "State practice *generally seems* to support this rule that..." as compared to "It *is* a rule of customary international law, *supported* by state practice, that..." "It *could* be concluded" vs "it can be concluded" "The facts *suggest*" vs "the facts *show*".
- In short: make assertions, be confident, and don't prevaricate: judges can smell fear!
- You must adopt a position on the law or facts in circumstances where they are ambiguous. However, if facts are ambiguous, then be careful to use the same as a licence to invent new facts. The mooter can proffer explanations for why certain facts might exist. However, if the problem questions do not say so, he cannot assert it. For example, if, in a contract case, two parties agree on a construction contract for what is stated in the problem as 'a ridiculously low price', and the judge proceeds to ask "Why did your client agree to such a low price?', One should be honest and reply "The record doesn't indicate why my client did so, Your Honour. Possible reasons may

be that she knew the contractor, or was unaware of a reasonable retail price, but ultimately we do not know." This proffers an explanation, without inventing facts.

- The mooter should know the limits of his argument and the effect of findings against him (including the implications for your co-counsel).
- Identify his strong from your weak arguments.

As for the appropriate functional norms and behaviour in the moot court, a few useful tips are as under:—

- Be deferential but natural.
- Show flexibility and enthusiasm.
- Strive for clarity – put your argument as succinctly as feasible and don't be verbose.

Benefits of Mooting

Mooting in the initial stages may appear difficult for the freshers but with practice it can become an enjoyable and exhilarating activity. Participating in mooting during the early part of law studies is particularly important because it will be beneficial to the students in their studies. It helps in comprehension of complex topics in criminal and civil laws. It would also help them to develop their legal research skills, training them to investigate in-depth and think outside the box to accommodate other points of view. Such a position will become particularly useful when the students work for their dissertation topics. Mooting will help them to develop advocacy skills essential for a number of legal and non-legal careers. Further, it inculcates in them confidence for public speaking, time management and the ability to think on their feet.

Showing commitment to mooting through participation in the internal competition will look great on a student's CV and will provide a talking point in job interviews.

The Moot has other benefits too. Networking during the events and the meeting of like-minded students across the country help prepare them to operate in a globalised world. Friendships are formed amongst students, long lasting relationships forged between participating law schools and useful contacts made through this competition.

How to Organise a Moot

The initial after invitation about a moot could be sent on the following lines. This may be sent by the institution concerned or by its Moot Court Society.

Respected Sir/Madam

With due regards we are glad to inform you that Amity Law School, Noida, India is organizing the 2nd Amity International Moot Court Competition from 10th-12 October, 2012.

The moot competition is being organised with a view to general awareness and competition on the international aspects of the legal world. The problem is designed to test the students on their legal acumen and the practical application of their knowledge of International Law.

We are looking forward for participation from your prestigious institution and are forwarding you the invitation. Please find attached files containing the Rules, Invitation, Moot Problem and Registration form for the competition.

We look forward to a positive response from your institution at the earliest Thanking you,

Best wishes,
Director, Convener, Moot Court Society
Law School, ... University,
Distt.
Pin Code
Tel :
Mob :
Visit our site at www.amity.edu/alsn

The relevant papers concerning a moot court competition, as reproduced below, can be useful reference material for the mooters.

Judges' Name: .... **Date/ Time:** ....

Courtroom: .... **Round No:** ....

INSTRUCTIONS:

It has to be borne in mind by the evaluator that in assessing each or a list he she should take into account his/her:

(1) Knowledge of law
(2) Facts and application of law thereto
(3) Ingenuity, wit, presence of mind, language and ability to answe questions.
(4) Style, poise, courtesy and demeanor and
(5) Time management and organization

Rules for Scoring

1. Each team shall argue twice in the preliminary round. At the end of th preliminary rounds, the first eight teams will qualify for the Quarter Final The first 8 teams will be selected on the basis of cumulative scores in th preliminary rounds. A Team shall be credited with a win if its total mark in the respective session are higher than its opponents team's. Further fo the purpose of calculation, the memorial marks of the teams in th preliminary rounds shall be added to the marks secured out of 200 awarde by the Judges for the oral pleadings. The total scores in the prelimina rounds shall be out of 300. In order to secure a win a team's score must b greater than its opponent's score out of 300.
2. If the situation of tie exists, then the **total oral marks** of the Teams from bo sessions will be considered. The Team with the higher score will advan to the Quarter Finals.
3. The quarter finals/semi finals and finals will be knock-out rounds. A tea will be credited with a win in the Quarter Finals if their total marks, a higher than its opponent's team's.

4. In case of a tie, the total oral marks of the Teams in the previous round(s) will be considered. The Team with the higher score will win.
5. The oralists will be judged on the pre-decided ***criteria:***

General Procedures

- Each preliminary oral round of competition consists of sixty (60) minutes of oral pleadings. Prosecution and defence each allotted thirty (30) minutes.
- Oral presentations during the round must be made by two (2) members, prior to the beginning of the oral round, each team must indicate to the bailiff how it wishes to allocate its 30 minutes among (a) its first oralist, (b) its second oralist and (c) rebuttal (for Prosecution) or sub-rebuttal (for Defense).
- The team may not allocate more than twenty (20) minutes, including rebuttal or sub-rebuttal, to either oralist. Time allocated for but not used by one oralist may not be used by another oralist, or in the rebuttal or sub-rebuttal.
- Judges may, at their discretion, extend total Team oral argument time beyond the thirty (30) minute allocation. Oralists asked to further expand upon arguments may, in such instance, argue for more than the twenty (20) minute individual limit.
- The order of the pleadings in each Oral Round at all levels of the Competition is: Prosecution 1 —> Prosecution 2 —> Defense 1 —> Defense 2 —> Rebuttal (Prosecution 1 or 2) —> Sub-rebuttal (Defense 1 or 2). Once an oralist has completed his or her main leading, that oralist may not make any additional argument except for rebuttal or sub-rebuttal. This applies irrespective of whether the pleading team uses all of the time it has allocated for the main pleading. Further, any time that is not used in the main pleading may not be used to extend the time allocated to rebuttal or sub-rebuttal.

- **Rebuttal and Sub-rebuttal**
  - Each Team may reserve up to five (5) minutes for rebuttal or sub-rebuttal. As a courtesy to the judges, teams should announce whether they intend to reserve time for rebuttal or sub-rebuttal at the beginning of their oral argument, and how much time they intend to reserve. Failure to announce will not waive the right to rebuttal or sub-rebuttal. Only one team member may deliver the rebuttal or sub-rebuttal. The rebuttal or sub-rebuttal must be delivered by one of the two oralists participating in the Oral Round. A rebuttal shall immediately follow defendant 2, and the sub-rebuttal shall immediately follow the rebuttal. The team need not indicate prior to rebuttal or sub-rebuttal which of the pleading team members will deliver rebuttal or sub-rebuttal. Teams may waive their rebuttal or sub-rebuttal.
- **Scope of Pleadings**
  - A team's oral pleadings are not in any way limited to the scope of the team's memorial. The scope of the prosecution's rebuttal is limited to

responding to the defendant's primary oral pleadings, and the scope of the defendant's sub-rebuttal is limited to responding to the prosecution's rebuttal. If the prosecution waives rebuttal, defendant may not appear for sub-rebuttal.

- **Court Room Communication**
  - Written communication during the oral round shall be limited to written communication among team members seated at the counsel table. No other written communication may take place.
- **Scouting**
  - Team members or persons directly affiliated with any Team may only attend preliminary rounds in which their team is competing. Violation of this rule should be brought to the attention of the court room officers immediately, without disturbing the oral round, or immediately after the oral round has finished.
  - A Team which commits Scouting in any form shall be disqualified from the competition.

Final Scores

Prosecution team code

No. .... Defendant team code No. ....

1st Prosecution Code No. 1st Defendant Code No.

Score(50-100) Score(50-100)

2nd Prosecution Code No. 2nd Defendant Code No.

Score (50-100) Score(50-100)

Name: ....

Signature: .... *(score sheet cannot be validated without signature)*

INTERNATIONAL MOOTS

S. No.	*NAME OF THE COMPETITION*	*HOST INSTITUTION*	*USUALLY HELD DURING*	*TOPIC*
1	*Philip C. Jessop International Moot Court Competition*	*Subject to change*	*January*	*Humanitarian Law*
2.	*Stetsons International Environment Moot Court Competition*	*SNDT University, Mumbai/ Department of Legal Sciences, University of Madras*	*January*	*Environment Law*
3.	*Oxford IP Law Moot Court Competition (World Rounds)*	*St. Catherine's College, Oxford*	*March*	*Media Law*

S. No.	NAME OF THE COMPETITION	HOST INSTITUTION	USUALLY HELD DURING	TOPIC
4.	*Red Cross International Humanitarian Law Moot Court*	*University of Hong Kong*	*March*	*Humanitarian Law*
5.	*Frankfurt Investment Arbitration Moot Court Competition*	*Frankfurt, Germany*	*March*	*Investment Arbitration*
6.	*Philip C. Jessop International Moot Court Competition, World Rounds*	*Washington DC (USA)*	*March*	*Humanitarian Law*
7.	*Stetsons International Environment Moot Court Competition*	*Stetson University, College of Law, Gulfport, Florida*	*March*	*International Environment Law*
8.	*ELSA WTO Moot Court Competition, Asian Rounds*	*Taiwan, Taipei*	*March*	*WTO Law*
9.	*William C. Viz International Commercial Arbitration*	*Vienna*	*March*	*International Commercial Arbitration*
10.	*William C. Viz International Commercial Arbitration (East)*	*Hong Kong*	*March*	*International Commercial Arbitration*
11.	*ICC Trial Moot Court Competition*	*ICC Headquarters Paris*	*April*	*International Criminal Law*

List of moots where venue is subject to change

Philip C. Jessop International Moot Court Competition – *January*

Bar Council of India Moot Court Competition – *February*

List of National Moots

SR. No.	NAME OF MOOT	HOST INSTITUTION	USUALLY HELD DURING
1	2	3	4
1.	*Annual Raj Anand Intellectual Property Moot Court Competition*	*Symbiosis Law School, Noida*	*August*
2.	*School of Law, Christ University Moot Court Competition*	*Christ College of Bangalore*	*September*

1	2	3	4
3.	*K.R. Ramani Memorial Moot Court Competition*	*School of Excellence in Law, Chennai*	*September*
4.	*Surana Trial Advocacy Moot Court Competition (North/South Rounds)*	*NUALS, Kochi*	*September*
5.	*Annual NALSAR – Justice B.R. Sawhney Memorial Moot Court*	*NALSAR, Hyderabad*	*September*
6.	*Surana International Minority Rights Moot Court Competition*	*AKK New Law Academy, Pune Rizvi Law College, Mumbai*	*September*
7.	*Rizvi Law College National Moot Court Competition*	*Rizvi Law College, Mumbai*	*October*
8.	*Hidayatullah Memorial National Moot Court Competition*	*HNLU, Raipur*	*October*
9.	*Nani Palkhivala Memorial National Tax Moot Court Competition*	*GLC, Mumbai*	*October*
10.	*Baroda School of Legal Studies Moot Court Competition*	*Baroda Institute of Legal Studies*	*October*
11.	*S.C. Javali Memorial National Moot Court Competition, 2012*	*University Law College, Dharwad*	*October*
12.	*National Moot Court Competition*	*Faculty of Law, University of Delhi*	*November*
13.	*International Infrastructure and Construction Law Arbitration Moot Court Competition*	*National Law University, Delhi*	*November*
14.	*NLIU Juris Corp Moot Court Competition*	*NLIU, Bhopal*	*November*
15.	*All India Moot Court Competition*	*GLC, Ernakulam*	*November*
16.	*Annual Amity International Law Moot Court Competition*	*Amity Law School, Noida*	*November*
17.	*Oxford Media Moot Court Competition (India Rounds)*	*NLU, Delhi*	*November*
18	*B.R. Krishna Memorial National Intellectual Property Rights Moot Court Competition, 2013*	*Symbiosis Law School, Pune*	*January*

1	2	3	4
19.	*M.C. Chagla Memorial Government Law College National Moot Court Competition, 2013*	*GLC, Mumbai*	*January*
20.	*Anti Trust Law Moot Court Competition*	*Christ University, Bangalore*	*January*
21.	*NALSAR – Gurcharan Singh Tulsi Memorial Criminal Law Moot Court Competition, 2013*	*NALSAR, Hyderabad*	*January*
22.	*K.K. Luthra Memorial Moot Court Competition*	*Campus Law Centre, Faculty of Law, University of Delhi*	*January*
23.	*Lex Novitas, National Law Moot Court Competition*	*V.M. Salgaocar College of Law, Panaji, Goa*	*January*
24.	*Stetsons International Environment Moot Court Competition (North/South Rounds)*	*SNDT University, Mum/ Department of Legal Sciences, Univ. of Madras*	*January*
25.	*Annual M.M. Singhvi Memorial – BCI International Law Moot Court Competition*	*NLU, Jodhpur*	*January*
26.	*Fiat Justicia National Moot Court Competition*	*Dr. Ambedkar Government Law College*	*February*
27.	*NLIU-INADR South Asian Inter Law School Mediation Tournament*	*NLIU, Bhopal*	*February*
28.	*All India Moot Court Competition*	*GLC, Thiruvananthapuram*	*February*
29.	*UILS National Client Counselling Competition*	*The University Institute of Legal*	*February*
30.	*National ADR Mechanism Competition*	*Christ University, Bangalore*	*February*
31.	*Surana Corporate Moot*	*Surana & Surana International Attorneys*	*February*
32.	*NUJS Herbert Smith National Corporate Law Moot Court Competition*	*WBNUJS, Kolkata*	*February*
33.	*Surana and Surana Memorial Information Technology Moot Court Competition*	*Symbiosis Law School, Pune*	*February*

1	2	3	4
34.	*Bar Council of India Inter-University Moot Court Competition*	*Subject to change*	*February*
35.	*Justa Causa National Moot Court Competition*	*Dr. Babasaheb Ambedkar College of Law, Nagpur*	*February*
36.	*Prof. S.P. Sathe Memorial National Moot Court Competition*	*ILS Law College, Pune*	*February*
37.	*All India Moot Court Competition*	*University Law College, Bangalore*	*February*
38.	*NLU Delhi All India Corporate Law Moot Court Competition*	*NLU, Delhi*	*February*
39.	*RGNUL, National Moot Court Competition*	*RGNUL, Patiala*	*March*
40.	*Amity National Moot Court Competition*	*Amity Law School, Delhi*	*March*
41.	*NLU Antitrust Law Moot Court Competition*	*NLU, Jodhpur*	*March*
42.	*Bar Council of India Inter-University Moot Court Competition*	*Subject to change*	*March*
43.	*Annual National Moot Court Competition*	*KC Law College, Mumbai*	*March*
44.	*Army Institute of Law Moot Court Competition*	*Army Law Institute, Mohali*	*March*
45.	*D.H. Law Associates National Moot Court Competition*	*CNLU, Patna*	*March*
46.	*Louis Brown Client Counselling Competition (Western Regional Rounds)*	*V.M. Salgaocar College of Law, Goa*	*March*
47.	*National Moot Court Competition*	*G.H. Raisoni Law School, Nagpur*	*March*
48.	*All India Moot Court Competition*	*Dr. Ambedkar Government Law College, Puducherry*	*Unconfirmed*
49.	*Dr. Paras Diwan Energy Law National Moot Court Competition*	*UPES, Dehradun*	*April*
50.	*NLIU Tankha Moot Court Competition*	*NLIU, Bhopal*	*Unconfirmed*

1	2	3	4
51.	*NFGC NALSAR Moot Court Competition*	*NALSAR, Hyderabad*	*April*
52.	*National Moot Court Competition*	*Sastra University*	*April*

2nd Amity International Moot Court Competition, 2012

AMITY INTERNATIONAL LAW MOOT COMPETITION-2012

INTERNATIONAL CRIMINAL COURT AT THE HAGUE

MOOT PROBLEM

PROSECUTOR V. MAJOR GENERAL NAIRA BLAKOUSA

FACTS OF THE CASE

1. The continent of Barbaria was under the dominance of colonial rule in the 19th and early 20th century. The countries which were a part of the continent gained their independence mostly in late 1960s and 1970s. The continent comprises of eight countries which are very diverse in their cultural heritage, religion, traditions, language. In the peninsular region of southern Barbaria lies Triala which share its borders with the States of Nivansha and Gargola.

2. The general populace of Nivansha belong to Nivanshi ethnicity that constitutes 89% of its population whereas Gargola comprises of gargolians who constitute 84% of the State's population. Both such States are governed by democratically elected political parties representing the majority in the respective States. On the other hand, Triala is a small country with a population of 15 million whereby 69% of its population belongs to gargolians ethnicity and 23% belongs to Nivanshi ethnicity. Triala is a republican State, currently governed by Triala Association of Revolutionary Workers (TAR), a multi ethnic political party led by gargolian leader named Mr. Ivanovic.

3. Tanits, a river flowing from the south western part of the continent passes through Gargola and the borders of Triala to Nivansha. The river has critical importance to all three nations due to its natural, geographical and cultural significance. It is closely situated to the international borders and is also one of the major sources of drinking water, fishing, agriculture and navigation in the southern countries of Barbaria, besides being a rich source of sea life.

4. The river meanders over the fertile plain of Nivansha which is one of the largest exporters of timber and fisheries. In fact, 67% of the timber exported by the country per annum thrives on the yield of the land irrigated by waters from the river Tanits. Similarly, the river offers an excellent fishing ground that contributes to 71% of the fisheries exported by the country. Gargola, on the other hand, has its strong economy based on automobile and steel industries. The country has been dependent on its imports from Nivansha and Triala for agricultural products. To meet its increasing demand for food and electricity, Gargola planned erection of two hydro electric dams across the river Tanits. The first dam was proposed for greater ulilisation of the agricultural lands through high yielding seeds and efficient irrigation while other dam was ordained to be used for the purpose of generating hydroelectricity.

5. The river Tanits being an international waterway, originates from a confluence of tributaries, most important being Forcados, which flows within the territory of Triala. According to a report published by an independent geological agency, this tributary is abundant in Uranium (U-235/238) ores. The formation of the tributary is attributed to Lord Nivansh, who sought to save the Nivanshis from a major disaster that occurred over 2500 years ago, as narrated by the ethnical epics and myths prevalent within the community. Also, a temple is located at the end of the tributary, which is considered to be the place from where the Lord Nivansh chanted his prayers for the survival of his people.

6. Concerned with its increasing needs, Gargola's ambassador Mr. Atkin met Mr. Zavrito, the gargolians President of Triala to execute an agreement for trade of U-235/238 ores from Triala to Gargola. However, such an agreement would not have been in economic interests of a certain part of the State. The proposal was opposed by the Government of Nivansha since the stage of negotiations. Nivansha presented its objections before the Barbaria Regional Cooperation Association. BRCR, is an organisation dedicated to socio-economic development and political stability as well as on regional and international peace and cooperation emphasising collective self-reliance, in their annual summit but their representatives were disregarded.

7. On 29th July, 2010, Triala and Gargola concluded the proposed agreement. The terms of the agreement chiefly stipulated that for the next three years, Triala would supply 2500 tons of U-235 to Gargola. The proposal made by the Triala for the agreement's execution involved the diversion of a significant part of the tributary. Such move on part of the Triala and Gargola infuriated the Nivanshis in Triala. There were incidents of attacks on several cultural centres of gargolians and also at party head quarters of TAR. The troops of Triala further retaliated and attacked many Nivanshis killing 45 people in an ambush on 17th August, 2010. This incident led to a series of counter attacks from the Nivanshis who indulged in widespread violent attacks against the government and its officials. There were bomb blasts in several places including the Matheri Railway Station, markets, and other public places in eastern part of Triala. The Nivanshi Progressive Youth Foundation (NPYF) formed under the leadership of Mr. Fuziama claimed responsibility for these bombings in which 102 people lost their lives and the bombing at Matheri Railway Station which further claimed 98 lives according to a press communiqué released to a local newspaper.

8. The TAR led government of Triala, unable to handle the situation called upon Gargola to help them in restoration of peace in their country. Gargola along with Mochamma, Phillimore and Latifundia decided in a meeting on 15th October, 2010 conducted by the BRCR to intervene with their troops to restore peace in the region. Gargola denounced the move. But the other countries claimed that they had a responsibility to protect the people of Triala from violence and were obliged to intervene. To this end, the BRCR sent a request seeking permission of the Security Council. The permission was soon accorded to Barbaria for intervention in the matter and for the restoration of peace as expeditiously as possible. The Council, *vide* its resolution No. 1994-E/2011 dated 12th November, 2011 ordered strict adherence of international humanitarian law. Thereafter, BRCR requested Gargola

to send in its troops to restore peace in Triala which in response sent 1200 troops into Triala led by Major General Naira Blakousa along with Brigadier Smith.

9. On 29th December, 2010, a crowd of 350 Nivanshis marched towards the Parliament of Triala in protest against the government's decision to launch its program for extraction of U-235 ores. The troops of Gargola acting under orders to stop the protest asked the protestors to disperse off quietly. Suddenly a stone hurled from the crowd hit Colonel O. Riley, the commander of battalion X, on the head. Aggravated with this act, the commander ordered his men to open fire at the crowd. Nearly 123 people were killed and 280 people were injured in the protestors' rally, most of whom were women and children. The newspaper headlines of the next day read as 'Gargola troops shoot 123 down in self defence'.

10. Enraged by the excessive use of force exercised by the troops, the NPYF bombed the houses of several ministers of Triala including the house of Mr. Styx, a cousin of Major General Blakousa, killing his wife, 2 children and 3 guards. This was followed by several arrests of people belonging to Nivanshis ethnicity including several leaders of APYF. The national newspaper 'Daily Times', with the large circulation in the region, reported that the troops had arrested almost every male member of the Nivanshi ethnicity above the age of 18. Women who protested against the same were also brutally injured and arrested. According to the news items, several arrests were made by plain clothed men representing to be agents of 'Peacekeepers' an independent peacekeeping and intelligence agency allegedly formed by Mr. Styx. It was also rumoured that two plain clothed men carried illegal weapons which was provided to them by Gargolian troops.

11. Following the widespread arrests, several storage houses and warehouses were taken over by the troops to keep the detainees. The persons under custody were guarded by plain clothed men as well as officers across several regions in the country. However, both plain clothed men and officers were not seen guarding such detention cells together.

12. After a span of one month, it was reported by a local Human Rights Agency named 'Protector of Rights' that these prisons and detention cells had witnessed widespread and grave breaches of Human Rights and International Humanitarian Law. It was reported by the agency that women were forced to have sex for food and were inhumanly treated. Other women were tied up in chains and given food only once a day. The agency further reported that the supply of food to the prisons was not increased although the increased number of the prisoners led to sporadic acts of violence amongst the prisoners for food. It was also revealed that 17 people had died in the course of such activities. The incidents involving death were admitted by the officials. However, the cause of death was attributed to clashes between two groups amongst the prisoners.

13. On 28th May, 2011, one of the prisons in North Triala was bombed allegedly by a band of insurgents. The confusion led to the escape of 420 prisoners. Exasperated by the event, Major General Naira Blakousa ordered the search of all prisoners who escaped in the mass break. It was a task on which both the troops and the plain clothed men embarked. Within a span of two weeks dead bodies were found in the eastern region of Triala. Examination of the dead bodies

indicated that all of them were the people who had escaped from the prison. It was rumoured that men in uniform were seen around the region two days ago.

14. On 12th June, 2011, the troops had received information from an anonymous source that as many as 80 prisoners who had escaped were hiding at the 'Cheshire Homes' a home for the disabled situated in the western part of Triala. Major General Blakousa ordered his troops to cordon the locality for capture of all prisoners at all costs. When his soldiers reached the place, one of their vehicles was attacked and firing came from the direction of the home which caused no injuries. The troops returned fire towards the home. However, no injuries were reported. The firing continued for almost a period of one hour in spite of lack of retaliation. Finally, when the troops broke open the house, 270 people were found dead, of which 22 were those who had escaped from the prison and the rest were inhabitants of the shelter home.

15. On 20th June, 2011, Mr. Styx in an interview to local newspaper denied all affiliation to the 'Peacekeepers'. However, the plain clothed men continued to act in the name of Mr. Styx. Further, in one of their prisons it was rumoured that the personal assistant of Mr. Styx had come and ordered that shock treatment be given to Mr. Fuziama who was responsible for triggering the explosion of Mr. Styx's house.

16. Within next two months, many surveys were conducted and the 'Daily Times' reported several killings of Nivanshis in Triala. In the aforesaid span of time, as many as 370 killings of Nivanshis men and women were reported both within and out of prisons.

17. The Government of Nivansha through its embassy in Triala conducted an independent investigation. It reported that over 1200 Nivanshi men and women had died at the hands of the military. The Government requested the prosecutor of the International Criminal Court to investigate into the matter.

18. On 11th September, 2011, Major General Blakousa announced that peace was restored in Triala and the terrorist activities of NPYF and its supporters had been brought under control. According to the official release the troops had killed 69 terrorists of the APYF in their activities and their major leaders and other members were behind the bars and would be tried before Federal Court of Justice at Triala.

19. The prosecutor of the International Criminal Court conducted his investigation. The following charges were framed against Mr. Styx, Major General Blakousa, Brigadier Smith and Colonel Riley herein stated below:

- The commission of the crime of 'Genocide' for killing members of Nivanshi ethnicity in Triala from 17th August, 2010 till the end of August, 2011 under article 6(a) of the Rome Statute of the International Criminal Court.
- The war crime of 'wilful killing' committed during the incidents that took place against the escaped prisoners and civilians in Triala between 28th May and 12th June, 2012, as per article 8(2)(a)(i) of the Rome Statute of the International Criminal Court.

- The act of Extermination against civilians in Triala on 12th June, 2011 as stipulated under article 7(1)(b) of the Rome Statute of the International Criminal Court.
- The war crime of sexual slavery committed against women in Triala as per article 8(2)(b) of the Rome Statute of the International Criminal Court.

20. The State of Gargola has objected to the jurisdiction of the International Criminal Court on the ground that the military law of their State shall apply to the instant situation whereby the military courts shall deal with these issues rather than the International Criminal Court. It must be noted that Gargola, Triala and Nivansha are parties to the Rome Statute of International Criminal Court.

ANNEXURE – I

Gargola Department of Army Field Manual

(Relevant extracts)

BGM 93-10
HEADQUARTERS
DEPARTMENT OF THE ARMY
Burgundy, 15 July, 1976

By virtue of the authority vested in me as President of the Gargola by the Constitution and laws of the Gargola and as Commander-in-Chief of the Armed Forces of the Gargola, it is hereby ordered as follows:

BGM 93-10 is promulgated with a view to consolidate and amend the law relating to the government of the Defence Forces of the State.

(1) This manual may be called the Gargola Field Manual.

(2) It shall be applicable to the Gargolian Defence Forces within and outside the territory of the State.

Section III

CRIMES UNDER INTERNATIONAL LAW

391. *Crimes under International Law*

Any person, whether a member of the armed forces or a civilian, who commits an act which constitutes a crime under international law is responsible therefore and will be liable to punishment. Such offences in connection with war comprise:

a. Crimes against peace.

b. Crimes against humanity.

c. War crimes.

Although this manual recognizes the criminal responsibility of individuals for those offenses which may comprise any of the foregoing types of crimes, members of the armed forces will normally be concerned only with those offences constituting "war crimes."

396. *War Crimes*

The term "war crime" is the technical expression for a violation of the law of war by any person or persons, military or civilian. Every violation of the law of war is a war crime.

398. Conspiracy, Incitement, Attempts, and Complicity

Conspiracy, direct incitement, and attempts to commit, as well as complicity in the commission of, crimes against peace, crimes against humanity, and war crimes are punishable.

412. Responsibility for Acts of Subordinates

In some cases, military commanders may be responsible for war crimes committed by subordinate members of the armed forces, or other persons subject to their control. Thus, for instance, when troops commit massacres and atrocities against the civilian population of occupied territory or against prisoners of war, the responsibility may rest not only with the actual perpetrators but also with the commander. Such a responsibility arises directly when the acts in question have been committed in pursuance of an order of the commander concerned. The commander is also responsible if he has actual knowledge, or should have knowledge, through reports received by him or through other means, that troops or other persons subject to his control are about to commit or have committed a war crime and he fails to take the necessary and reasonable steps to ensure compliance with the law of war or to punish violators thereof.

416. Other Types of War Crimes

In addition to the "grave breaches" of the Geneva Conventions of 1949, the following acts are representative of violations of the law of war ("war crimes"):

- *a. Making use of poisoned or otherwise forbidden arms or ammunition.*
- *b. Treacherous request for quarter.*
- *c. Maltreatment of dead bodies.*
- *d. Firing on localities which are undefended and without military significance.*
- *e. Abuse of or firing on the flag of truce.*
- *f. Misuse of the Red Cross emblem.*
- *g. Use of civilian clothing by troops to conceal their military character during battle.*
- *h. Improper use of privileged buildings for military purposes.*
- *i. Poisoning of wells or streams.*
- *j. Pillage or purposeless destruction.*
- *k. Compelling prisoners of war to perform prohibited labour.*
- *l. Killing without trial spies or other persons who have committed hostile acts.*
- *m. Compelling civilians to perform prohibited labour.*
- *n. Violation of surrender terms.*

Section IV

PUNISHMENT OF WAR CRIMES

418. Trials

- *a. Nature of Proceeding. Any person charged with a war crime has the right to a fair trial on the facts and law.*
- *b. Rights of Accused. Persons accused of "grave breaches" of the Geneva Conventions of 1949 are to be tried under conditions no less favourable than those provided by Article 105 and those following.*

c. *Rights of Prisoners of War. Pursuant to Article 85, GPW (par. 161), prisoners of war accused of war crimes benefit from the provisions of GPW, especially Articles 82-108 (pars. 158-184).*

d. *Jurisdiction. War crimes are within the jurisdiction of general courts-martial (JCMJ, Art. 18), military commissions, provost courts, military government courts, and other military tribunals (G C J, Art. 21) of the Gargola, as well as of international tribunals.*

e. *Applicable Law. As the international law of war is part of the law of the land in the Gargola, enemy personnel charged with war crimes are tried directly under international law without recourse to the statutes of the Gargola. However, directives declaratory of international law may be promulgated to assist such tribunals in the performance of their function.*

Section VI
PROVISIONS COMMON TO THE TERRITORIES OF THE PARTIES TO THE CONFLICT AND TO OCCUPIED TERRITORIES

443. General

Protected persons are entitled, in all circumstances, to respect for their persons, their honour, their family rights, their religious convictions and practices, and their manners and customs. They shall at all times be humanely treated, and shall be protected especially against all acts of violence or threats thereof and against insults and public curiosity.

Women shall be especially protected against any attack on their honour, in particular against rape, enforced prostitution, or any form of indecent assault. Without prejudice to the provisions relating to their state of health, age and sex, all protected persons shall be treated with the same consideration by the Party to the conflict in whose power they are, without any adverse distinction based, in particular, on race, religion or political opinion. However, the Parties to the conflict may take such measures of control and security in regard to protected persons as may be necessary as a result of the war.

Section VIII
WOUNDED AND SICK

467. Protection and Care 2nd Amity International Moot Court Competition, 2012

a. Treaty Provision

Members of the armed forces and other persons mentioned in the following article, who are wounded or sick, shall be respected and protected in all circumstances. They shall be treated humanely and eared for by the Party to the conflict in whose power they may be, without any adverse distinction founded on sex, race, nationality, religion, political opinions, or any other similar criteria. Any attempts upon their lives, or violence to their persons, shall be strictly prohibited; in particular, they shall not be murdered or exterminated, subjected to torture or to biological experiments; they shall not wilfully be left without medical assistance and care, nor shall conditions exposing them to contagion or infection be created.

Only urgent medical reasons will authorize priority in the order of treatment to be administered.

Women shall be treated with all consideration due to their sex. The Party to the conflict which is compelled to abandon wounded or sick to the enemy shall, as far as military considerations permit, leave with them a part of its medical personnel and material to assist in their care.

Section XI

GENERAL PROTECTION OF PRISONERS OF WAR

489. Respect for the Person of Prisoners

Prisoners of war are entitled in all circumstances to respect for their persons and their honour. Women shall be treated with all the regard due to their sex and shall in all cases benefit by treatment as favourable as that granted to men. Prisoners of war shall retain the full civil capacity which they enjoyed at the time of their capture. The Detaining Power may not restrict the exercise, either within or without its own territory, of the rights such capacity confers except in so far as the captivity requires.

ANNEXURE – II

[This is a fictional document for use in the ICC Trial Competition]
Amity International Moot Court Competition SC Res 1994-E/2011
Security Council Resolution 1994-E, 12th November, 2011.
Adopted by a unanimous vote of the Security Council at its 169th meeting on 12th November, 2011

The Security Council,

Taking note of the a meeting on 15th October, 2010 conducted by Barbaria Regional Cooperation Association (BRCR) to intervene in the situation prevailing in Triala with respect to the agreement for trade executed by Triala and Gargola, with their troops to restore peace in the region.

The Security Council,

Mindful of the principles of cooperation enshrined in the BRCR Charter,

Finding that international tension exists on a dangerous scale,

Having called for an immediate cessation of hostilities,

1. *Reaffirming the importance of the exercise by the Security Council of its primary responsibility for the maintenance of international peace and security, and the duty of the permanent members to seek unanimity and to exercise restraint in the use of the veto,*
2. *Conscious that failure of the Security Council to discharge its responsibilities on behalf of all the Member States, particularly those responsibilities referred to in the two preceding paragraphs, does not relieve Member States of their obligations or the BRCR of its responsibility under the Charter to maintain international peace and security,*
3. *Invites each Member of the BRCR to survey its resources in order to determine the nature and scope of the assistance it may be in a position to render in support of any recommendations of the Security Council for the restoration of international peace and security,*
4. *Recommends to the States Members of the BRCR that each Member maintain within its national armed forces elements so trained, organized and equipped that they could promptly be made available, in accordance with its constitutional processes, for service as a BRCR unit or units, upon recommendation by the Security Council,*

5. *Requests the Secretary-General to appoint, a panel of military experts who could be made available, on request, to Member States wishing to obtain technical advice regarding the organization, training, and equipment for prompt service as BRCR units,*
6. *Urges Member States to respectfully, and to intensify, joint action, in co-operation with the BRCR, to develop and stimulate universal respect for and observance of human rights and fundamental freedoms, and to intensify individual and collective efforts to achieve conditions of economic stability and social progress, particularly through the development of under-developed countries and areas,*
7. *In witness whereof the undersigned, being duly authorized thereto by their respective Governments have signed this Convention.*

JORDAN LACROUSA	*ORTON KEBANO*
Minister of Foreign Affairs	*Minister of State for External Affairs*
People's Republic of Triala	*Republic of Mochamma*
JEFF HARSON	*URIAH QUAKES*
Minister for Foreign Affairs	*Minister of Foreign Affairs*
His Majesty's Government of Latifundia	*Kingdom of Phillimore*
TESCO VAN PERSIE	*MARCUS DEMAN*

ANNEXURE – III
STATUTE OF THE INTERNATIONAL CRIMINAL COURT
ELEMENTS OF CRIMES

Article 6(a)

Genocide by killing:

1. *The perpetrator killed one or more persons.*
2. *Such person or persons belonged to a particular national, ethnical, racial or religious group.*
3. *The perpetrator intended to destroy, in whole or in part, that national, ethnical, racial or religious group, as such.*
4. *The conduct took place in the context of a manifest pattern of similar conduct directed against that group or was conduct that could itself effect such destruction.*

Article 7(1)(b)

Crime against humanity of extermination:

1. *The perpetrator killed one or more persons, including by inflicting conditions of life calculated to bring about the destruction of part of a population.*
2. *The conduct constituted, or took place as part of, a mass killing of members of a civilian population.*
3. *The conduct was committed as part of a widespread or systematic attack directed against a civilian population.*

4. *The perpetrator knew that the conduct was part of or intended the conduct to be part of a widespread or systematic attack directed against a civilian population.*

Article 8(2)(a)(i)

War crime of wilful killing:

1. *The perpetrator killed one or more persons.*
2. *Such person or persons were protected under one or more of the Geneva Conventions of 1949.*
3. *The perpetrator was aware of the factual circumstances that established that protected status.*
4. *The conduct took place in the context of and was associated with an international armed conflict.*
5. *The perpetrator was aware of factual circumstances that established the existence of an armed conflict.*

Article 8(2)(b)

War crime of sexual slavery:

1. *The perpetrator exercised any or all of the powers attaching to the right of ownership over one or more persons, such as by purchasing, selling, lending or bartering such a person or persons, or by imposing on them a similar deprivation of liberty.*
2. *The perpetrator caused such person or persons to engage in one or more acts of a sexual nature.*
3. *The conduct took place in the context of and was associated with an international armed conflict.*
4. *The perpetrator was aware of factual circumstances that established the existence of an armed conflict.*

CHAPTER 5
Legal Aid

Legal Awareness Classes

The law students should be encouraged to organize legal awareness classes. These should be held for small groups say, one village, or a group of four to five houses or 10 to 15 people. These could also be targeted at old age homes or orphanage etc. These may be held in the form of informal gatherings.

Law students should identify the issues or problems warranting legal awareness. To illustrate, these could relate to right to education, dowry prohibition, domestic violence, house rent, old age pension, public distribution system etc.

No fee, whether in cash or in kind, is to be charged from the beneficiaries of legal aid clinics.

One of the functions of a State Bar Council is to organize legal aid to the poor in the prescribed manner. Similar expectation is from the Bar Council of India[1]. The Bar Council of India as also the State Bar Councils may constitute one or more funds for the purpose of giving legal aid or advice in accordance with the rules made in this behalf.[2]

The rules making power of a Bar Council extends to 'organisation of legal aid and advice to the poor, constitution and functions of committees and sub committees for that purpose and description of proceedings in connection with which legal aid or advice may be given[3].

Do's and Don'ts

1. Legal aid clinics should be held only after the students have been imparted instructions in the substantive and procedural laws relating to the subject chosen.
2. Each clinic should preferably be held to deal with one particular law and connected topics. To illustrate:
   (a) **Family Law** – marriage, divorce, adoption, domestic violence, custody etc.
   (b) **Traffic Laws** – Motor accidents, compensation, driving licences.
   (c) **Tenancy Laws** – Conflict between house owners & tenants, problems of water, electricity, right of way.

---

1. Sections 6(ee) and 7(2)(ib) respectively of the Advocates Act, 1961.
2. Sections 7(2)(b) and 6(2)(b) respectively of the Advocates Act.
3. Section 15(2)(gb) of the Advocates Act.

(d) **Consumer Laws** – Complaints about deficiency in service, inadequacy or damage in any consumer relationship.

(e) **Labour Laws** – Wages, compensation, security of tenure, accidents compensation, casual and temporary workers.

(f) **Land Laws** – Issues of land revenue, water and irrigation, cess, electricity, land holdings, food distribution, ration card.

(g) **Municipal Laws** – Ration cards, voters identity cards, old age or disability pension, water, electricity, hygiene and sanitation aspects, medical facilities.

Legal Aid

The legal education has to take the students out from the class room into the society so as to be fully prepared to undertake their professional duties. They would then understand with the societal needs and see the live problems of the real people. An exposure to the way how the law interplays and responds to real life situations that would bring out the practical application to the legal education.

A student undergoing training as a lawyer is expected to also work for the interests of the poor, for the marginalized and for the vulnerable groups. Such an obligation can be met by rendition of legal aid. Legal education should also work towards empowerment of the poor. Therefore, the law students should become poor friendly, pro-marginalized and do some *pro bono* work for the interest of the down trodden.

Legal aid is the provision of assistance to people who are otherwise unable to afford legal representation and access to the court system. A person may not be able to defend himself adequately due to his poverty. Poverty should not be a reason for denial of adequate opportunity to defend and resultant 'injustice'. No indigent should be deprived to get justice. Legal aid is pivotal to provision of access to justice. It ensures equality before law, the right to counsel and the right to a fair trial. It is a welfare provision by the State to people who are beyond the access to the legal representation.

Article 39A of the Constitution of India provides for free legal aid to the poor and weaker sections of the society and ensures justice for all. The right for free legal aid further finds strength from section 304 of the Criminal Procedure Code, 1973. "Where on a trial before the court of session, the accused is not represented by a pleader, and where it appears to the court that the accused has not sufficient means to engage a pleader, the court shall assign a pleader for his defence at the expense of the State. Order XXXIII of the Civil Procedure Code, 1908 exempts indigenous people from paying the court fee prescribed for the plaint if they don't have sufficient means to do so.

Articles 14 and 22(1) of the Constitution also make it obligatory for the State to ensure equality before law and a legal system which promotes justice on the basis of equal opportunity to all. Equal justice for all is an essential feature of our Constitution.

Article 39A – The said Article promotes equal justice and free legal aid. "The State shall secure that the operation of the legal system promotes justice, on a basis of equal opportunity, and shall, in particular, provide free legal aid, by suitable legislation or schemes or in any other way, to ensure that opportunities for securing justice are not denied to any citizen by reason of economic or other disabilities."

A major drawback of the existing system is lack of training in relevant skills to meet the ever changing demands of the modern world. Lack of the ability is manifest to facilitate access to basic human rights to the poor and marginalized. Most of the Indian lawyers are yet to acquire the status of effective social engineers capable of empowering the society.

The Supreme Court of India while articulating its vision on legal aid has remarked "legal aid is required in many forms and at various stages, for obtaining guidance, for resolving disputes in courts, tribunals or other authorities. It has manifold facets. The explosion in population, the vast changes brought about by scientific, technological and other developments, and the all round enlarged field of human activity reflected in modern society, and the consequent increase in litigation in courts and other forums demand that the service of competent persons with expertise in law is required in many stages and at different forums or levels and should be made available. The need for a continuing and well-organized legal education is absolutely essential reckoning the new trends in the world order, to meet the ever growing challenges. The legal education should be able to meet the ever growing demands of the society and should be thoroughly equipped to cater to the complexities of the different situations."

Rendition of free and competent legal service to the weaker sections of the society would militate against the denial of opportunities for securing justice to the citizens by reason of economic or other disabilities.

The Advocates Act has used the words 'legal aid' in its text while dealing with the functions of the State Bar Councils, Bar Council of India and their Rule-making powers. However, the Act is silent as to what exactly is meant by and covered by 'legal aid'. It does not indicate the object for such a venture. Nor it states how and to whom such legal aid is to be imparted.

The object of the Legal Services Authorities Act, 1987 is to establish legal service authorities to provide free and competent legal services to the weaker sections of the society along with the organization of Lok Adalats. The Act has drawn up a scheme to implement such a vision. Chapter II of the Act caters for setting up of a National Legal Services Authority. Chapter III provides for constitution of State Legal Service Authority and Chapter VI deals with organization and powers of Lok Adalats. The legislation provides for rendition of legal aid to all members of a scheduled caste or scheduled tribe, to all women and children irrespective of their financial status, to victims of trafficking in human beings to persons with disabilities, to persons who are victims of man made disasters, ethnic violence, flood, drought, caste atrocity etc., an industrial workmen; persons in custody and those in receipt of income less than Rs. 9000.

Legal Aid Clinics

Law students may actively associate and form groups to establish legal aid clinics. These may be organized so as to be focused at specific villages, remote areas and slums etc. Where feasible, help of competent lawyers may be sought as legal consultants. Wide publicity about the clinics may be arranged by soliciting help of media including vernacular press, local self-government institutions, NGOs, local courts, bar associations and social-cum-service organizations like Rotary Club and Lions Club etc. A list of some of such agencies is provided elsewhere in this book.

The students may be divided into small groups and deputed to the assigned areas. Each group should be guided by a team of senior faculty.

It is very essential for the students to win the confidence and trust of the local people. Rapport between the legal aid team and their 'clients' is of prime importance for the success of the scheme. Student volunteers will be advised to exhibit patience and sympathetic attitude towards the aid seekers.

There are vast type of cases in which legal aid can be granted. To illustrate, all cases of civil nature such as property disputes, matrimonial and custody matters, labour or service grievances, claims for compensation in motor accidents, consumer complaints, different type of criminal cases and matters involving denial of fundamental rights.

To begin with, the students may not find any issues requiring legal assistance. The aid seekers may, however, have a number of difficulties or grievances of civil nature. These could, for instance, relate to issue of ration card, or Aadhar, opening of bank account, driving licence, SC/ST/OBC certificate, old age pension, issue of gas connection, disbursement of bank loans or consumer complaints and the like. The legal aid cells may render suitable help and take up cases on their behalf with the department/agencies concerned.

There are a few category of cases in which legal aid is not to be imported, for example, malicious prosecution, defamation, perjury, contempt of court, election disputes, economic offences and crimes against social laws like complaints against untouchability or caste basis or prejudices.

How to Organise

Legal aid clinics should first be organized within the law school itself. To practice by the student the class should be divided into one or more teams consisting of clients, lawyers and observers. The clients would approach the lawyers to discuss legal problems seeking their opinions about remedies available. The observers should carefully watch each session and then present their assessments. Their reports should be discussed in a frank and objective manner dispassionately.

In the next stage, such clinics may be organized within the law school campus for the class four staff, casual workers or others falling in the category of old, disabled or weaker sections. At this stage also, each session should be supervised by a faculty who must monitor the actual rendition of legal aid.

It would be advisable for the legal aid society of law schools/colleges to function within the overall patronage of the District/Taluka Legal Services Authority. Such a practice would bring due recognition and legitimacy to the activities of law students. This would also facilitate access to and acceptability by the practicing counsels.

In the next stage, legal aid clinics may be held beyond the law schools. Venues may be carefully chosen in the neighbouring villages, slum areas or industrial sites or old age homes, shelters for migrant workers etc. Legal aid camps may also be held in prisons, reformation homes for the juveniles or women homes.

Necessary Infrastructure

Each clinic may have a banner sign board or poster indicating a clinic in progress.

The venue should have requisite furniture in the form of tables, chairs where the clients may be interviewed.

The students must carry required literature *i.e.*, bare Acts, law forms and stationery.

Proper record must be kept of the particulars of the clients, brief gist of the problems/issues warranting advice together with a short description of the advice rendered.

Where feasible, active cooperation and guidance of the local judiciary and bar association must be requested and arranged.

Extension

Legal aid facility can be extended to also cover following activities:

- **Prison Advocacy Projects** – The basic aim is to ensure systematic implementation of the existing legal provisions that guarantee the prisoners their rights, especially of being released on bail and having a speedy trial.
- **Development of Legal Literacy Literature** – In the form of books, manuals, posters, short films and other publications for easy dissemination to those in need.
- **Adoption of a Village**, slum, colony, camp, prison or such other areas for providing legal aid. Such a policy would develop strong bonds and give continuity of legal aid. Improvements in statics and better harmony would then be discernible leading to encouragement to other law schools to follow similar approach.
- **Street Plays** – With a view to spread awareness among the communities. Simple programmes produced with imagination and on actual case studies would duly upgrade legal awareness of the segment concerned. This can be a useful tool to attract the attention of the young and old alike.
- **Community Radio** – This option can be gainfully exploited by seeking access to local radio networks. Problems and issues of relevance to particular geographical entities can be suitably addressed. The efforts can then be expanded by seeking licence for local area small range radio networks.
- **Helpline** – Such a mode can be tried either by way of toll-free number on telephone or physically manned windows to be operational at pre-selected publicized timings. Students can carefully and patiently listen to the problems and then render proper advice to suggest suitable legal remedies.

- **Filing of RTI Application in different causes** – Law students can play a positive role for community service by inviting attention to common issues having first been duly armed by requisite facts and details. Seeking information from the concerned public authorities can provide valuable information. To illustrate, information about funds released for construction of waterlines, roads, tube-wells or drains or for supply of medicines can then be utilized to highlight shortages or misappropriations, etc.

CHAPTER 6

Cross Examination

The evidence of witnesses is usually taken in open court in the presence and under the personal direction and superintendence of the judge. After a witness is sworn or affirmed, he is first examined by the party calling him. This is known as examination-in-chief. A witness is expected to speak to facts and not to opinions, beliefs or inferences. The object of this examination is to get from the witness all material facts within his knowledge.

Cross-examination is the interrogation of a witness by one's opponent or the opposite counsel. It is preceded by examination-in-chief and may be followed by a re-examination.

A right to cross-examination, apart from being a natural right is a statutory right under section 137 of the Indian Evidence Act.

The cross-examination usually follows immediately upon the examination-in-chief. The main object of cross-examination is to bring out the falsity and to find out the truth. Cross-examination is directed *firstly* to the credibility of the witness, and *secondly* to the facts to which he had deposed in-chief, including the cross-examiner's version thereof; and *lastly* the facts to which the witness had not deposed but to which the cross-examiner thinks he is able to depose.

Cross-examination is an art. The object of cross-examination is two fold – to weaken, qualify, or destroy the case of the opponent; and to establish the party's own case by means of his opponent's witnesses.*

The objects are to impeach the accuracy, credibility, and general value of the evidence given in-chief, to sift the facts already stated by the witness to detect and expose discrepancies or to elicit suppressed facts which will support the case of cross-examining party. The exercise of this right is justly regarded as one of the most efficacious tests, which the law has devised for the discovery of the truth.

Paul Brown's Golden Rules:

1. Except in indifferent matters, never take your eye from that of the witness.
2. Be not regardless, of the voice of the witness; next to the eye, this is perhaps the best interpreter of the witness.
3. Be mild with the mild – shrewd with the crafty – confiding with the honest – merciful to the young, the frail, or the fearful – rough to the

---

* Sarkar: Law of Evidence (17th Edn., 2010) Vol. 2, p. 2.713.

ruffian, and a thunderbolt to the liar. But in all this, never be unmindful of your dignity.

4. Ask few questions, and be certain – never to ask any, the answer to which, if against you, may destroy your client.
5. An equivocal question is almost as much to be avoided and condemned as an equivocal answer. Singleness of purpose, clearly expressed, is the best trait in the examination of witnesses, whether they be honest or the reverse.
6. If the witness determines to be witty or refractory with you, you had better settle the account with him at first, or its items will increase with the examination.
7. Like a skillful chess-player, in every move, fix your mind upon the combinations and relations of the game – partial and temporary success may otherwise end in total and remediless defeat.
8. Never undervalue your adversary, but stand steadily upon your guard.
9. Be respectful to the court – kind to your colleague – civil to your antagonist, but never sacrifice the slightest principle of duty to overweening defence towards either.

Timothy A Pratt; www.thefederation.org/documents/Pratt-SP03.htm

The Ten Commandments of Cross-Examination.

1. Thou Shalt prepare
2. Thou Shalt Know Thy Objective
3. Thou Shalt Take Baby Steps
4. Thou Shalt Lead the Witness (Usually)
5. Thou Shalt Know Thy Style and Adopt It to the Occasion
6. Thou Shalt Know When to Quit
7. Thou Shalt Know What to Take to the Podium
8. Thou Shalt Know Thy Audience
9. Thou Shalt Know the Rules of Evidence
10. Thou Shalt Know Thy Judge

Facts of the Case

According to Mahatma Gandhi, facts are three fourths of the case. If we take care of the facts of a case, the law will take care of itself. (Realise) this importance of facts. Facts mean truth, and once we adhere to truth, the law comes to our aid naturally.*

Illustrations of Actual Cross-Examination

1. *Are you a British subject?*
2. *Were you in the Transvaal before the War?*

* The Law and the Lawyers by K.K. Gandhi (Navjivan Publishing House, Ahmedabad, Revised Edn., January 1999) pp. 46-47.

3. *Did you pay the Dutch government Euro 3?*
4. *You have not taken out a registration certificate under this law.*
5. *Why not?**
6. *You have received a list of exemption?*
7. *Will you produce that list?*
8. *But it must be a public document. Have you been prevented by the authorities?*
9. *Have you been prevented by the authorities?***

---

* The Man Before the Mahatma by Charles DiSalvo (Random Houses India, 2012, Edn.), p. 241.

** *Ibid.*, p. 280.

CHAPTER 7
Mock Trial

What it is

A Mock Trial is an act or imitation trial. It is a simulated exercise to train potential lawyers, judges or court officials. Lawyers preparing for an actual trial might first prepare for and go through a mock trial with the help of volunteers as role players. It would help them to experiment with each other or try new theories. It may also be used by an experienced lawyer to train and prepare his associates or juniors with a view to let them gain confidence.

Mock Trial can also be usefully employed as a part of Clinical Legal Education to train law students to educate them about procedural rules to practice. To save time some of the rules can be telescoped. In a mock trial normal rules of procedure are often abbreviated with a view to emphasize a particular portion of the trial. Time may be cut short by reducing number of witnesses, objections or by limiting time for address. The term 'trial advocacy' is also used for mock trial. Case evidence is presented both from the plaintiff and defendant's perspective to a group of mock judges.

Objective

The aim of mock trial is to promote skills of trial advocacy and familiarize students with the trial process as well as the nuances of cross-examination of witnesses. While mooting as a technique relates to appellate stage, a mock trial is based on the trial portion of a legal case.

Methodology

The setting in a mock trial could relate to any of the following or an entirely different case:

(a) A criminal prosecution

(b) Matter involving bail

(c) Case for divorce

(d) Matter relating to cheque dishonoured

(e) Rent control matter

(f) Service conditions case of a public servant

- Decision should be taken with regard to the statutory law and rules of procedure to be studied.
- At the first stage, students should be made to understand the trial procedure and the various trial stages through the workshops.

- In the next step the students should be given a chance to select the role which they aspire to assume in the competition *i.e.;* the prosecution counsel, the defense counsel, the researchers, witness and accused or the judge etc.
- A plot should be carefully chosen with a pre-determined scope of the exercise.
- Screening from the interested students must be done to select the best students to portray each role.
- Selected students should be further coached for the final performance.
- Prior to the start of the mock trial, an opening address should explain the outline of the plot and lessons intended to be imparted.
- The mock trial should be staged in front of the relevant audience.
- At the conclusion of the trial, the audience may be encouraged to ask questions to clarify the doubts.
- Where feasible, video films may be screened of mock trials staged earlier.

Competition Structure

- Each team should be given a predetermined time to present their case. A suggested division of time could be as follows:—
  - Opening statement by the prosecution – 5 minutes
  - Examination-in-Chief by the prosecution – 15 minutes
  - Cross-Examination by the defense – 25 minutes
  - Opening statement by the defense – 5 minutes
  - Examination-in-Chief by the defense – 15 minutes
  - Cross-Examination by the prosecution – 25 minutes
  - Closing statement by the defence – 10 minutes
  - Closing statement by the prosecution – 10 minutes

Selection Criteria

- For prosecution and defense counsels:
  - Knowledge of facts.
  - Logic, reasoning and clarity.
  - Persuasiveness & deference to court.
  - Proper, articulate and systematic analysis of the issues arising out of facts.
- For Researchers:
  - Originality in analysis of issues.
  - Logical progression of ideas and clear, precise and unambiguous writing style.
  - Proper and articulate analysis of strengths and weakness of the case.
  - Understanding of the legal principles directly applicable to the issues.

Example from Mahatma Gandhi

Address and Response to the Court

1. *I hope you will allow me to make an explanation. I do not want to make a long explanation, but I think it is necessary, seeing that I am an official of the Court, that I should render an explanation as to why I have not submitted to this Act.*
2. *I don't want to make any political speeches.*
3. *That is perfectly true.*
4. *I ask the indulgence of the Court for five minutes.*
5. *Very well, Sir, then I have nothing more to say.*[1]
6. *I do, Sir, and I am going to try and argue that before the Court, if I get the opportunity.*[2]

AN ILLUSTRATIVE PLOT ON TRIAL ADVOCACY

State of Delhi v. *Jagdish*

In the Court of Metropolitan Magistrate, New Delhi

C.C. No. 435 of 2009

1. *Bruno is a huge chain of super markets having branches all over India with its main branch in Connaught Place, New Delhi. In the metros they had branches in main shopping areas. Bruno sold everything from cosmetics, electronics, fashion accessories, garments and household items. The premier items like perfumes, liquor and electronic were imported from many countries. They were reputed for genuine products and had a fairly good business throughout the year.*
2. *During festival, marriage season and on important occasions shops saw heavy crowd as they offered special discounts. All imported goods arrived in containers at Indira Gandhi National Airport periodically. It is then segregated and re-packed and electronic price tags with bar-coding are fixed for easy billing and audit. The fixing of the tags was done manually at the main branch and transported to different branches as and when required.*
3. *This work was assigned to Jagdish, supervisor in the main branch. During the season it was difficult for the employees to handle work pressure and on many occasions tempers were frayed. Bruno paid their employees fairly well but as usual the employees always wanted more and felt that special allowances given at such times were not adequate. The attrition rate among employees was high and resulting additional work pressures came on to existing employees.*
4. *Besides the supervisory work for two to three days in a week. Jagdish doubted up as a sales manager interacting with customers and assisting sales personnel in the electronics and cosmetics section. He had two assistants John and Kuldeep. Jagdish is a science graduate. The other two were high school drop outs. But they had an average ability to read, write and speak Hindi, Punjabi and English.*
5. *Jagdish was considered a good employee by Bruno management. Mr. Khanna joined as the new manager in-charge of Connaught Place branch. He was an*

1. p. 239.
2. p. 276.

ex-serviceman and imposed and expected strict discipline among staff. Though he was considered a good person by most of the employees, at times he was open and vocal in his observations, which caused resentment among many. He held the supervisors responsible for the mistakes of the staff under them.

6. *Jagdish colleges mates regularly visited Bruno. When Jagdish was on supervisory work they enquired about his whereabouts from staff and also Mr. Khanna at times. They came to buy a few things and used to have long chat with Jagdish and other nearby sales staff, mostly girls. Mr. Khanna did not like ethics and warned Jagdish many times. One day Mr. Khanna was out on some work. On his return he saw Jagdish chatting with some friends along with the sales girls and they were laughing loud. Mr. Khanna was furious and he shouted at Jagdish in the open hall. He also warned his friends that if it happened again he would have to take some stern steps.*
7. *After this incident Jagdish was very quiet and did not mingle well with the rest of the staff. To his dismay he found that he did not get the expected special increment, which was promised to him earlier. Around the same time preparations for Diwali sales began. An all staff meeting was arranged regarding additional work to be done. Mr. Khanna had brought in a representative from Dubai to explain to the supervisors how to check with product code list and fix the new Barcode pricing list to respective products. Barcode technology & infrared reading guns were explained to billing clerks.*
8. *At Bruno new security measures were adopted. Close circuit cameras were installed in the business areas. New consignments started arriving. Jagdish was to supervise fixing of barcodes with the help of John and Kuldeep for electronic and cosmetic items. It was a laborious job that needed lot of concentration. If the price sticker is switched, there could be considerable loss/gain depending on the sale of the product. As there will be large, diverse crowd during Diwali, it would be near impossible to contact customers after the product is sold.*
9. *The printing of the barcode stickers was done by Mr. Pancham, Accounts Manager and handed over to the supervisors. There were separate cartons for the local consumption and for transporting to other branches. Jagdish was working overtime and was very tired. As Diwali was just a month away, work was very heavy and they were working very late. At the back of his mind he was also perturbed about the incident and his failure to get special increment. When asked about it, he was told, "we'll consider it after Diwali". He was seething and wanted to teach them a lesson. He took leave for two days and joined office on 24 September, 2012.*
10. *On 25 September, 2012 Jadgish asked for the entire batch of stickers, to finish the job at one go. When Mr. Pancham was about to print, he received a call from Mr. Khanna to meet him immediately. Jagdish sat on Mr. Pancham's seat, selected the items on the list, and gave the print command. Mr. Pancham returned and saw Jagdish taking the printed stickers from the printer tray. Though he was surprised, he did not say anything as he did not notice anything unusual. After a few hours he found that the cost price list he had printed earlier missing. Remembering that Jagdish had come to his room, he asked him. Jagdish hastily returned the sheet apologizing that he had mistakenly taken the sheet along with price stickers.*

11. *On 26 September, 2012 he again went on leave on the pretext of being unwell. He even contemplated quitting during the peak season. On his return next day, Mr. Khanna scolded him in front of everybody and also informed that he can forget his special increment. Jagdish did not report for duty from 28 September, 2012. Diwali was just two week away. His colleagues informed Mr. Khanna that he was seen near the tea shop with friends.*

12. *Mr. Satish was Jagdish's classmate right from preliminary school to college. Satish was quite affluent and was the one who often visited Jagdish at Bruno. He looked after his father's grocery shop. Satish went to Bruno but did not find Jagdish. He was informed that Jagdish had stopped coming to work. Satish met Jagdish at the usual tea shop. Jagdish explained to him the incidents that led him to quit.*

13. *Later Jagdish and Satish went along with his friends for a drink. After a few rounds, Jagdish started abusing Mr. Khanna and said that he will pay dearly for treating him shabbily. When Satish questioned him further, he said he might have issued wrong pricing code stickers to be fixed in electronic products and luxury cosmetic items. With the Diwali crowd nobody would have the time to check.*

14. *After a few days on a Sunday (7 October, 2012), just two weeks before Diwali (Saturday, 13 October 2012), Satish went to Bruno. He regularly used to buy cosmetic and other items from Bruno. He was aware of the pricing of the products. He checked out for items and found that perfumes and some electronic MP-3 players were underpriced. He told people around that he was getting married and would like to pick up presents for his friends, as festival discount offered is good. He picked up some items and paid for it in cash. He purchased goods worth about Rs. 69,920 mostly perfumes and MP-3 players. At the billing counter, the sales girl just beamed the gun at the products and received the cash. Since Satish was well known, nobody suspected anything.*

15. *Next day Jagdish met Satish in the tea shop. Jagdish teased Satish being too smelly albeit good. Satish took it jocularly and offered Jagdish a spray can. Satish had removed the price stickers from all the items he purchased. He also informed that he is getting engaged shortly and had bought some gifts for his close friends and cousins. Jagdish was hesitant but Satish insisted and put it inside Jagdish bike's side box.*

16. *After Diwali, there was much less crowd and the staff was in a relaxed mood. On 20 October, 2012, one of the customers took two Chanel perfume bottles and gave it for billing. The billing clerk mechanically beamed the reading gun on the barcode and extended the bill for payment. On receipt of the bill, he noticed that one was priced high (Rs. 10,995) and the other very low (Rs. 3,995). He asked the billing clerk whether it was a spurious stuff. It was brought to the notice of Mr. Khanna.*

17. *Mr. Khanna first thought it must be some mistake. He immediately checked the price list and found that Rs. 10,995 was the correct price. He offered to pick up a new bottle for the customer, but could not find it on the shelf. He was mildly surprised and told the customer that he would inform him when he gets the product or get it sent to his residence.*

18. *Later he asked Mr. Kumar, another supervisor to stay back for the night. On checking out the sales chart and figures he saw the anomaly in pricing mainly of*

few premium cosmetics and electronic items. Next day he engaged five staff members and checked for correctness of the price stickers for the listed items on the shelves. He found a few products of the description on the shelf. The rest had been sold.

19. *He informed the management, who engaged auditors to take out the entire list of items sold and compared it with the price list. It was found that Bill No. 666, Sunday, 4 October, 2012 billed at 6.00 p.m. that had all the listed items with lowest price. The items were premium perfumes and MP-3 players of reputed brands. The bill amount was Rs. 69,920 paid by cash. The items purchased were five bottles of Chanel 5 perfume, five sony MP-3 players, five Davidoff Eu de cologne bottles.*
20. *The auditing team headed by Mr. Ranga, immediately ordered for the recorded video of the camera facing the sales, counter and bill counter. On reply they found that Satish had picked up the items and paid the bill.*
21. *On 23 October, 2012 Mr. Vohra filed a criminal complaint with Tilak Nagar Police Station against Mr. Jagdish and Mr. Satish. The Inspector in-charge of Tilak Nagar Police Station, Mr. Ganesh recorded the FIR at 10.45 a.m. on 23 October, 2012.*
22. *On completion of the investigation, Mr. Ganesh, Inspector, Tilak Nagar Police station, arrested Jagdish and Satish on 24 October, 2012 and took them into custody. The case was thereafter committed to the Court of the Metropolitan Magistrate Court and the Magistrate framed charges against the accused Jagdish (A1) in respect of offences under sections 420, 408, 109 and 120B read with section 34 of IPC and sections 65 and 66 of Information Technology Act, 2000 as amended by IT (Amendment) Act, 2008 and Satish (A2) in respect of offences under sections 420, 109 and 120B read with section 34 of IPC. The case thereafter was posted on trial.*

Witness :

1. *Jagdish (DW1) – (recorded under application from the accused).*
2. *Satish (DW2) – (recorded under application from the accused).*
3. *John (DW3).*
4. *Mr. Khanna (PW1).*
5. *Mr. Pancham (PW2).*
6. *Mr. Ranga, Auditor (PW3).*

Exhibits

1. *Bill No. 666 dated 4 October, 2012 (Exhibit 1).*
2. *Price list showing the actual price of confiscated items (Exhibit 2).*
3. *Barcode Tags showing price of products (Exhibit 3).*
4. *Two cassettes (CCTV recording of 4 October, 2009) (MO).*
5. *Confiscated perfume bottles, MP-3 players, Eu de cologne (5 bottles each) (MO).*

Documents

1. *FIR (Annexure 1).*
2. *Panchnama / Mahazar (Annexure 2).*
3. *Charge Sheet (Annexure 3).*
4. *Statement of witness (Annexure 4).*

ANNEXURE 1

FIRST INFORMATION REPORT

(Under section 154, Cr. P.C.)

1. District: New Delhi PS: Tilak Nagar Year : 2012 FIR No. 435
2. Act: I.P.C. — Sections 420, 408, 109 and 120B read with section 34, IPC and sections 65 & 66 of the IT Act, 2000, as amended by IT (Amendment) Act, 2008
3. Occurrence of Offence. — Day: 4 October, 2012 (Sunday) Date from: 25 September, 2012 Date to : 04 October, 2012 Time from : 5.00 p.m. Time to 6.00 p.m. Information recorded as PS. Date 23 September, 2012 Time : 12.00 Noon Entry No. 1246 Information recorded by : Inspector Ganesh
4. Type of Information: — Written/Oral : Written
5. Place of Occurrence: — Direction/Distance from PS : At Bruno Super Store – about one km South, from Police Station.

   Beat Number:

   Address:

   In case outside this PS, then the name of PS : District
6. Complainant/Informant,: Mr. Jolly Khanna, Father's name: Late Mr. Name Rajesh Khanna, Date of birth: 20 April, 1967. Nationality Indian Passport No. : Date of Issue : Place of Issue:

   Occupation: Manager Address: 17 Darya Ganj, New Delhi
7. Basis on which FIR is lodged: Information given in person, by Mr. Jolly Khanna
8. Details of Known/Unknown/Suspected accused with full particulars:

   Jagdish (A1) 25 years old; and Satish (A2) 25 years old.
9. Reasons for delay in reporting by the complainant/information : Crime noticed on 20 October, 2012 only.
10. Particulars of injuries sustained: NA
11. Particulars of Post Mortem Report: NA
12. Post Mortem Report done by: NA
13. Inquest report/Unnatural death Case No. if any......NA

ANNEXURE 2

PANCHNAMA / MAHAZAR

On 23 October, 2012 at 1.00 p.m. the investigating officer, visited the spot of the occurrence of the crime in Crime Number 435 of Tilak Nagar Police Station. After observing the place, the computer and the CCTV camera in the business and billing area he prepared a sketch.

The following were taken into possession and sealed in front of witnesses.

1. *Recorded tape of the security camera near cash counter.*
2. *Recorded tape near the cosmetic/electronic counters.*
3. *Copy of Bill No. 666 dated 4 October, 2012.*

Mr. Bala and Ram are sales and billing clerks at Bruno. They agreed to act as witnesses and have attested the panchnama.

Sd/-
SI Ganesh
Investigating Officer

Witness:

Signed

Mr. Bala, age 24 years, Residing at No. 124 Out House Quarters, 26, Akbar Road, New Delhi.

Signed

Mr. Ram, age 31 years. Residing at : No. 20, Railway Colony, New Delhi.

On 24 October, 2012 at 11.30 a.m. the investigating officer, visited the residence of Mr. Satish, one of the accused, at 11, Lincoln Street, New Rajender Nagar and took into possession the following and sealed in front of witnesses.

1. *5 nos. MP-3 players (Sony)*
2. *One no. used and four unused Chanel 5 perfume bottle*
3. *Four nos. Davidoff eu de cologne*

Sd/-
SI Ganesh
Investigating Officer

Witnesses:

Signed

Mr. Kali, age 24 years, residing at No. 14, Lincoln Street, New

Delhi.

Signed

Mr. Siva, age 30 years, residing at No. 16, Lincoln, New Delhi

On 24 October, 2012 at 10 p.m., the investigating officer, visited the residence of Jagdish, the accused at 21, Pahar Ganj, New Delhi and took into possession the following and sealed in front of witness.

One number used Davidoff eu de cologne.

Sd/-
SI Ganesh
Investigating Officer

Witness:
Signed

Mr. Ustaad, age 29 years, residing at No. 13 Pahar Ganj, New Delhi

Signed

Mr. Bhola, age 38 years, residing at No. 26, Pahar Ganj, New Delhi

ANNEXURE 3

Charge Sheet:
(Under Section 173, Cr. P.C.)

In the Court of the Metropolitan Magistrate Court,
Patiala House, New Delhi

Final Report in Cr No. 435/2009

Complainant

State of New Delhi

v.

Mr. Jagdish and Mr. Satish

Accused

1. *Mr. Jagdish, S/o Mr. Brahma, aged 25 years, residing at No. 21, Pahar Ganj, New Delhi.*
2. *Mr. Satish, S/o Mr. Siddharth, aged 25 years, residing at No. 11, Lincoln Street, New Rajendra Nagar, Delhi.*

   Mr. Jagdish (A1) under sections 420, 408, 109 and 120B read with section 34 of IPC and sections 65 and 66 of Information Technology Act, 2000 as amended by IT (Amendment) Act, 2008 and Mr. Satish (A2) in respect of offences under sections 420, 109 and 120B read with section 34 of IPC.

Summary of Facts

Mr. Jagdish (DW1), a science graduate was an employee of Bruno, a supermarket giant dealing with an array of consumer goods with its headquarters in New Delhi which used the barcode pricing system for its goods. He was primarily a supervisor but had to look after sales manager post in cosmetics and electronic departments due to high attrition rate amongst employees. He showed great resentment towards his new manager Mr. Khanna, an ex-serviceman primarily because Mr. Khanna (PW1) objected to Jagdish friends visiting the store during the work hours and even blasted Jagdish one day with regard to this. After this Jagdish was further perturbed because his increment was denied due to these issues and extra work was piling up for Diwali, wherein the barcode pricing stickers had to be fixed upon all products for sale. A representative was brought to explain this as if was done incorrectly there could be great loss or gain of profits.

Mr. Pancham, Accounts Manager, handled printing of the barcode stickers and distributed to supervisors who had to oversee fixing with help of assistants. On 25 September, 2012 Jagdish asked for the entire batch of sticker to finish the job and took the printout on his own ini Mr. Prasad's absence. On 26 September, 2012 Jagdish skipped work, joined briefly on 27 September, 2012 and quit job from 28-9-2012.

Satish (DW2) was one of Jagdish's close friends who was also affluent. While they were having a drink Jagdish abused Mr. Khanna and hinted to Satish switching of the pricing stickers on some of the electronic and luxury perfume goods. After this Satish visited the store on a Sunday when Diwali crowd was at it peak and picked up the precise under priced luxury items to the tune of Rs. 69,920 under the pretext of his marriage. He presented a bottle to Jagdish later.

After Diwali the switching of price stickers was discovered by a customer who happened to buy two Channel 5 perfumes that were dual priced. Mr. Pancham (PW2) after with the help of the auditor Mr. Ranga (PW3) traced the bulk of sales to Bill no. 666 and from CCTV evidence to Satish. Thus Mr. Jolly Khanna (PW1) filed a criminal complaint against DW1 and DW2 on 23 October, 2012 in Tilak Nagar Police Station.

ANNEXURE 4

STATEMENT OF WITNESSES

Persons examined

1. *Mr. Jolly Khanna*
2. *Mr. Kannan*
3. *Mr. Ranga (Auditor)*
4. *Mr. Pancham*
5. *Mahazar witness*
   Bala & Ram – Employees of Bruno
   Kali & Siva – Neighbours of Satish
   Ustaad & Bhola – Neighbour of Jagdish
6. *Investigating Officer*

1. *Mr. Jolly Khanna*

I am the newly appointed manager of Bruno and an ex-serviceman. I am very strict with employees as we deal with different types of high profile customers. Jagdish's cavalier behaviour along with his friends does not suit our working style. I reprimanded him in front of everyone one day when I found him having merry time with friends and other staff during working hours. I had advised to management to put on hold his special increment till Diwali. He deliberately skipped work without reason when work is at peak. I had warned his friends too. I recognized Satish as Jagdish's friend, who frequents Bruno on the CCTV footage.

2. *Mr. Kannan*

I have been working as a supervisor in Bruno for the last two years and knew Jagdish from the beginning. He was in-charge of the electronics and luxury perfumes section and before diwali he was assigned the task of supervising the placing of barcode stickers upon the items. Mr. Khanna informed me about the sudden irregularities with regard to the price of Channel 5 perfume after Diwali. Upon investigation I discovered that all items under Jagdish's supervision were wrongly priced.

3. *Mr. Ranga*

I handle the auditing and accounts for Bruno and have been working there for three years. I was one day notified about certain irregularities in the pricing of the electronic and luxury perfume items by Mr. Khanna. I was asked to trace all purchases of items in respect of electronic and premium cosmetic items. I thoroughly checked the entire accounts and traced a bulk purchase of the said items to Bill No. 666 made on the 4th of October, 2012.

4. Mr. Pancham

I am an employee of Bruno and am in-charge of the printing of barcode stickers. I handover the stickers to the respective supervisors who arrange to stick them on the products. On 25 September, 2012. Jagdish wanted the printout of all the barcodes to finish the job at one go. I got them ready in the digital format. Before I could print them out I got a call and had to leave. When I returned, Jagdish had already printed them and later found the price list for different products also missing. When I asked Jagdish, he returned the list apologizing that he had accidentally taken it along with the stickers. Later I was informed about the switch.

5. Mahazar Witness

Bala & Ram – *On 23-10-2012 the police inspector requested us to check the list of things he prepared that were taken from Bruno. We checked and they were matching. Thereafter he sealed the packets with the contents.*

Kali & Siva – *On 24 October at 11.30 a.m., the police inspector requested us to check the list of things he prepared that were recovered from the house of Mr. Satish. We checked and they were matching. Thereafter he sealed the packets with the contents.*

Ustaad & Bhola – *On 24 October at 1.00 p.m., the police inspector requested us to check the list of things he prepared that were recovered from the house of Mr. Jagdish. We checked and they were matching. Thereafter he sealed the packets with the contents.*

6. Investigating Officer

I, Ganapathy, am the Inspector at Tilak Nagar Police Station and the investigating officer in this case. On 24th October after ascertaining certain facts from people investigated, have taken A1 & A2 into custody and charged with Mr. Jagdish under sections 420, 408, 120B read with section 34 of the IPC and sections 65 & 66 of the IT Act, 2000 as amended by the IT (Amendment) Act, 2008 and Mr. Satish under sections 420, 408 and 120B read with section 34 of the IPC.

EXHIBIT-1

BRUNO

Bruno Group of Supermarkets Pvt. Ltd.
No. 15, Asaf Ali Road, New Delhi
TIN No. 5677489393

Cash Bill

Bill NO. 666 *Date : 4 October, 2012* *Time :*

Description	*Amount*	*Quantity*	*Rate (Rs.)*
Sony MP-3	*2995*	*5*	*14,975.00*
Davidoff – Eu de cologne	*2995*	*5*	*14,975.00*
Channel 5 Perfume	*3995*	*5*	*19,975.00*
Other items			
Amount Total		*15*	*49,925.00*

VAT @ 12.5%
Total tax – Rs. 5,548
Amount received – Rs. 70,000
Amount returned – Rs. 80

Thank you & visit again
No cash refund

EXHIBIT-2

BRUNO
Bruno Group of Supermarkets Pvt. Ltd.
No. 15, Asaf Ali Road, New Delhi
TIN No. 5677489393

Price List

1. Channel 5 perfume	:	*Rs. 10,995*
2. Sony MP-3 player	:	*Rs. 5,995*
3. Davidoff en de cologne	:	*Rs. 4,995*

All prices inclusive of VAT @ 12.5%

MOCK TRIAL
SUGGESTED RULES AND REGULATIONS

I. Aim and Purpose

The Mock Trial problem has been conceived with the aim of promoting skills of trial advocacy and familiarize students with the trial process as well as the nuances of cross-examination of witnesses.

II. Venue & Date

The mock trial advocacy shall be held on ....(date) from ....to .... (time) at ....(venue).

III. Language

The competition shall be in English/....... (state language)

IV. Dress Code

Advocates attire (including neckband and gown)

V. Eligibility

The mock trial advocacy is open to all students of the School wanting to excel in trial advocacy.

VI. Team Composition

(a) Each team shall consist of a maximum of .... Members (indicate)

(b) There can be a maximum of two counsels and one researcher designated for each team.

VII. Recording of Evidence

The team members should take notes of the question and answers during chief/cross-examinations.

VIII. General Rules

(a) Exhibits of the case are already before the Hon'ble Court

(b) There are six witnesses in the case to be examined upon.

(c) Each team will get a total of 55 minutes to present their case. The division of time shall be as follows:—

- Opening statement by the prosecution – 5 minutes
- Examination-in-Chief by the prosecution – 15 minutes
- Cross-Examination by the defence – 25 minutes
- Opening statement by the defence – 5 minutes
- Examination-in-Chief by the defence – 15 minutes
- Cross-Examination by the prosecution – 25 minutes
- Closing statement by the defence – 10 minutes
- Closing statement by the prosecution – 10 minutes

(d) Each of the speakers shall conduct either the chief or the cross-examination and deliver either the opening or closing statement. Therefore, each speaker shall compulsorily conduct an examination and deliver either the opening or closing statement.

CHAPTER 8

Case Method

Case method is a mode based on the practice wherein student volunteers and their community partners share their experiences or discuss a given situation. The case method is a teaching approach that consists in presenting the students with a case and explaining how it was handled and thereafter putting them in the role of a decision maker facing a problem. The response may present out different method how the case should have been handled.

A case study is a document that illustrates handling of a legal matter and inviting comments on its handling. The situation depicted may relate to the stage of pre-trial, actual trial or post-trial when different law issues have emerged.

This mode is a situation to be critically examined and commented upon. It provides useful and interesting information for class room discussion and academic studies. The situation does not have an obvious single solution. There may be a number of approaches each with accompanied advantages and disadvantages. The case provides a scope to stimulate an absorbing dialogue on possible approaches and outcomes. Each case has one central angle to keep the discussion on a focused matter.

Case method should be adopted in a progressive manner. At the initial stage, case study selected should be based on simple and straight forward facts. Subsequently the studies chosen should gradually indicate more complex data. However, the aim of each case method should be clear and incapable of multiple themes. The class may be supplied with all necessary details of the problem and then afforded time to come up with their responses.

According to Justice M. Jagannadha Rao, a former Judge of the Supreme Court of India, "The advantage of 'case studies' in any branch is that one can grasp the practical aspects of a law. In fact, even in law schools, the 'case method' was one of the successful methods employed for purpose of teaching. In departmental enquiries or in court martial proceedings, those whose responsibility it is to conduct inquiries or proceedings, get better guidance by going through 'case studies' rather than by reading a section or rule in the abstract".

Sample of a few case studies are given below.

Engineer Works

The matter relating to award of a contract for quarrying boulders and their crushing/ re-crushing by a Chief Engineer was needed to be probed. The original contract amount was for Rs. 98.67 lakh but total final bill had amounted to Rs. 1.87 crore and thus far exceeded in scope.

The enquiry revealed that by use of wrong tender form the contractor had managed to get the benefit of escalation to which he was otherwise not entitled. Market rate analysis was not obtained by the authorities from the Surveyor of Works. It was carried out arbitrarily by the GE. An inordinate high escalation factor was allowed which caused gain to the firm.

While calling for fresh tenders, inadequate time was given and thereby only one firm could submit its bids. Though reflecting higher rates, the option of re-rendering was ignored. An amendment to the contract was issued improperly in a hurried manner in two days without mentioning relevant details. It did not disclose financial implication. Subsequently another amendment was circulated. Sanction to proceed on a single tender action was not sought. Payments were made to the contractor beyond laid down deviation limits.

A high level court of inquiry brought out these lapses but termed them procedural irregularities inadvertently committed.

Observations

(a) Use of correct tender form could have guarded against likelihood of excess payment done.

(b) Detailed market analysis should have been obtained from the SSW.

(c) Market analysis should have taken into account details of plant or equipment required, labour component, transportation elements, contractors overhead and profits.

(d) Realistic rates should have been determined.

(e) Adequate time should have been given for tender response.

(f) Re-tendering should have been resorted to when needed under the laid down orders.

(g) All relevant details and specific figures should have been shown in the amendment issued.

(h) This was a clear case of fraudulent lapses warranting suitable disciplinary action rather than lenient disposal.

Investigations

An officer was tasked to lay an ambush on a road to stop the move of some Naga militants. The ambush party intercepted and searched a civilian jeep carrying three males, three women and two children. Out of the persons stopped two males were detained and put through an interrogation on the site. One of the civilians was blindfolded and made to lie down on the road. Petrol was poured on him. He denied his involvement in any underground activity and pleaded for mercy. Some one lit a matchstick and soon he was engulfed in fire. The civilian suffered burn injuries on his neck, hands and legs. There was delay in his evacuation to the hospital.

The matter was investigated by a Court of Inquiry. The Court found that the burn injuries were consequent to manhandling and maltreatment of the civilian. The Court found the officer to have caused the fire accidentally. The officer was administered a warning by his brigade commander. Later he was awarded a Severe Displeasure (Recordable) for his lapses by a higher commander.

Observations

(a) The provisions of rule 180 were not invoked at the inquiry. The same should have been done.

(b) The warning by the brigade commander for the lapse should have been given merely to caution and not as a disposal of the case.

(c) The show-cause notice did not bring out specific lapses and was thus vague.

Death in Cross Fire

'C' Copy of a Gorkha Bn was deployed on a prominent road axis emanating from Bhutan and was responsible for the conduct of CI ops in Chirang and Kokrajhar district of lower Assam. There had been reports of militants intending to strike at Bhutanese convoys. The area was IED prone with a number of bridges and culverts. The anti-nationals had resorted to mass extortion drives.

In the wake of the militants declaring a unilateral cease fire, the security forces were under strict instructions not to fire upon any militant unless fired at. The sub unit had also received instructions to use 'loud hailers' to warn the militants cadres to surrender in case sighted and an attempt to apprehend them without resorting to firing.

This patrol noticed some movement in a haystack and informed the officer accordingly. At this juncture a woman who was sitting next to the fire got up and started moving towards the bamboo grove. On seeing the NCO, she was startled and ran back shouting.

This served as a warning to the two militants who were hiding in the haystack. They immediately got up and started running towards the centre of the village. The officer immediately alerted his patrol as well as the JCO led party and ordered them to close in towards the centre of the village in order to trap the terrorists.

One of the terrorists running had an AK-47 in his hand. Sensing the dragnet closing in on them, the terrorist fired a burst at the troops following closely at his heels. Taken completely by surprise, the troops dived for cover and instinctively returned fire. At this juncture screams and cries of pain were heard from one of the nearby houses which diverted the attention of the troops towards them. At the end of the encounter, two civilians were found to have died due to the cross-fire.

Observations

(a) Contingencies in which civilians could be involved in cross-fire should have been deliberated upon.

(b) The rules of engagement though clearly laid down are difficult to implement on ground, especially when a terrorist is sighted armed with a weapon. To await till the terrorist opens fire is a difficult situation.

(c) Knowledge of local language is a must while operating in such conditions.

(d) Incorporation of a Police Representative in such operations is of utmost importance and is a legal necessity.

(e) The troops did not exhibit a proper control and expertise in firing this was evident when they missed the terrorists and civilian casualties occurred due to the cross-fire.

Custodial Death

An infantry unit patrol of HER Battalion deployed near Udalguri, Majbat and Organg areas picked up two persons including one person named JACK from the house of one PETER on 5 August, 1998. The provisions of Armed Forces (Special Powers) Act, 1958 were in force. Arms and ammunition were also recovered during the encounter. During interrogation the two civilians confessed their links to a militant organization. However, JACK was not handed over to the police authorities and nor produced before a Magistrate. A Habeas Corpus *petition was filed by his relative in the High Court.*

In its affidavit the Army claimed to have handed over JACK to the police station on 6 August, 1998 at 17.30 hrs. The same was denied in the affidavit filed by the police authorities. According to them, an exchange of fire between CHEETAH Battalion and the extremists, had taken place near the site of an ambush laid by the Army unit. After the firing subsided, a dead body of an unidentified militant was found lying nearly. It was photographed, finger prints taken and then cremated. A teacher of the local school later identified the picture to be that of JACK.

The High Court ordered the Union of India to pay a compensation of Rs. 1.50 Lac for the custodial death besides the cost of litigation.

Observations

- *(a) There was no independent evidence to support the Army version about capture of ILL FATED JOE having led to recovery of large quantity of arms and ammunition.*
- *(b) The situation report submitted by local authorities contradicted the military claim.*
- *(c) There was no evidence to indicate that ILL FATED JOE was taken to village MALGUDI for recovery of arms and ammunition as contended by the Army.*
- *(d) There was no satisfactory explanation for the delay in handing over the dead body after the so-called encounter.*
- *(e) There was no convincing reply why dead body was not handed to the nearest police station but instead to one located far away.*

Lenient Disposal

An officer posted in HQ Eastern Command was attached to a training establishment in Central Command. He was ordered to undertake the invigilation duties for the entrance test for admission to a professional college located at a station in Central Command. He manipulated to be assigned duties in the same room where his son was writing the question paper. He was found tampering with the answer sheet of his son in an attempt to assist him to qualify the exam.

The investigations were held in a careless manner. The probe was unnecessarily delayed. The charge framed was not proper. Rather than bringing the officer to trial by Court Martial, he was let off with the minimum punishment.

Observations

- *(a) The matter should have been investigated by a staff court of inquiry with clear terms of reference.*
- *(b) Formal legal advice should have been sought.*
- *(c) The lapse being in the nature of moral turpitude should have been dealt by a Court Martial.*

CHAPTER 9

Opinion Work

Lawyers are often called upon to discuss, examine and then render their opinion on any given matter. Usually, the client's aim is to ascertain options available to him in the situation and find out the best legal remedy available within the constraints like time, resources and finances etc.

It would be advisable for the law student to practice rendition of opinion. The important points to note are as enumerated below.

The opinion must marshal and recapitulate relevant facts.

The law points/issues involved must be clearly identified.

Applicable laws, both statutory and procedural must be indicated.

Relevant and applicable case law should be sequentially discussed.

In the event of an apparent unfavourable ruling, an effort should be made to indicate how far are the facts and legal situation different in the instant case.

Available options should then be discussed bringing out accompanied consequences, risks or other difficulties apart from an estimation of financial implications and the legal process.

The opinion must record that it is based on the documents and files submitted for perusal. If any facts, legal rules and judicial records were not made available to the counsel, obviously the conclusions and opinion would not be correct.

Sample

IN THE MATTER OF :

M/s. ABC ...*QUERIST*

I. The Querist has sought my opinion on the following issues:—

(i) In view of the judgment passed by the Hon'ble Supreme Court in Booz Allen & Hamilton Inc. v. *SBI Home Finance Ltd., (2011) 5 SCC 532, would be Querist (who is a Mortgagee), be able to invoke the arbitration clause contained in the various Loan Agreements, for recovering the dues owed from its various Mortgagors and for enforcing the security?*

(ii) Would be Querist be entitled to claim both – money decree as well as enforcement under arbitration?

OR

Should the Querist proceed under arbitration and limit its claim only to a money decree, and simultaneously file a separate suit in High Court for enforcement of decree under Order XXXIV of C.P.C.?

(iii) *The Querist has recently in another separate arbitration, filed its Statement of Claim, wherein a prayer has been made for a money decree for the amount due, and also for a decree for enforcement of mortgage. If the subject-matter is not arbitrable, should the Querist file an Application before the Arbitrator for amending the Statement of Claim and withdraw the remedy for enforcing the mortgage to make the subject-matter arbitrable?*

OR

Should the Querist withdraw the entire arbitration action, and file a separate suit in the Civil Court for both money decree and for enforcing the security?

II. The Querist has supplied me with the following documents in order to enable me to opine on the queries raised:—

(i) *Statement of Claim of M/s. ABC* v. *PQR Pvt. Ltd.; and*

(ii) *Case for opinion*

III. The aforesaid documents indicate the following factual background in which the queries are raised:—

(a) *The Querist is a Non-Banking Company ("NBFC") registered with the Reserve Bank of India, and is incorporated under the Companies Act, 1956. The Querist is, engaged* inter-alia *in the business of providing loans and advances.*

(b) *In or about 2010, the Querist was approached by one Mr. V.N. Kumar on behalf of PQR Pvt. Ltd. (hereinafter referred to as "the Borrower") requesting for a Loan against mortgage of property, for an amount of Rs. 2.25 crores, for a period of 72 months. The aforesaid Loan was duly sanctioned by the Querist Company. In order to secure the aforesaid Loan, Chadda Homes Pvt. Ltd. (hereinafter referred to as "the co-borrower") executed Memorandum of Entry – First Time Mortgage by Deposit of Title Deeds on 14-7-2010, and deposited the original title deeds with the Querist Company. The Borrower and Co-Borrower also provided secondary security in the form of Post Dated Cheques.*

(c) *That several documents were executed at the time of obtaining the Loan* i.e., *Loan Agreement, demand Promissory Note, Letter of Continuity etc. Under the aforesaid Loan Agreement, the parties agreed that all disputes arising out of the loan would be referred to a Sole Arbitrator to be appointed by the Querist Company. Further, the agreement would be governed by Indian Law with respect to any dispute between the parties, and the venue of arbitration would be Mumbai.*

(d) *The Borrowers were persistently irregular in payment of the monthly installments. As a consequence, the Querist Company was constrained to recall the entire loan by way of Loan Recall Notice dated 4-2-2012. As on August, 2012, an aggregate sum of Rs. 2.62 crores became due and payable to the Querist Company from the Borrowers.*

(e) *The Querist invoked the arbitration clause contained in the Arbitration Agreement and filed a Statement of Claim, praying* inter-alia *for a money decree of Rs. 2.62 crores, failing which, the mortgaged properties be sold to realize the unpaid dues.*

IV. My opinion on the Queries raised are as under:—

(a) With respect to query (i) mentioned hereinabove, in view of the Judgment of the Hon'ble Supreme Court in the case of Booz Allen, (2011) 5 SCC 532, the Querist Company would now not be able to invoke Arbitration proceedings in terms of the Arbitration Clause, since Supreme Court has in paras 46, 48.1 and 48.2 held that a mortgage being a transfer of a right in rem, *a Suit for enforcement of a mortgage, not being a mere Suit for recovery of money, will have to be decided by the Courts of law, and not by Arbitral Tribunals. The Court has concluded in para 51 that a mortgage Suit is not only about determination of the existence of the mortgage, or determination of the amount due. It is about enforcement of the mortgage with reference to an immovable property, and adjudicating upon the rights obligations of several classes of persons who have the right to participating in the proceedings relating to the enforcement of the mortgage. The Court has clearly held that even if some of the issues in a mortgaged suit are arbitrable, or could be decided by a private forum, the issues in a mortgage suit can not be decided.*

The remedy available to the Mortgage would be to file a substantive Suit in the civil courts under the provisions of Order XXXIV, C.P.C. and seek the remedy of a money decree inter-alia *through sale of the mortgaged asset, etc.*

(b) With respect to query (ii) mentioned hereinabove, it is opined that it would not be advisable for the Querist Company to bifurcate the cause of action by invoking arbitration proceedings for a money decree, and file a separate suit for enforcement of the Mortgage. The Supreme Court in the Judgment of Sukanya Holding v. *Jayesh Pandya, (2003) 9 SCC 531 has held that it would not be proper to bifurcate the subject-matter of a Suit. Furthermore, the principles contained in Order II, rule 2 of the CPC stipulate that the whole claim is to be filed as one, and in case the Plaintiff does not include the whole claim, the same would amount to relinquishing the portion of the claim not included. Hence, it would be appropriate to file a substantive suit praying for various reliefs in common proceedings. Furthermore, as per Order XXXIV, C.P.C. which pertains to suits relating to Mortgages of Immovable Property, where before a Final Decree for redemption/foreclosure is passed, the Court is required to Order that an account be taken of what was due to the Plaintiff and pass a preliminary decree calling upon the Mortgagor to make payments of the amount due. The passing of the aforesaid preliminary decree in the Suit would make it wholly unnecessary to file a separate claim for a money decree before the Arbitral Tribunal.*

(c) With respect to query (iii) mentioned hereinabove, since the dispute is not arbitrable, by virtue of the Judgment of the Supreme Court, the Querist is advised to withdraw the claim before the Arbitrator/Tribunal with liberty to agitate the claim before a Civil Court of competent jurisdiction.

V. Iopine accordingly.

JAMSHED JI PALKIWALA
SENIOR ADVOCATE

CHAPTER 10
Legal Entrepreneurship

Clinical Legal Education can play a significant role in preparing law students to set up law offices to offer diverse services concerning legal implications to the community.

A wide range of legal needs and documents warrant, adequate awareness of applicable laws and procedures. These would need due scrutiny of eligibility criteria.

The range of services in this sphere would include

- Preparation of wills,
- Consumer complaints and disputes,
- Loan and mortgage documents,
- Due diligence procedure,
- Court marriages and registration of marriage certificates,
- Matrimonial disputes including divorce and custody,
- Preparation of notices and affidavits,
- Motor accident compensation cases,
- Change of name process,
- Preparation of partnership deeds, or other conveyances,
- Registration of society, trust or foundation,
- Setting up of an NGO, etc.,
- Cases relating to dishonouring of cheques,
- Adoption,
- Immigration,
- International Commercial Arbitration,
- Loss of share certificates, nomination division and succession,
- Queries under the Right to Information Act.

No doubt the legal profession undertakes above needs of the clients through the existing mode of lawyers. However, the absence of any organized system of law professionals, trained and equipped to handle such cases with specialization results in delay and adhocism. Lack of specialization always presents a handicap in the area of adequate experience to deal with a wide range of situations. Hence, setting up of proper law offices geared to provide such services would introduce a systematic, organized and expert process to offer a timely and legally appropriate service to the clients.

Presently the body of lawyers provide above services depending upon their availability and resources. In majority of cases they lack any special expertise and competence by way of thorough study experience in any specific field.

Setting up of law office manned by young, energetic and dedicated law graduates can successfully provide above services to the community. This field is specially suited for law students who would like to set up their own offices and who are imbued with a spirit of entrepreneurship, adventure and courage. They belong to the category of those who have self-confidence and are not averse to taking some risks. Some of them may have family support. Most of them would be free from any financial worries or family obligations.

The students would expect suitable guidance from their faculty and experienced professionals to properly sensitize them with regard to the under mentioned aspects.

(a) Premises as regards selection, location and size, layout and organization, furnitures and other infrastructure.

(b) Staff.

(c) Library and search engines.

(d) Loan.

(e) Marketing.

(f) Advertisement.

(g) Partnership.

(h) Applicable legal regime.

(i) Legal regime pertaining to provident fund, gratuity, labour and employment.

It would be advisable for the law college to set up a clinic for legal entrepreneurship. The body should be open to all the students who would like to set up law offices individually or jointly with others.

The students would require to be duly informed and educated about the aspects like market survey, seed capital, essential and desirable scale of infrastructure and logistics, relevant rules and procedures. They should also be apprised about the Bar Council of India norms applicable to right to continue in practice and advertisement etc.

It may be prudent for the students to approach law departments of the corporate houses to explore the feasibility of work they would like to outsource. This may give a space for the new entrepreneurs to gain entry.

Given below are the documents needed to progress a claim seeking compensation in a motor accident case.

BEFORE THE PRESIDENT MOTOR ACCIDENTS CLAIMS TRIBUNAL NEW DELHI (Patiala House)

Shri Rohan Tejpal, S/o Sh. Amrit Tejpal, R/o 25/21 1st Floor, East Patel Nagar, New Delhi – 110 008

..... Petitioner/Claimant

Versus

1. Shri Barjang Beli Tiwari, S/o Sh. Jagdamba Parshad Tiwari, R/o H.No. 393, 5th Pushta, Sonia Vihar P.S. Khajuri Khas; Poorvi Delhi-94. Driver of the offending Truck TATA 407 NO-DL-ILE-6607.
2. Shiv Kumar Tiwari, S/o Sh. Tatan Deen Tiwari, H.No. E-393, Mandir Marg, Sonia Vihar, New Delhi – 94.
3. National Insurance Company, Division XIV; 13/32 WEA Arya Samaj Road, Karol Bagh, New Delhi – 110 005.

Respondents

Claim Application for compensation of a sum of Rs. 1.25 crores (One crore twenty-five lacs) due injuries suffered by the Claimant in a vehicular accident U/S 166 of MVA 1988 duly amended from time-to-time.

Sir,

I, Rohan Tejpal/S/o Shri Amrit Tejpal, R/o 25/21, 1st Floor, East Patel Nagar, New Delhi do hereby apply for the grant of compensation under Motor Vehicles Act for the injuries suffered by me. Necessary particulars are given below:—

1.	Name of the person injured	– Rohan Tejpal, S/o Shri Amrit Tejpal
2.	Full address of the injured	– 25/21 1st Floor, East Patel Nagar, New Delhi – 110 008
3.	Age of the person	– 30 years approx. at the time of accident, DOB (7-9-1978)
4.	Occupation of the person injured	– Employed as a Senior Manager, Administration and Business Development with R. Vision Pvt. Ltd.
5.	Name and address of the employer of the deceased	– Not Applicable
6.	Monthly income claimant	– Total emoluments paid were Rs. 59,000 p.m. with other allied benefits p.m. (last income-tax return attached); after the accident he is paid Rs. 15,000/- p.m.
7.	Does the person in respect of whom compensation is claimed pay income-tax	– -yes- (last income-tax return attached)

8.	Place, date and time of accident	– Place : on Mata Road (Gurgaon) A little ahead of Kataria Chowk, offending truck came in the wrong lane and caused accident. Date : 10 April, 2009 Time : At about 4 AM
9.	Name and address of Police Station in whose jurisdiction the accident took place or was registered	– Police Post/PS Civil Lines, Gurgaon *vide* FIR 154 dated 13-4-2009
10.	Was the person in respect of whom compensation is claimed travelling by the motor vehicle involved in the accident? If so, give the name of place of starting of journey and destination	– Yes, was proceeding from Gurgaon to Patel Nagar, New Delhi in Car DL-9CJ-5912 Alto. Offending truck came from opposite direction but in the wrong lane.
11.	Nature of injuries sustained	– Multiple serious and grievous injuries all over the body; in particular right leg was totally fractured and crushed. Car was totally smashed and petitioner became unconscious.
12.	Name and address of Medical Officer who attended the injured	– The injured claimant was evacuated to nearby medical clinic 'Kalyani Hospital Pvt. Ltd.' Gurgaon in an unconscious state. He had suffered multiple injuries and fractures and was profusely bleeding. A team of doctors headed by Dr. Mathur attended on him.
13.	Period of treatment and expenditure incurred thereon	– Remained admitted as an indoor patient for 12 days. A number of operations were performed and the petitioner was advised to take complete bed rest with number of medicines prescribed and to undergo regular physiotherapy. All this is still continuing. His leg is shortened about one inch and he moves about with the help of wooden staff. A sum of Rs. 2.35 Lacs was paid to Kalyani Hospital, Gurgaon and another sum of Rs. 28,000 has been spent till date on X-rays, medicines, physiotherapy. A sum of Rs. 1,000 p.m. is anticipated expenditure through out the life span of petitioner.
14.	Registration number and type of vehicle involved in the accident	– Offending vehicle Tata Truck 407 DL-1LE-6607

15. Name and address of Insurer of motor vehicle involved in the accident	–	National Insurance Co., WEA, Arya Samaj Road, New Delhi of offending Truck 407-DL-ILE-6607
16. Name and address of owner of the motor vehicle	–	As per head note above
17. Has any claim been lodged with owner/insurer, if so, with what results?	–	No
18. Name and address of applicant	–	As per head note above
19. Relationship with the deceased	–	Not applicable
20. Title to the property of deceased	–	Not applicable
21. Amount of compensation claimed	–	A sum of Rs. 1.25 crores
22. Any other information that may be necessary or helpful in the disposal of the case	–	More than Rs. 3 Lacs has already been spent. His treatment will continue through out his life. With disability suffered, his matrimonial life will be badly affected.
23. Reasons or grounds for late submission of claim petition	–	There is social stigma as he is limping affecting him psychologically.
24. Cause of accident with brief description:—	–	Not applicable.

That the petitioner on 10 April in the morning was coming back from Gurgaon to New Delhi in Car No. DL-9CJ-5912 driven by him. He was driving in his own lane of the road. Petitioner had crossed Kataria Chowk and was proceeding in his lane on Mata Road towards Delhi; when, the offending truck driven rashly and negligently without light or horn came from opposite direction driven in the wrong lane struck forcefully against the car. The impact was so heavy that the car was totally smashed and the petitioner was sandwiched between the engine/steering of car and the rear seats. His right leg was totally crushed, stomach got punctured and he suffered multiple injuries all over his body with profuse bleeding. He became unconscious and was removed to a nearby hospital *viz.* Kalyani Hospital Private Limited. The driver of the offending vehicle ran away leaving the vehicle at the accident sight.

The petitioner is the only earning member as his father retired in 2003 and his elder brother Navish is disabled with 71% global disability. He was thus looking after his entire family consisting of five members.

Petitioner for enhancing his career prospects had left his earlier employers *viz.* Citi Bank and had been offered a better assignment with R Vision Pvt. Ltd., New Delhi as one of the Deputy Directors with an increase of Rs. 25,000 p.m. as additional emolument. This accident has sealed his fate and he is presently being paid Rs. 15,000 p.m. only as he is unable to undertake outside assignments and is stuck to desk work.

CHAPTER 11

Client Counselling

Undoubtedly one of the most relevant aspects for a legal practitioner to be acquainted with and attain proficiency is client counselling.

Client counselling is the next and final stage. It is preceded by client interviewing.

Client interviewing involves giving access to a client and ascertaining his problems and needs. The client interview is a dialogue which may take place face-to-face, by the way of a telephonic interview, in the form of a letter communication or even by teleconferencing. This may at times be held through a third party, or by taking help of interpreters.

The process of client interviewing would require gaining information about who the client is, his name address, age, educational qualification, vocation and financial status.

This would then require ascertaining the problem, difficulty or matter for which a remedy is needed. Account would be necessary to find out the relevant dates in a chronological order. A perusal of all documents, records or material exhibits would also be inescapable. A list of all these should be meticulously prepared.

In certain situations like marital discord, domestic violence or sexual assault etc., it may necessitate co-option of psychological experts to render the desired emotional support.

The venue should be free from disturbance or distractions.

Client counseling should be carried out in a language that is simple and easy to understand. As far as possible, it should be in the language known to the client. The use of technical or complex words should be avoided. To make the advise meaningful, suitable examples may be given.

Counselling must be carried out having due regard to privacy and confidentiality. Its contents must not be divulged to third party. Even with others it may be shared only on the basis of 'need to know'.

For maximum effect and to achieve due accountability, the substance or gist may be handed over to the client in writing. However, as far as possible rendition of advice on telephone or through third party must be avoided.

The counselling must indicate options or courses of action available to the client. The advantages or disadvantages of each option should also be indicated.

An honest estimation of time and expenses involved, apart from fee, and inconveniences envisaged should also be honestly spelt out. Similarly, adverse consequences, if any, should be discussed *e.g.* likelihood of denial of bail or interim relief or loss of a job or confiscation of goods etc.

The counselling must also point out the need for urgency and applicable limitation aspects.

CHAPTER 12

Due Diligence

This is a term used for a number of concepts involving either an investigation of business or person prior to signing a contract, or an act with a certain standard of case, *e.g.* sanction of a loan by a bank or financial institution. The term refers to the case a reasonable person should take before entering into an agreement or a transaction with another party.

Persons desirous of acquiring, selling, lending or borrowing real estate, whether residential or commercial, routinely need to undertake a variety of due diligence.

Given below is the assignment letter issued by a bank instructing a lawyer to undertake a due diligence task. The same is followed by the format in which report is to be furnished after due scrutiny and completion of the task.

STATE BANK OF ....

RETAIL ASSETS SMALL ENTERPRISES CREDIT CELL,
NEW DELHI Branch

Mr.	KR
Advocate,	No. RASECC/DZ/
24, Model Colony,	Date 19-8-2012
New Delhi	
Mobile :	

Sir,

Housing/Mortgage/Home Cash/Education/Rent Plus

New/Enhancement/Renewal

RA/M/

Smt. Abha Rawal & Sh. Vijay Rawal at Amar Colony, Lajpat Nagar III, New Delhi

SEARCH AND VERIFICATION OF TITLE DEEDS/DOCUMENTS

You are requested to make an investigation of title to the properties to enable us to obtain a valid and enforceable mortgage of the property(ies) more fully described in Annexure 'B' Annexure 'E' enclosed herein is required to be filled up by you with full details. To enable you to make a proper search report, a checklist in the form of guidelines *vide* Annexure 'D' is enclosed. The certificate of search may please be given on format given in annexure F.

Please note that the responsibility of making search of the records required for the purpose of various Government/revenue office/ Company Registrar etc., is entirely on you and you shall be liable for any loss caused to the bank due to negligent search on your part or on the part of the agent/servant engaged by you for this purpose.

Please do not hesitate do demand any document/record/material required by you for the purpose of making proper investigation into the title to the property of the mortgager.

The search for title/encumbrances is normally required to be made for a period of 30 years. If this is not possible for unavoidable reasons, please note that the search should be at least for 15 years, provided you are entirely satisfied that the 15 years search would be sufficient in the particular facts and circumstances of the matter in hand. If you are not fully satisfied regarding the title to the property by making on investigation/search for a period of 15 years only, you should invariably ask for further period as you feel necessary, for records, documents, and should verify them also.

Please note that you are required to verify the original title, deeds only, particularly title deeds, which are the subject-matter of the mortgage. If the original title deeds/documents are not available and certified extracts are produced, kindly examine whether that should be sufficient for creation of a valid and enforceable mortgage and state what precautions are to be taken for the purpose.

In case of agricultural lands offered as security, please advise as to whether there are any restrictions under the local laws for creation and enforceability of the mortgage of agricultural lands.

In case of lending by Consortium members/Multiple Lenders and/or extension of mortgages, priority of charges existing in favour of other charge-holders, intervening charges created if any will have to be verified in detail, and please advise the Bank as to the restrictions/limitations/impediments, and remedial measures if any.

Please ensure that all legal formalities/procedures required under laws are complied with for valid creation of mortgage in favour of the Bank. If there are any legal impediments/restrictions, kindly advise as to whether such impediments can be cured and if so, what procedure is to be followed.

Please sign the duplicate of this letter acknowledging the receipt of this letter and also confirming the terms and conditions under which you will be providing the required search report and certificate. The format of the certificate to be provided is in terms of Annexure 'F'.

Please acknowledge receipt and ensure submission of TIR within three days receipt of this letter, failing which penalty may be imposed as per MoU.

Yours faithfully, Received

For ASSTT. GENERAL MANAGER

ENCLOSURE TO CIRCULAR NO. P/50/2006-07 DATED 22-11-2006

Annexure B

Details of property/titles to be verified

1. To be filled by the Branch/Unit.

A.	Name of the Branch/Business Unit	Amar Colony, New Delhi
B.	Branch/BU Letter Reference & Date	
C.	Name of the title holder of the property (ies)	Smt. Abha Rawal
D.	Whether Borrower/s or Guarantor/s	
E.	Constitution of the Borrowers/Guarantors	
F.	Description of documents scrutinized	
S. No.	Documents	Whether Original/Certified copy
	Date Name	
2.	**Description of Properties**	
	Survey/Door NO.	E-346
	Extent	Dayabagh Colony
	Location	Lajpat Nagar – III
	Boundaries/	New Delhi
	East West	South North
3.	**List of documents delivered to advocate for verification (specify/certified extracts/copies etc.)**	
4.	**Location Details**	
(i)	Name of the Applicant/Borrower	
(ii)	Prominent landmark	
(iii)	Bus route	
(iv)	Bus stop	
5.	**Complete Address : E-346, Dayabagh Colony, Lajpat Nagar-III, New Delhi**	
(i)	Approach sketch to the location	
(ii)	Exact location of construction/ purchase and working plan	
	Please mention details about the builder (if applicable)	
(a)	Name of the Firm	
(b)	Address of the Firm	
(c)	Telephone No./Mob No.	
(d)	Contact person	Sh. Vijay Rawal

(e) Is the builder/project in the Bank's latest approved list. Mention the date of approval of the builder and validity of the current approval.

ROUGH LOCATION SKETCH:—

Date :

Signature :

Name:

Designation :

Branch/Unit

CHAPTER 13

Community Lawyering

Community lawyering is the work undertaken at the needs and interests of a particular community. The term 'community' may relate to a housing colony, community (e.g. teachers, skilled workmen, labour unions or victims and so on) or a group. It is also known as 'cause lawyering'. It is based on the concept of value system. To those already in legal profession, it offers a scope for pro bono work.

Community lawyering is essentially giving a hand to solve neighbourhood problems. An underlying objective is to inculcate amongst future law professions a commitment towards service to the society. This focuses on the potential in a lawyer to problem solving. The problems or difficulties may concern a variety of functions such as crime prevention, improvement in quality of life, enhanced security and so on. The students would have the satisfaction for having worked for the poor, neglected and disempowered. Further, they would contribute for effective measures towards anti poverty goals.

Law students can work in the area of community lawyering by taking up legal needs and interests of a particular community. To illustrate,

(a) Pensioners

(b) Resident Welfare Association

(c) Group Housing Societies

(d) Trade Unions

(e) Old age homes

(f) Domestic worker's groups

(g) Child beggars

(h) Sex workers

(i) Disabled or handicapped persons

(j) Inmates of a prison

(k) Juvenile remand homes

(l) Survivors of natural or other disasters

(m) Support groups for alcoholics or drug abuse victims

(n) Widows

(o) Immigrants

The law schools may wish to set up Community Lawyering Clinics (CLCs). The first component of their work would be class room discussions to understand the needs, applicable laws and also to devise strategy to provide legal services. They would work under the guidance and supervision of a faculty.

The classroom discussion must also cover the ethical considerations with regard to privacy aspects, conflict of interests, and advertising restrictions under the Advocates Act. This would also impinge on need for law reforms, if any and simplification of procedural laws. Such group activity may be supplemented by guest lectures by social activists, public interest lawyers, judges and media personnel. Need for community sensitization programmes by way of articles, seminars, posters and video films may also be considered.

Another topic for classroom discussion may concern consensus on effective legal remedies. These may appear in the form of injunctions, stay orders and custody orders etc. Where feasible use of mediation, negotiation or conciliation etc. may be helpful.

The classroom discussion may be followed by active steps outside law schools. These may include:

(a) Client counselling

(b) Negotiations and mediations for custody, restrain, compensation etc.

(c) Litigations

(d) Special education

(e) Arrangements for psychiatric or psychological assistance.

(f) Seminars, conferences, workshops

(g) Media interaction

An example of a very useful case study with regard to community lawyering was the initiative taken by the Federation of Resident Welfare Associations Ghaziabad District of Uttar Pradesh from 2005-06 onwards. The programme has been continued thereafter. A pragmatic initiative by the residents to present a collective voice resulted in vast improvements in civic facilities like repair of roads, provision of street lights, cleaning of Hindon river, city transport, maintenance of drains, water supply and increased green cover in residential colonies. They succeeded in getting medical care by way of eye camps. Their demand materialized for repair of national highway. The move was a laudable example of 'good governance by public participation'. The residents benefited enormously by acquiring a capacity upgrade with regard to laws relating to the administration and municipal functioning.

It would be useful for the law students to be familiar with the contents of a cause list. Reproduced below are the extracts from a cause list of High Court of Delhi bringing out a few type of cases that may appear on such a list.

HIGH COURT OF DELHI
ADVANCE CAUSE LIST

LIST OF BUSINESS
FOR
WEDNESDAY, THE 2ND JANUARY, 2013

INDEX

(APPELLATE JURISDICTION)

(Note : Unless otherwise specified, before all appellate side courts, fresh matters shown in the supplementary lists will be taken up first).

COURT No. 1
(DIVISION BENCH-I)
HON'BLE THE CHIEF JUSTICE
HON'BLE MR. JUSTICE V.K. JAIN

(NOTE-I COUNSELS ARE REQUESTED TO PAGINATE THEIR

FILES IN CONFIRMITY WITH THE COURT FILE IN ADVANCE)

(NOTE-II COUNSELS ARE REQUESTED TO PROVIDE LIST OF BOOKS/ACTS ON WHICH THEY ARE RELYING IN ADVANCE)

(NOTE-III PASS OVER FRESH MATTERS SHOWN IN THE SUPPLEMENTARY LIST WILL BE TAKEN UP AGAIN AT 2.15 PM)

FOR ADMISSION

1.	W.P. (C) 3146/2012	JOSE ABRAHAM	RITU KUMAR, N. WAZIRI v. GOVT. OF NCT OF DELHI

AFTER NOTICE MISC. MATTERS

2.	W.P. (C) 29/2010 CM APPL. 10351/2011 CM APPL. 13506/2011 CM APPL. 19904/2011 CM APPL. 19978/2011	COURT ON ITS OWN MOTION v. GOVT. OF NCT DELHI AND ANR	REENA GEORGE, J.S. BAKSHI, GEETANJALI MOHAN, AK SINGH, OP SAXENA, MEERA BHATIA, MANINDER ACHARYA, JAYANT BHUSHAN, GAUTAM TALUKDAR, N. WAZIRI
3.	W.P. (C) 4535/2010 CM APPL. 10105/2012 CM APPL. 12199/2012	COURT ON ITS OWN MOTION v. GOVT. OF NCT OF DELHI AND MCD	ASHOK AGARWAL, VINOD, N. WAZIRI, MANINDER ACHARYA, S.K. DUBEY, VINOD WADHWA, R.K. SINGH, ZUBEDA BEGUM

4. W.P. (C) 1618/2012	JAGMOHAN v. UOI	A.K. SINGH
5. W.P. (C) 6324/2012 C.M. APPL. 16884/2012	ARYAWART JANGAGRITY WELFARE ASSO v. DIRECTORATE OF EDUCATION	M.M. HASHMI
6. FAO (OS) 559/2012 CM APPL. 19527/2012	BHARATHI RAMAKRISHNAN v. RAVI KANTA	R.N.S. ASSOCIATES

COURT No. 3

(DIVISION BENCH-3)

HON'BLE MR. JUSTICE BADAR DURREZ AHMED

HON'BLE MR. JUSTICE R.V. EASWAR

FRESH MATTERS & APPLICATIONS

7. ITA 693/2012	COMMISSIONER OF INCOME TAX-XII v. RAJINDER KUMAR	N.P. SAHNI
8. ITA 694/2012	COMMISSIONER OF INCOME TAX-X v. CHANDER SINGH SEHRAWAT AND ASSOCIATES	N.P. SAHNI AND RUCHESH SINHA

FOR ADMISSION

9. W.P. (C) 6023/2012 CM APPL. 16294/2012 CM APPL. 16295/2012 CM APPL. 16296/2012	CIT CENTRAL II v. BURR BROWN INDIA LTD.	RASHMI CHOPRA

COURT No. 5

(DIVISION BENCH-6)

HON'BLE MR. JUSTICE S. RAVINDRA BHAT

HON'BLE MR. JUSTICE SUDERSHAN KUMAR MISRA

(NOTE-I COUNSELS ARE REQUESTED TO FILE DOCUMENTS, PAPER BOOK ETC. AS FAR AS POSSIBLE, IN E-FORM AND AVOID FILING THEM IN PAPER FORM.

COUNSEL ARE ALSO REQUESTED TO MAKE USE OF THE HIGH COURT WEBSITE TO ASCERTAIN THE STATUS OF PENDING MATTERS.

FOR DIRECTIONS

10. RFA (OS) 121/2012	MR. VIJAYANANDAN REDDY v. PRADEEP K. DHINGRA	K.R. CHAWLA, SACHIN SOOD

AFTER NOTICE MISC. MATTERS

11. W.P. (C) 1909/2008 CM APPL. 3723/2008 CM APPL. 19691/2012 WITH CW 5573/2002	SRIMANT SANGRAM SINH PRATAP v. UOI	RAJIV SHANKAR DVIVEDI, TRIVENI POTEKA, B.S. RAJESH AGRAJIT, ANUJ SINGH

Bibliograph

1. The Law and the Lawyers, M.K. Gandhi, Navjivan Publishing House, Ahmedabad, Revised Edition 1999.
2. Partition of India, Legend and Reality, HM Seervai, Universal Law Publishing Co. Pvt. Ltd., 2nd Edn., Reprint, 2012.
3. Before Memory Fades, Fali S. Nariman, Hay House India, 1st Edn., 2010.
4. Making of a Good Lawyer, Jagdish Swarup, Universal Law Publishing Co. Pvt. Ltd., 2nd Edn., 2005.
5. Legends in Law, our Great Forbears, V. Sudhish Pai, Universal Law Publishing Co. Pvt. Ltd, 2013 Edn.
6. Clinical Legal Education, N.R. Madhava Menon, Eastern Book Company, 1st Edn., 1998.
7. Turning Point, The Story of a Law Teacher, N.R. Madhava Menon, Universal Law Publishing Co. Pvt. Ltd., 2009 Edition.
8. Nani Palkhivala, A Role Model, Maj. Gen. Nilendra Kumar, Universal Law Publishing Co. Pvt. Ltd., 4th Edn., 2012.
9. Case Studies on Military Law, Maj. Gen. Nilendra Kumar, Universal Law Publishing Co. Pvt. Ltd., 2nd Edn., 2011.
10. The Advocates Act, 1961.